Workers and politics
in occupied Austria
1945–55

Manchester University Press

Workers and politics in occupied Austria 1945–55

Jill Lewis

Manchester University Press

Published by Manchester University Press
Altrincham Street, Manchester M1 7JA, UK
www.manchesteruniversitypress.co.uk

British Library Cataloguing-in-Publication Data is available

Library of Congress Cataloging-in-Publication Data is available

ISBN 978 0 7190 7351 9 paperback

First published by Manchester University Press in hardback 2007

This paperback edition first published 2015

Printed by Lightning Source

Contents

Acknowledgements

For help in preparing this book my thanks are due to the staff of the Archiv der Republik, Vienna, headed by Professor Lorenz Mikoletsky, the Verein der Geschichte der Arbeiterbewegung, the Kammer für Arbeiter und Angestellte, Vienna, in particular Dr Madeleine Wolensky, and the Institut für Wissenschaft vom Menschen, Vienna, the National Archive at Kew in London, and the National Archive in Washington and especially Dr Amy Schmidt. I am indebted to Ingrid Fraberger for undertaking research on my behalf in the Russian archives. Among other academic colleagues and friends, grateful mention should be made of Professor Gerhard Jagschitz, Professor Oliver Rathkolb, Professor Karl Stuhlpfarrer, Professor Julian Jackson, Professor Reinhold Wagnleitner, Professor Mark Cornwall, Dr Robert Knight, Dr Heinz Renner, Dr Maria Mesner, Dr Matthew Berg, Dr Tim Kirk, Dr Dan Healey, Dr Gareth Pritchard and Dr Hans Safrian. The members of my own department at Swansea University, students as well as staff, have given me ongoing encouragement and intellectual stimulation. Generous grants have been forthcoming from the British Academy, Leverhulme Trust and the Arts and Humanities Research Council. Throughout the project, Dr Eleonore Breuning provided scholarly and moral support in no small measure.

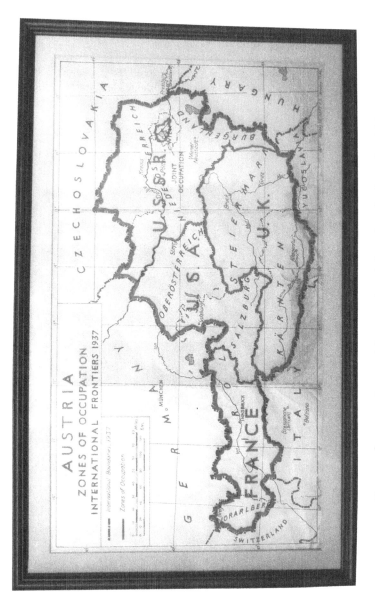

Zones of occupation and international frontiers in Austria, 1937

Introduction

The purpose of this book is to examine the complex origins of the political culture of the Second Republic. Whereas several books have concentrated on the diplomatic complexities of Austria's position under Allied occupation, and its relation to the Cold War, few have considered how these factors affected domestic politics, especially the new political system that was emerging.[1] In particular, there is a gulf between analyses of the means by which Austria achieved independence in 1955 and studies of the effects which continued occupation had on class and political relations. On the basis of an examination of post-war labour politics, it will be shown that under occupation the Austrian government, aided by the leadership of the labour movement, quelled dissent and centralised authority by exploiting the new state's greatest weakness – its precarious political situation. By exaggerating the significance of the recurrent episodes of labour unrest, Austrian politicians were able to achieve three successes in one: they marginalised domestic Communist opposition, reduced Soviet influence within the Allied Control Council, and increased their bargaining power vis-à-vis the United States in relation to Marshall Aid, thus safeguarding economic growth. In the process, the foundations for the Social Partnership were laid and with them the basis for that curious mixture of corporate and democratic politics which for the last four decades of the twentieth century was to characterise the 'Austrian model'.

Of late years, this Austrian model has been challenged. Before embarking on our examination of what were, in effect, the origins of the Social Partnership, it may be as well to pause to examine and consider whether they were misconceived.

In the Austrian general election of October 1999, 27 per cent of voters chose to support Jörg Haider's right-wing Freedom Party (*Freiheitliche Partei Österreichs* – FPÖ), reducing the Socialist Party (*Sozialistische Partei Österreichs* – SPÖ) to 34 per cent and pushing the conservative People's Party (*Österreichische Volkspartei* – ÖVP) into a neck-and-neck finish for second place, with only 415 votes more than the FPÖ. After many weeks of frenzied negotiations, the leader of the ÖVP, Wolfgang Schüssel, overturned an earlier commitment to stay out of government if his party was forced into third place, and invited the FPÖ to join a coalition government. The grand coalition of SPÖ and ÖVP, which had either directly or indirectly controlled the Second Austrian Republic for most of the previous fifty years, was shattered. The SPÖ was still the largest party in parliament, but, for only the second time since 1945, it was no longer part of the government.[2]

The election result did not come as a complete surprise. Since 1986, when Haider became the leader of the Freedom Party and ousted its liberal wing, the party had systematically increased its electoral base from a meagre 5 per cent in 1983 to 24 per cent in the European elections of 1998. Haider's overtly aggressive political style, combined with a carefully stylised youthful charisma, contrasted starkly with that of the bland grey politicians who had dominated Austrian political life since the days of Bruno Kreisky. He was portrayed as the slim, lithe, athletic young leader, who could climb mountains, run marathons and talk to ordinary people at their own level, using simple language rather than the jargon of Austrian political discourse. His campaigns emphasised youth, vitality and directness.[3] But he was also an extreme right-wing politician, with connections to German neo-Nazi groups, who frequently applauded the bravery of the soldiers of his father's generation who had served in the *Wehrmacht* during the Second World War. He publicly praised Nazi employment policies for being 'orderly', later justifying this by saying : 'To avoid any misinterpretation – all I said was based on facts. That the Third Reich created a great number of jobs through an intensive policy of employment, and thus eliminated unemployment.'[4] In a television interview in 1988 this man who would be chancellor described the (Second) Austrian Republic as a 'monstrosity':

> You know as well as I do that the Austrian nation has been a monstros-
> ity, an ideological monstrosity, because ethnicity (*Volkszugehörigkeit*) is
> one thing and citizenship (*Staatszugehörigkeit*) is another and if one
> person is allowed to identify himself as Slovene-Austrian, or Hungarian-
> Austrian or Croat-Austrian, then it must also be possible for someone to
> identify themselves as German-Austrian. And that is what is laid out in
> our programme.'[5]

Seven years later he went on to claim that 'liberation from Hitler did not mean freedom for us for long. It was the freedom of the Soviets, the freedom of rape, the freedom of Stalin and perhaps with that also the freedom of those who have a say in the ORF.'[6] This reinforced the image which many Austrians still held of themselves as victims of occupation both during and after the war, but with an added smear attack on one of Haider's prime targets, the broadcasting media.

Haider's provocative political statements played a major role in his political campaigning, providing him with lavish publicity and media coverage. They also sometimes rebounded upon him. In 1991 he was forced to stand down as provincial leader of Carinthia after his endorsement of Nazi labour policies. But this did not curb his language. In a book published in 1993 he once again denounced the Austrian political system, declaring that 'we *Freiheitlichen* want a new, a Third Republic'.[7] Two years later, in a speech in 1995, he was reported to have said that 'the classical form of representative democracy has had its day'.[8] It was statements like these which led the Austrian President, Thomas Klestil, to take an unprecedented step in February 2000 and demand that, before he swore it in, the newly elected coalition government should make a formal declaration promising to uphold democracy. The inclusion of the right-wing FPÖ in government provoked outrage abroad. The Israeli government took the radical step of withdrawing its ambassador to Vienna, while the United States government decided on a more cautious move and recalled its ambassador for consultations. The European Union (EU), of which Austria had been a member since 1995, announced that bilateral relations with the new Austrian government would be suspended: Austria could remain a member of the EU and take part in policy and decision-making, but there would be no one-to-one negotiations between Austria and her fellow members. It was the most severe punishment that the EU had imposed on a member country.[9]

This was not the first time that Austrian domestic politics had provoked international condemnation. In 1986, the former Secretary-General of the United Nations, Kurt Waldheim, was elected President of Austria, despite fresh revelations that his own account of his activities during the Second World War was inaccurate. Waldheim had maintained that he had been invalided out of the German Army in 1942 and had spent the remaining war years as a student in Vienna. When it was revealed that, instead, he had been seconded for service as an intelligence officer in occupied Yugoslavia, his defence changed from denying any role in the Nazi war machine to arguing that 'he had only been doing his duty'.[10] The international community was not convinced. The United States government added his name to the Watch List of undesirable aliens and banned him from setting foot on its soil and, despite his earlier diplomatic reputation, Waldheim was ostracised and spent the remainder of his political life confined to his native land, with very occasional state visits to countries in the Middle East.

The 1986 presidential election and the 1999 national election had certain aspects in common which are of direct relevance to the present book. In both cases an underlying feature for foreign observers has been the reluctance of the Austrian people to engage in open discussion of their recent history. In consequence, few defensible explanations of the path taken by Austria are available, apart from dubious stereotypes about the nature of the Austrian national character. Indeed, there are strong grounds for arguing that its system of constraining historical debate at both the popular and the professional level has been a salient feature of Austrian culture since the end of the Second World War. This culture did not arise organically from the genetic or social make-up of Austrian society, but was consciously constructed in the first decades of the Second Republic. Since 1945 Austrian politicians have sought to develop a national identity based on consensus politics, identifying commonly held goals and fostering a vision of a new Austrian nation alleged to have emerged from the ashes of war, its people bound together by their shared suffering under first Nazi and then Allied, and specifically Soviet, occupation. According to the official line, this new Austrian nationalism was born in the concentration camps, where former political opponents shared the sufferings of incarceration under the Third Reich and from which they emerged in 1945 having purged their internal differences and become united in their faith in Austrian nationalism.[11] It was then consolidated by ten years of Allied occupation, during which time those same politicians were forced to prove their country's democratic credentials. Austrians had, so went the reasoning, suffered collectively not once, but twice under the yoke of foreign occupation.

The use of a myth of resistance to Nazism in the construction of post-war state ideologies was not unique to Austria, as Tony Judt has shown.[12] However, in the Austrian case the apparent support for integration into the Third Reich in 1938, Austria's subsequent position as a part of that Reich, and the role of many of its people in the Nazi political and military machine, raised specific problems for an analysis which sought to prove that Austrians had been victims of Nazism. But Austrian politicians had little need of that analysis, for in the Moscow Declaration of 1943 the Allied Powers themselves had described Austria as the first victim of 'Hitlerite aggression', in a bid to encourage internal resistance to the Nazi regime. In the early years of the Cold War, Allied attempts to implement a policy of denazification in Austria faltered, as the Soviets and Western Allies alike strove to increase their influence over the country. For Austrians themselves, the actual role of Nazism in their country became a taboo topic of discussion, replaced by the image of Austria as the victim of Nazism, and remained so for the duration of the Cold War and as long as the culture of consensus prevailed. To this in the 1950s was added a new myth – that of Austria, the small democratic state which, uniquely, had successfully resisted a Soviet putsch, to become the only 'neutral' state to emerge in Central Europe.

The absence of any general discussion of culpability in relation to the Second World War is one explanation for the popular responses in Austria to the Waldheim Affair and to Jörg Haider. There are, however, differences between the two cases. The general response of Austrians in 1986 to outside condemnation was to rally behind Waldheim. Most newspapers supported the President and some provoked further outrage abroad by complaining about foreign interference in domestic issues and positing an international, if not a Jewish, conspiracy to denigrate their country.[13] The most common response on the streets was that Waldheim, and with him Austria, was being unfairly condemned. Repeating the mantra which had been adopted by both Austrian and Allied politicians, Austrians argued that they were not guilty on account of their part in the Second World War, but had, rather, been the first victims of 'Hitlerite aggression'. Without a hint of irony, Austrians saw their country, in the words of Pope Paul VI, as *'der Insel der Seligen'* (the island of the blessed), and they later went on to re-elect Waldheim as president for a second term.[14] The Austrian government, which in 1986 was a Socialist-led coalition, tried publicly to distance itself from the international furore and set up a commission of enquiry, but one which was given limited terms of reference. Behind the scenes government ministers strove to minimise the damage done to their country's reputation. A British historian, Robert Knight, was attacked in Austrian newspapers for an unsympathetic review relating to the Waldheim Affair which appeared in the *Times Literary Supplement*.[15] Shortly afterwards, the Austrian Foreign Minister addressed letters marked 'private and confidential' to prominent Austrian historians, enclosing Knight's review and exhorting them to establish contacts with foreign colleagues in order to correct the 'false' image of Austria which was developing abroad.[16]

The reaction of the Austrian public to the 1999 election was very different. The announcement of the ÖVP/FPÖ coalition on 11 February 2000 was marked by hostile demonstrations in Vienna and other cities, organised by unaffiliated opposition groups which used the Internet to establish contacts and spread information. The demonstrations culminated on 19 February in a mass rally of 250,000 people on the Heldenplatz, where Hitler had staged his ceremonial entrance into Vienna in March 1938. Actors, artists, writers and musicians made public statements condemning the inclusion of the FPÖ in the government and accusing Schüssel of pursuing his personal ambition to become chancellor at the expense of Austria's international reputation. Much of the Austrian media was also critical of the new government and of Jörg Haider's role in it. When Haider announced that he was withdrawing as leader of the FPÖ, the ORF and many newspapers reacted with scepticism, pointing out that, whatever his formal position, he would remain the de facto leader as long as the party hierarchy was dominated by people whom he had appointed.[17] The FPÖ would remain Haider's party as long as he remained at its centre of power. Days after this announcement a scandal forced the resignation of the newly appointed FPÖ Minister of Justice, who was then replaced by Haider's personal lawyer.[18]

Whereas the Waldheim Affair led to limited debate within Austria, the Haider controversy sparked a degree of political activity and discussion which was without precedent in the Second Republic. The reason for this was not just the political character of Haider or that of his party, but the fact that Haider had promoted his career by challenging the underlying corporatism on which the political culture of the Second Republic was built, the culture which had been consciously fostered in the early post-war era and which advocated political consensus not only as the basis of Austrian identity, but also as the bedrock of a stable and prosperous state. The framework for this was the Austrian Social Partnership and *Proporz* (proportionality). These concepts involved the formalised sharing out of political power and decision-making between the two dominant political parties, the SPÖ and the ÖVP, from the early 1960s onwards, creating a system in which policy was framed by a labyrinthine structure of committees and subcommittees in which affiliation to one of these two parties determined appointments at all levels.[19] Debate took place in closed sessions, after which decisions were ratified by the government and presented to the public as unanimous. Throughout the 1970s and 1980s, the Austrian model of democracy and Social Partnership was praised internationally for delivering sustained economic growth and social stability, in an exceptionally successful version of 'controlled capitalism'. But it also stifled political debate and limited participation in the exercise of power to an oligarchical elite.

It was this system which Jörg Haider sought to smash. Denouncing it as undemocratic, his right-wing party was able to articulate dissent and to fracture the traditional pattern of Austrian voting, cloaking its anti-liberal and xenophobic philosophies in the rhetoric of populism. In so doing it gave rise to international caricatures of the Austrian people as self-satisfied, small-minded, introverted and racist, stereotypes which themselves sometimes smack of that self-same racism and lack of analysis which the FPÖ attributed to its political opponents.[20] But although Haider may have capitalised on Austria's refusal to confront its past, which allowed him and his political cohorts to articulate extreme right-wing views without losing popular support, his electoral success was also due to the already declining influence of the Austrian Social Partnership. It is clear that the kaleidoscope of Austrian politics has recently been given a vigorous shaking, and we have yet to see what new pattern will emerge.

All metaphor aside, however, it is unlikely that future developments in Austria will be wholly benign if the past is not at long last subjected to a thorough and dispassionate scrutiny. It is hoped that the present book will succeed in making a contribution to this process, which, though already begun, has by no means yet been completed.

Notes

1 See Günter Bischof, *Austria in the First Cold War 1945–1955: The Leverage of the Weak* (Basingstoke: Macmillan, 1999); Audrey Kurth Cronin, *Great Power Politics and the Struggle over Austria, 1945–1955* (Ithaca, NY: Cornell University Press, 1986); William Bader, *Austria between East and West, 1945–1955* (Stanford, CA: Stanford University Press, 1966).

2 Armin Thurnher, *Heimniederlage. Nachrichten aus dem neuen Österreich* (Vienna: Zsolnay Verlag, 2000), ch. 2.

3 Armin Thurnher coined the term '*Feschismus*' to describe Haider's style. This is a word play on the Austrian word '*fesch*', meaning trendy, cute or stylish. Armin Thurnher, *Das Trauma, ein Leben. Österreichische Einzelheiten* (Vienna: Zsolnay Verlag, 1999), ch. 5.

4 Asked about his views on the *Wehrmacht* in an interview with the Austrian news magazine, *profil*, on 21 August 1995, he answered, 'I have said that the soldiers of the "Wehrmacht" made possible the democracy which we now have in Europe. If they had not resisted, if they had not been in the East, then, [. . .]'. *profil*: 'What do you mean by "resistance"? It was an invasion campaign by the German "Wehrmacht".' Haider: 'Then we must now start to ask what it really was.'
   The comment on Nazi employment policies was made in the Carinthian provincial parliament in June 1991.

5 'Das wissen Sie so gut wie ich, dass die österreichische Nation eine Missgeburt gewesen ist, eine ideologische Missgeburt, denn die Volkszugehörigkeit ist die eine Sache und die *Staatszugehörigkeit* ist die andere Sache, und wenn

man es jemandem freistellt, sich als slowenischer Österreicher zu bekennen, als ungarischer, als kroatischer, dann muss es auch möglich sein, sich als deutscher Österreicher zu bekennen. Und das ist auch das, was in unserem Programm formuliert ist.' Broadcast on ORF (Austrian Broadcasting Authority/ Österreichischer Rundfunk) *Inlandsreport*, 18 August 1988.

6   Part of a speech Haider made in the Palais Ausperg on 26 April 1996, quoted in *Stern* magazine (7/2000), 148.

7   Jörg Haider, *Die Freiheit, die ich meine. Das Ende des Proporzstaats. Plädoyer für eine Dritte Republik* (Frankfurt/Main: Ullstein, 1993).

8   'Die klassische Form der repräsentativen Demokratie hat sich überlebt', quoted in *Stern* (7/2000), 148.

9   The sanctions were lifted following the publication on 8 September 2000 of an EU report on Austria produced by the 'three wise men'. This report exonerated the Austrian government, but not the FPÖ, which it described as a 'right-wing populist party with extreme expressions . . . which has exploited and enforced xenophobic sentiments in campaigns . . . and has also tried to suppress criticism by the continuous use of the libel procedures'. Report by Martti Ahtisaari, Jochen Frowein and Marcelino Oreja (Paris: 2000), 27, 32–3.

10 Richard Mitten, *The Politics of Antisemitic Prejudice: The Waldheim Phenomenon in Austria* (Boulder, CO: Westview Press, 1992), 62–81, 106.

11 The official version first appeared in the *Rot-Weiss-Rot-Buch: Darstellungen, Dokumente und Nachweise zur Vorgeschichte und Geschichte der Okkupation Österreichs (nach amtlichen Quellen)* (Vienna: Verlag der österreichischen Staatsdruckerei, 1946). An English language version was printed in 1947: *Red-White-Red-Book: Descriptions, documents and proofs to the antecedents and history of the occupation of Austria from 'official sources'. Part One* (Vienna: Verlag der österreichischen Staatsdruckerei, 1947).

12 Tony Judt, 'The Past is another Country: Myth and Memory in Postwar Europe', in István Deák, Jan T. Gross and Tony Judt (eds), *The Politics of Retribution in Europe: World War II and its Aftermath* (Princeton, NJ: Princeton University Press, 2000), 83–118. See also Robert Knight, 'Narratives in Post-war Austrian Historiography', in Anthony Bushell (ed.), *Austria 1945–1955* (Cardiff: University of Wales Press, 1996), 11–36.

13 Mitten, *The Politics of Antisemitic Prejudice*, ch. 8. There were pointed comments about the World Jewish Congress and other international bodies 'dictating' Austrian domestic policy.

14 The statement was made during a Papal visit to Austria in 1967.

15 Robert Knight, 'The Waldheim context: Austria and Nazism', *Times Literary Supplement* (30 October 1986).

16 Friedrich Weckerlein, 'Armes Österreich; erst Opfer Hitlers, dann der Historiker', *Frankfurter Rundschau* (13 March 1987). *The Waldheim Report submitted to Federal Chancellor Dr Franz Vranitzky by the International Commission of Historians designed to Establish the Military Service of Lieutenant/Ist Lieutenant Kurt Waldheim* (Copenhagen: Museum Tusculanum Press, 1993).

17 On 21 February 2000, Haider announced on television that he would stand down as leader of the FPÖ from 1 May 2000.

18 *profil* (28 February 2000), 36–8.
19 For a discussion of the Austrian Social Partnership, see Jill Lewis, 'Austria in Historical Perspective: From Civil War to Social Partnership', and Emmerich Tálos and Bernhard Kittel, 'Austria in the 1990s: The Routine of Social Partnership in Question?', in Stefan Berger and Hugh Compston (eds), *Policy Concertation and Social Partnership in Western Europe. Lessons for the 21st Century* (New York/Oxford: Berghahn, 2002).
20 The *Guardian* editorials of 5 October 1999 and 8 November 2000 are examples of this.

1

The *Anschluss*

On the evening of Friday 11 March 1938 Nazi supporters took to the streets of Vienna, unleashing a cacophony of chants, shouts and screams. The British journalist G. E. R. Gedye described the scene as follows:

> It was an indescribable witches' sabbath – storm-troopers, lots of them barely out of the school-room, with cartridge-belts and carbines, the only other evidence of authority being Swastika brassards, were marching side by side with police turncoats, men and women shrieking or crying hysterically the name of their leader, embracing the police and dragging them along in the swirling stream of humanity, motor-lorries filled with storm-troopers clutching their long-concealed weapons, hooting furiously, trying to make themselves heard above the din, men and women leaping, shouting and dancing in the light of the smoking torches which soon began to make their appearance, the air filled with a pandemonium of sound in which intermingled the screams of: 'Down with Jews! *Heil Hitler! Heil Hitler! Sieg Heil!* Perish the Jews! Hang Schuschnigg! *Heil Seyss-Inquart . . .*'[1]

A Viennese Jew, Carl Zuckmayer, went further:

> On that evening all hell broke out. Hades had opened its gates and let loose its lowest, most terrible and foulest spirits.[2]

Later that night and in the early hours of Saturday the German Eighth Army crossed the border between Bavaria and the Austrian provinces of Salzburg and Tyrol.[3] The Second Panzer Division reached Linz by midday and twelve hours later its armoured vehicles were rolling along the Ringstrasse, the main boulevard in central Vienna.[4] On the same day German army columns moved north to secure the border with Czechoslovakia and south-west to occupy the Brenner Pass, closing the border with Italy. The military occupation of Austria took little more than a day and was carried out, as ordered, with the minimum of force: shortly before the invasion Adolf Hitler had instructed his army to overlook 'minor acts of provocation' where possible, for 'it is in our interest that the entire exercise should proceed without the use of violence and should take the form of a peaceful advance welcomed by the people'.[5] However, his order went on, if resistance were to break out, it was to be smashed by the ruthless use of force of arms.[6] In the event, there was little 'provocation' and even less concerted resistance. The German armed convoys were met by large cheering crowds lining the roads and streets of Austria. On the evening of that first day of the invasion, Hitler himself travelled across the river Inn, was driven into Braunau, his birthplace, and moved on to Linz, the provincial capital of Upper Austria and the city in which he had gone to school, arriving at 7.30 p.m. Once there he addressed a mass of people, estimated at between 60,000 and 80,000, from the balcony of the town hall, telling them that Providence had taken him from this, his home town, to Germany to become leader of the Reich and had entrusted to him the task of handing his dear homeland back to the German Empire. He invited all those present to imagine the surge of emotion he was feeling at that moment as he stood in front of them in the knowledge that he would finally be able to fulfil his task. Film footage of this event leaves no doubt about the corresponding elation evinced by the members of the listening crowd.[7] The following day, 13 March, *Luftwaffe* planes dropped 300 million propaganda leaflets and transported troops into the southern provinces of Styria and Carinthia, who were met by yet more throngs of ecstatic supporters. There were rumours at the time that the enthusiasm of the Austrian crowds surpassed even Hitler's own expectations and that it was this which persuaded him to change his plans. That evening, on the very day on which the Austrian Chancellor, Kurt Schuschnigg, was to have held his plebiscite, Hitler made it known that Austria was to become part of the Third Reich rather than a separate Nazi state with its own administration and that the *Anschluss* would be validated by a plebiscite to be held one month later on April 10.[8]

Hitler had long envisaged the annexation of his homeland by its cultural sibling and more powerful neighbour. It had been the initial stage in his plan for the establishment of German supremacy which he had set it out in *Mein Kampf* in 1924.[9] Some fourteen years later this operation appeared to proceed without a hitch. However, the image of the super-efficient and well-oiled German military machine progressing inexorably on the first stage of its path towards European and then world domination is flawed. According to Gedye, Hitler's own progress was far from smooth. Having originally intended to carry on with the two-hour journey from his 'home town' to Vienna as soon as he had finished addressing the crowd in Linz, Hitler was forced to delay his departure for two days. Gedye, who was in Vienna as Central European correspondent for *The Times* and who had distinct sympathies with the Austrian Socialists, reported that the main problem lay with the German military machine itself, which had already 'begun to creak and lumber' on that first day of the invasion. Foreign military attachés in the capital told him that between thirty and fifty German tanks had been spotted 'lying helpless and paralysed' along the road between Linz and Vienna, having either broken down or run out of petrol.[10] In addition, Heinrich Himmler, the chief of the German police and the SS (*Schützstaffel*), had flown into Vienna on the preceding Friday to assume control of the Austrian Order and Security Police (*Ordnungs-und Sicherheitspolizei*). He had been appalled at the slapdash nature of the plans for the security and protection of the Führer and had rejected them. As a result, Hitler's motor cavalcade was delayed and did not set off from Linz until Monday 14 March, when it proceeded along the banks of the river Danube, stopped off to greet crowds in St Pölten and, finally entering Vienna, moved along the Ringstrasse to the sound of pealing church bells, arriving on the Heldenplatz in the centre of the city at just before 6 that evening.[11] One eyewitness painted the scene as follows:

> The whole city behaved like an aroused woman, vibrating, writhing, moaning and sighing lustfully for orgasm and release. This is not purple writing. It is an exact description of what Vienna was and felt like on Monday, 14 March 1938, as Hitler entered her.[12]

The next morning, standing on the balcony of the Imperial Palace before a jubilant crowd of approximately a quarter of a million people, Hitler proclaimed that 'the primeval Ostmark of the German people shall henceforth constitute the youngest bulwark of the German nation and thus of the German Reich'.[13] Austria was dead and the *Ostmark* had been born.

The final act in this political drama had begun one month earlier, on 12 February, when Kurt Schuschnigg arrived at Hitler's mountain retreat at Berchtesgaden, having been unceremoniously summoned there by his German counterpart and former compatriot. Having greeted his guest with a flow of insulting rants, Hitler hurled a set of eleven demands at Schuschnigg, each of which constituted an intrusion into Austrian domestic politics and violated that country's independence.[14] The most important of these were a general amnesty for all Nazis in Austria, including those who had been found guilty of attempting to overthrow the government, and the appointment of a known Nazi – Arthur Seyss-Inquart – as Austrian Minister of the Interior with authority over the

police and internal security.[15] After some hesitation, Schuschnigg capit-
ulated on three points, but procrastinated on the others in the hope
that he would be able to obtain a more general personal statement from
Hitler guaranteeing Austria's independence. In addition he wanted firm
assurances from the German Chancellor that the Austrian Nazis would
be ordered to comply with Austrian law on their release. Hitler's answer
came one week later, when Austrian Nazis in the southern province of
Styria seized control of Graz, the provincial capital. The following
day, Sunday 20 February, Hitler made a radio speech to the German
public which was also broadcast, by agreement, on the state-owned
Austrian radio, RAVAG. Rather than confirming his intention to uphold
the independent status of Austria, Hitler referred to the 'German
minority' who lived outside the German state frontier and whom he
deemed to have been denied 'the general right of racial self-determination
simply because they are Germans'. The inference was that it was the
responsibility of the 'Fatherland' to protect the '*Volk*' irrespective of
borders. He concluded by condemning Schuschnigg specifically as a
'torturer of the German people'.[16]

Schuschnigg responded four days later in a speech in parliament.
Having given a brief account of the difficulties which had confronted
the Austrian state since the founding of the republic, and the successes
the country had achieved, he ended with the words, 'I trust in the Lord
God, who will not desert our country. He helps only those who are
determined to concentrate for the cause all their strength, all their will-
power. And because we are so determined, our final victory is beyond
question. "Until death, Red-White-Red!" *Österreich*!'[17] Austrians were
finally being asked to stand up to German intimidation.[18] It is almost
certain that by this time Schuschnigg had taken the decision to hold a
plebiscite on the question of Austrian independence, but if so the decision
remained a secret for over two weeks longer in order to allow arrangements to be made with the minimum danger of Nazi interference.
It was not until the evening of 9 March that he informed the Austrian
people in a radio broadcast from Innsbruck that the plebiscite would
take place just three days later, on Sunday 13 March, and that all
Austrians over the age of twenty-four would be eligible to vote. In the
heat of the moment, he forgot to tell them the exact wording of the
question. In the event they were to be asked to vote yes or no to what
might initially seem to be a relatively straightforward question, 'Are
you in favour of an independent and social, a Christian, German and
united Austria?'[19]

The Austrian government, or those members of it who remained loyal
to an independent Austria, used the period between the Berchtesgaden

meeting and the proposed date of the plebiscite to mend political fences and strengthen support. It was for this reason that, for the first time in four years, talks began between the government and members of the clandestine Free Trade Union movement (*Illegale Freie Gewerkschaften/* IFG), the underground successor to the Socialist Free Trade Unions. Schuschnigg was at first reluctant to enter into any negotiations. The entire Socialist movement had been outlawed in 1934 and its union federation had been replaced by the government-controlled Unity Union (*Einheitsgewerkschaft/*EG). The IFG had initially banned its members from participating in the new 'union', under the slogan 'not one man and not one penny for the system'. It had only abandoned this policy in 1936 when the government finally fulfilled a two-year-old pledge to hold elections to appoint shop stewards.[20] The IFG responded to this by instructing its supporters to stand for election in any plant where the majority of workers were members of the EG, providing that this had been previously sanctioned by the Revolutionary Socialist party (RS).[21] The new strategy was designed to allow Socialists to fight the EG, and hence the government, from within. As a result, in the larger Viennese plants in particular, a substantial proportion of the legally elected shop stewards were members of the illegal IFG as well as the EG. Schuschnigg's dilemma was that he would have to negotiate with these very shop stewards, for it was they who, on hearing in February of the reports of the Berchtesgaden meeting, took the initiative and organised a shop-floor petition pledging that workers would fight in defence of Austrian independence. But their support did not come without a price – they also laid down conditions that would undermine the very nature of the authoritarian Austrian state which Schuschnigg headed, and would restore specific political freedoms which had been lost with the overthrow of the democratic republic and the establishment of the Corporate State in 1934. Their list included the restoration of freedom of conscience and concessions to Socialists of rights of political organisation on a par with those already granted to the Nazi Party; the election rather than the appointment of trade union officials; a free and independent newspaper; and improved social welfare provisions.[22]

Despite the urgency of the situation, Schuschnigg initially balked at the idea of collaborating with his opponents and ignored the shop-stewards' request for a face-to-face meeting. He did sanction the distribution of the shop-stewards' petition when asked to do so by the EG, but at the same time ordered the EG leader, Johann Staud, to change the petition's wording to declare that Austrian workers were 'solidly aligned with their representatives behind the federal chancellor, for an independent, free, social, Christian and German Austria'.[23] By this one emendation, the petition was transformed from a defence of Austrian independence to a declaration of support for Schuschnigg, his government and the Corporate State. This strategy failed. At a series of plant meetings held at the end of February, workers refused to accept the change of wording and Schuschnigg was forced to relent; on 3 March he held a four-hour discussion with a delegation of shop stewards which included Friedrich Hillegeist, a leader of the IFG.[24] There was little rapprochement at the meeting.[25] The Chancellor was told that the shop stewards had agreed to meet him, but had come neither as friends nor as supporters, but as opponents, representatives of the mass of Austrian workers who had supported the Social Democratic Party (SDAP) in the days of democracy. They were searching for 'a way of bringing the workers into line – not behind you, for that is beyond our powers, but beside you, to fight the appalling danger now threatening our country and imperilling above all the class to which we belong'.[26] The delegation repeated their demands for political and press freedoms and for reform, which Schuschnigg appeared to accept in principle, but without making any specific concessions. He did, however, authorise the first legal meeting of IFG leaders in over four years in a bid to strengthen open popular support for his stand against Hitler. This was held in the workers' club in the Viennese suburb of Floridsdorf on 7 March. Hillegeist and other members of the delegation reported to an audience of over 350 trade unionists who then voted on three alternative courses of action – to support the government without reservation; to remain aloof from the dispute between the Corporate State and the Nazi dictatorship; or to support the government's battle against Hitler on condition that democratic rights were restored in Austria. The meeting voted in favour of the third alternative, with only the Communists advocating unconditional support for the government.[27] Two days later Schuschnigg announced his plebiscite to the Austrian people. But it was too late.

The Socialists have often been criticised for their refusal to give unreserved support to Schuschnigg in 1938, but their decision was based on their experience of political life under the First Republic and the Corporate State. Austria was a divided country in 1938 and the events which followed the weekend of 12–14 March 1938 were the culmination not only of international factors, but also of two decades of domestic conflict in which supporters of the SDAP had fought against the Christian Social Party and its allies and had lost. Consequently, they had little reason to put their faith in the Austrian Chancellor, despite their knowledge of what was taking place in the Third Reich. Hitler had abandoned democracy and destroyed the working-class movement in Germany, but Schuschnigg and his predecessor, Engelbert Dollfuss, had done the same in Austria.

Moreover, the Socialists alone could not have defeated Nazism in Austria. As has already been shown and will be further discussed, there was widespread popular support in Schuschnigg's Austria for Hitler's Germany. The reasons for this are not far to seek and will be explored in the rest of this chapter. They reflect the lack of consensus in inter-war Austria and can be broken down roughly into three main categories. The most important factor was the absence of a confident sense of Austrian national identity at the very time when popular nationalism was becoming the most powerful political concept across the rest of the continent. The First Austrian Republic had been born in 1918, the product of military defeat in the First World War and the subsequent destruction of the Habsburg Empire at the hands of the new creed of national self-determination. But there had been no specific Austrian nationalism before 1918 and none emerged in the inter-war years. Few welcomed the arrival of the First Republic: it was described as 'truncated' and as a 'dwarf state' even by Otto Bauer, one of its Socialist founders.[28] For many Austrians, the size of the new state and the demise of former Imperial glory were less important than its subsequent political and economic failures; plagued by inflation, unemployment and low productivity since its birth, as well as by deep-seated cultural and provincial rivalries, it had descended into violent political sectarianism by 1930. This period of unrest culminated in civil war in February 1934, just twelve months after Hitler's appointment as Chancellor of Germany. Second, the Corporate State which was erected on the debris of the First Republic was also a failure. Its leaders sought to consolidate their shaky power base by outlawing the Socialist opposition, overthrowing democracy and imposing an authoritarian regime. The Austrian Corporate State was modelled on fascism, but lacked basic popular support. In an age of militant nationalism, its official description as a 'Christian, German Federal State on a corporate foundation' was confused and confusing. It failed to distinguish clearly between the Austrian and German 'nations' at a time when the major threat to its existence came from expansionist German nationalism in the form of Nazism.[29] Third and finally, the government was unable to resolve the critical problem of unemployment which continued to embrace over 20 per cent of the labour force throughout the period. This was in stark contrast to the economic recovery which was taking place in Germany, where unemployment had fallen to 4.5 per cent by 1937.[30] Non-Jewish

Austrians, therefore, had every reason to believe that unification with Germany would result in a rapid improvement in their standard of living.[31]

To return to the question of the absence of a distinct concept of Austrian national identity throughout the inter-war period: two decades of domestic conflict began in 1918 when the First Austrian Republic crawled from the ashes of the Habsburg Empire, an unbalanced state with few supporters and little prospect of economic or political stability. One-third of its population of six million lived and worked in the capital, Vienna, which had served for over four centuries as the administrative, financial and political centre of a vast empire with, by 1914, a population of 54 million people. By contrast, the other two-thirds of the Republic's population lived in small towns and villages; although there were industrial pockets outside the capital, these were relatively small, and not one of the eight provincial capitals had more than 153,000 inhabitants.[32] The country was therefore economically and politically divided. It was also extremely vulnerable to fluctuations in the international economy. Austria's traditional trade routes had lain within the Empire and these had been severed after the First World War. As a result, its industrial economy stagnated and it was plagued by high levels of structural unemployment from 1922 onwards. Its political culture was also fractured. It was dominated by two movements that drew support from separate and increasingly antagonistic classes and which advocated conflicting and adversarial policies – the Christian Social Party held sway over most of provincial Austria and over the coalition government, while the Social Democratic Party controlled political life in Vienna to an exceptional degree throughout the lifetime of the First Republic, also enjoying significant support in the few industrial regions in the provinces.[33] Throughout the 1920s successive Christian Social national coalition governments pursued conservative political and economic policies under the watchful eye of the League of Nations and called on religion and the Church to justify their approaches. At the same time the SDAP built 'Red Vienna' as an experiment in applied socialism based on a system of high progressive taxation. The revenue from this was used to finance an extensive welfare programme, including large housing estates in which Socialist values and beliefs were extolled at every opportunity. The rival political parties accused each other of extremism – the Christian Socials called the Socialists 'Bolsheviks' and denounced their economic policy as 'tax sadism', while the Socialists condemned the Christian Socials for undermining democracy and threatened to resort to force in its defence. Both sides also maintained their own pet paramilitary groups. The antagonism was relatively contained until 1927, when, at the beginning of a general election campaign, supporters of a right-wing veteran soldiers' group, the *Frontkämpferverein*, shot and killed a Socialist war veteran and a child during a demonstration in Schattendorf in Burgenland. The accused were arrested and put on trial, but the announcement of their acquittal in July sparked off demonstrations and strikes in the capital. Fearing bloodshed, the SDAP leadership initially ignored calls by rank-and-file Socialists for a general strike, and when they did respond it was too late. Workers marched in columns into the city centre, where the demonstration quickly deteriorated into street violence. A battle broke out between demonstrators and the police in the inner city during which the Palace of Justice burned down and ninety people were killed.[34] The Christian Social Chancellor, Ignaz Seipel, who was also an ordained Roman Catholic priest, announced that his government would show 'no mercy' to the demonstrators, and the government increased its attacks on the labour movement. Over the next two years each side built up its paramilitary forces, the Socialists by expanding training of the *Schutzbund* while the Christian Socials relied increasingly on the fascist *Heimwehr* to patrol the streets.[35] Consequently, by the end of the decade, as the banking system collapsed, production and trade declined and unemployment soared to more than one-fifth of the total workforce, there was an escalation of political violence.[36] Each weekend the political parties and their respective paramilitaries went out to 'claim the streets' in demonstrations and marches, proclaiming their power and seeking to intimidate their rivals. Tensions increased further after the 1930 general election, when the SDAP became the largest party in parliament, but without the majority it needed to form a government. At the same time, the position of the Christian Social Party had deteriorated considerably: its proportion of the national vote had fallen to 35.7 per cent, over 5 per cent behind that of the SDAP. When the governing coalition with the German Nationalists collapsed in May 1932, the Christian Social Chancellor, Dollfuss, was forced to cobble together a fragile agreement with the small Agrarian League and the even smaller and less reliable *Heimwehr* group. The new government had a majority of just one.[37]

This was the situation in Austria at the end of 1932, only weeks before Adolf Hitler was appointed Chancellor of Germany. Faced with the prospect of continued parliamentary instability and the imminent collapse of his government, Dollfuss decided to abandon parliamentary democracy. He prorogued parliament on 4 March during a debate on a national railway strike and then exploited a legal technicality to argue that the session could not be resumed.[38] For the next fourteen months, until the introduction of a clerical-fascist constitution in May 1934, Austria was governed by emergency decree. Civil liberties, such as the right to strike, to demonstrate, to march and to parade, were removed. Press censorship was increased and the small and relatively insignificant Austrian Communist Party was banned, along with the *Schutzbund*, the Social Democrat paramilitary organisation. The right-wing paramilitary groups remained legal for the time being, as did the Austrian Nazi Party until June 1933 and the SDAP, but without a parliament.

The official explanation for abandoning parliamentary democracy, at least at that time, was that the system had become unworkable and that the relative strength of the Social Democrats was threatening the stability of the government. It was only later that Austrian politicians argued that their real intentions had been patriotic, to stem the 'Brown Wave' of Nazism which was emanating from Germany. And yet by 1933 there were very clear grounds for fearing that support for the Austrian Nazi Party was growing at an alarming rate.[39] The earliest sign of this appeared as early as 1931, when the Styrian section of the *Heimwehr*, Austria's weak and divided native fascist movement, defected to the Nazi camp after the failure of their attempted coup – the Pfrimer Putsch.[40] But the first solid evidence came in the results of the local and provincial elections held in April 1932. These were the first Austrian elections in which the Nazi Party put up candidates under its own name, and it won seats in each of the three provinces it contested, capturing almost 18 per cent of the Viennese vote, just 3 per cent less than the Christian Social Party itself.[41] The extent of support for Nazism became even more evident in March 1933 as the crisis in parliament was actually unfolding: on 5 March, the day after the railway strike debate and during the first stages of the move to authoritarian rule, twelve thousand people packed into the main hall of Vienna's North-West Railway station to celebrate Hitler's appointment as German Chancellor. At the close of the meeting they spilled out onto the streets, unfurling swastikas and chanting Nazi slogans. According to the Socialists, this development increased the panic in government circles and confirmed them in their decision to suspend parliament.[42] Three months later, following a sustained outbreak of street-fighting, Dollfuss announced a ban on the NSDAP, SA and SS, followed by the Nazi group within the Styrian *Heimwehr*, which was outlawed after it continued the campaign of localised violence. The German government retaliated by imposing a thousand-mark levy on German tourists entering Austria, in an attempt to undermine the latter's economy.[43]

The Austrian government abandoned the last pretence of democratic rule in May 1934 when it abolished all elected bodies and introduced

a corporate constitution. It is difficult to reconcile subsequent justifi-
cations for the destruction of democracy. If the chief purpose had been
to restrain Nazism, there is little doubt that Dollfuss and his government would have attempted to find a compromise with the SDAP, which
was still the largest political party in the country. Instead, following
advice from the Italian leader, Benito Mussolini, the attack on the
Socialists was intensified. Dollfuss had decided to fight a battle on two
fronts, against both socialism and Nazism, but in the first half of 1934
his focus was primarily on the SDAP. On 12 February 1934, police and
Heimwehr troops stormed SDAP buildings in Linz and Vienna, ostensibly in response to information they had uncovered about a planned
SDAP coup against the government. Martial law was declared and over
the course of the following two weeks, 131 civilians and 55 government
troops were killed, 21 Socialists were sentenced to death for 'rebellion'
and 9 actually executed. Many of the leading figures in the SDAP fled
into exile and those who lingered too long in the country were
imprisoned. The party was banned, along with its plethora of clubs and
societies and the Free Trade Union Federation, and all assets belonging
to the labour movement were seized. Dollfuss had chosen to consolidate
the power of his increasingly shaky coalition government by launching
a bloody attack on the largest opposition party at the very time that
the threat from Germany was intensifying. It was later, in May 1934,
that the government announced the new constitution establishing a
'social, Christian, German state, Austria, founded upon estates under
strong authoritarian leadership', in an attempt to construct an alternative
Austrian form of clerical fascism to counter the mounting internal threat
of Nazism.[44]

If the government had hoped to contain dissent by resorting to
authoritarianism, it failed. The opposition went underground. Sections
of the SDAP condemned their party's leadership for weakness and
turned to the Communists. Those who remained loyal to the party set
up the Revolutionary Socialists at the end of 1934 and mounted a campaign of armed resistance. But the main danger in the summer of 1934
came from the Nazis. In June and July they stepped up their campaign
to destabilise the country, supported by the government in Berlin.
While local groups planted bombs in railway stations, German planes
entered Austrian airspace and dropped millions of leaflets urging the
population to rise up against their government. The German radio
broadcast speeches inciting the Austrian army, police and civilians to
disobey orders, to refuse to pay taxes and to close savings accounts in
an attempt to set off a run on the Austrian banks. On 25 July 1934,
tactics changed from inciting rebellion to direct action. Nazi supporters

took to the streets in Graz and Salzburg, as a cohort of 154 members of the SS *Standarte 89* attempted to overthrow the national government in Vienna. The radio station in the capital was seized and lorries streamed into the government quarter, bringing in the armed SA paramilitaries, many dressed in Austrian army and police uniforms. The plan was to capture the entire government while the Cabinet was in session, but this backfired when a sweep revealed that only three Cabinet members had remained in the central government building. The Austrian Chancellor, Engelbert Dollfuss, who had stayed in his office, was shot and left to die.[45]

The putsch, it appears, had not been well planned. Within hours, the rebels realised that they had been disowned by the German government, which was unwilling or unable to deploy forces to support them, and they began to bargain for safe passage out of the country. Their actions had also provoked international condemnation: Austria's neighbours, particularly Italy, threatened to retaliate. Mussolini had been giving moral and financial encouragement to the Austrian government to abandon democracy in favour of corporatism as part of his plan to extend Italian influence in central Europe. He was not going to concede the country to Germany at the very moment that this had been achieved. On hearing of the murder of Dollfuss, who was not only a political ally, but also a personal friend, he moved 100,000 troops up to the Brenner Pass and the border with Carinthia and also let it be known that his soldiers would cross the border if the Austrians requested aid.[46] At this, the Yugoslav government deployed its soldiers on the Yugoslav-Austrian border to pre-empt an Italian invasion of Carinthia.[47]

In July 1934 both the Austrian government and the state survived, partly because Hitler was not yet ready to use force over the issue of unification, and partly because Mussolini, who still believed that Austria was within his sphere of interest, was willing to use force to protect that country's independence from Germany. It was not the last time that Austria's fate was to be determined by its geopolitical importance. But the putsch had revealed severe internal weaknesses, not least the substantial support that the Nazi Party enjoyed within Austria among some leading politicians, the police and the army. Nevertheless, at this point the new Chancellor, Schuschnigg, felt strong enough to take determined action. The promise of safe passage for the putschists, which had been witnessed by the German ambassador to Vienna, Kurt Rieth, was broken.[48] While leaving the chancellery 140 Nazis were arrested, 13 of whom were later hanged. Rintelen, the former governor of Styria and current Austrian ambassador to Rome, who had been named chancellor in Nazi radio broadcasts, was sentenced to thirty years in prison. In addition, the martyrdom of Dollfuss became a central theme in the political imagery of the Corporate State, symbolising heroism and piety – the putschists, it was reported, had left the diminutive Chancellor to bleed to death and had refused his plea for a priest to administer the last rites.[49]

The failure of the 1934 putsch led to a temporary but insecure reprieve for the Austrian government, for it depended largely on the continuing protection of Mussolini. By 1936, this support had evaporated as power relations between Italy and Germany shifted: in January Mussolini informed the German ambassador in Rome that he accepted that Austria was a German satellite. Six months later Schuschnigg signed the 'Gentlemen's Agreement' with Hitler. Although this included general statements in which each recognised the sovereignty of the other and Germany promised to refrain from intervening in Austrian domestic affairs, there were more worrying concessions: Austrian foreign policy would from then on mirror that of Germany, some twenty thousand persons being held by the Austrian authorities would be granted political amnesty and the German Nationalist Glaise-Horstenau was to be appointed as Austrian Minister without Portfolio (and was soon promoted to the post of Minister of Internal Affairs with control over law and order). A more ambiguous clause allowed the 'national opposition' to enjoy political representation: it later transpired that this referred to the Nazi Party in Austria, which remained formally illegal, but whose members were granted the right to freedom of conscience and to set up informal groupings. In return the German government removed the thousand-mark levy on its tourists visiting Austria.[50] But by this time the weakness of Austrian independence was glaringly obvious.

The Gentlemen's Agreement represented the major change in international politics which undermined Schuschnigg, but his regime also faced domestic problems. Austrian corporatism failed to unify the country between 1934 and 1938. The economy had recovered little since the depths of the international depression. Wages were low and although officially unemployment decreased by 100,000 between 1933 and 1937, this did not take into account changes in the legislation nor the fact that the long-term unemployed did not feature in unemployment figures. Figures for the consumption of foodstuffs show a decrease of 18 per cent between 1929 and 1934 and little change between 1934 and 1937, and the situation was yet more dire for the unemployed, for whom it fell by 31 per cent.[51] Politically, Nazism continued to thrive domestically and the international situation shifted, leaving the country increasingly vulnerable to German intervention. Moreover, one political movement which could have provided large-scale popular support for Austrian independence, the Socialist, had been decimated in 1934 and its successors, the Revolutionary Socialist, the Communists and the IFG, were all completely opposed to the Corporate State. Both the internal and the domestic situations had combined, resulting in the 'bloodless' demise of an independent Austria in March 1938.

The response of the Austrian people to the *Anschluss* is still a controversial subject, for Austrians have often been accused of failing to acknowledge their role in the Third Reich and of therefore abrogating any responsibility they may have had for the atrocities committed by it.[52] But the argument is not about moral responsibility and its abrogation alone, as important as these are. It also impinges on the very nature of post-war Austrian culture and consensus, for after the Second World War the 'victim' thesis was built into the new concept of Austrian national identity. According to successive political elites, Austria was not just a victim of Nazism, it was in fact the 'first victim of Hitlerite aggression'. Its people, they argued, had opposed Nazism in 1934 and had continued to oppose it thereafter, only to be sacrificed to Germany by international consent in 1938 in a futile exercise in appeasement. It was the people's shared experience of suffering endured under the yoke of the Third Reich that laid the foundations for the new culture of consensus and social harmony which emerged after the war. Repression bred consensus.

It has already been noted that a history of resistance in the Second World War added greater legitimacy to many of the newly liberated states of Europe and to their politicians. However, in Austria the 'victim' thesis came to lie at the very heart of the post-war political culture, and the notion that the Austrian people embraced the Third Reich in 1938 was irreconcilable with it. This was a dilemma which was clearly understood by Austria's immediate post-war political leaders. In 1946 (and with astounding alacrity in the circumstances) the new government published the *Red-White-Red-Book*.[53] The book is an extraordinary exercise in political propaganda, using newspaper clippings and official documents to advance what had swiftly become the official government line on the position of Austria and Austrians in the period from 1934 to 1945. The first volume, the only part that was translated into English, is subtitled *Descriptions, documents and proofs to the antecedents and history of the occupation of Austria from 'official sources'* and its underlying thesis is that in 1938 only a minority of Austrians had been committed Nazis, while the majority had been opposed to the *Anschluss*.[54] The chief culprits in the annexation were identified, obviously, as the Nazis who perpetrated the crime. More controversially, the Western Allies were also held responsible for condoning this first

exercise in German expansionism, by withdrawing Austria's membership of the League of Nations, closing their missions in Vienna and
transferring business to their Berlin embassies and missions. Austria
had been abandoned in the mistaken belief that this would satisfy
Hitler's imperial designs and ensure peace with the Third Reich.[55] The
Austrian people and their government were completely exonerated,
despite the absence of popular opposition to the *Anschluss* and the
failure of the Schuschnigg government's attempts to defend the country:
indeed, the main reason why Austrians themselves did not openly resist
the occupation of their country, the book argues, was that they realised
that such action would be futile without outside support.[56] This was
the first clear rendition of the wider 'victim thesis' whereby Austrians
ascribed to themselves the status of double victimhood, of being
subjected to foreign occupation and exploitation not just once in 1938,
but for a second time under the ten-year Allied occupation which
followed the end of the Second World War. Ironically, the genesis of
this very useful interpretation of the past was the statement issued by
the very same Allies in the Moscow Declaration of 1943 (which will
be discussed later). The victim thesis is still repeated in history books
to this day.[57]

Not even the compilers of the *Red-White-Red-Book* could find
evidence of either popular resistance or visible protest in Austria against
the arrival of the German army and its leader in 1938. It was indeed
difficult to ignore the contemporary film footage of the crowds on 14
March lining streets decorated with swastikas. But, as Kurt Tweraser
and Bruno Kreisky both point out, the impression that all Austrians
were in favour of the *Anschluss* is misleading.[58] Many Austrians had
much to fear from a Nazi takeover, not least the Jews, Communists,
Austrian patriots and many Socialists. The Revolutionary Socialists, the
underground Socialist movement whose member had been persecuted
by the Austrian government for over four years, printed leaflets urging
their supporters to vote in favour of Austrian independence in the
Schuschnigg plebiscite. They intended to distribute these on 12 March,
but hastily burned them when news came that Schuschnigg had resigned
and the plebiscite had been called off.[59] But, by 14 March, those people
who were opposed to the Nazis had become invisible. Some, fearing to
venture out onto the streets, stayed indoors and watched and waited.
Others turned to camouflage. One particularly poignant image is found
in the memoirs of George Clare, who was a young Viennese Jewish boy
of seventeen at the time. He recalled dressing in the Nazi garb of white
knee socks, a black raincoat and a Tyrolean hat in the days leading up
to the *Anschluss*, because 'looking like a Nazi as much as possible

instilled a feeling of toughness in oneself, and the more you looked and behaved and bore yourself as they did, the less likely were the Nazis to touch you'.[60]

As important as it may be to avoid over-estimating the support the Nazis had in Austria in 1938, it is also essential to avoid under-estimations. And yet a completely reliable figure is impossible to obtain, because there is no solid and objective evidence. Political statistics are of little use – political parties, including the Nazi Party, had been illegal or semi-legal for over four years and elections had been suspended for even longer. The last general election was held in 1930 before the Nazi Party adopted electoral politics. They had not put up candidates. The Nazi authorities did set up their own plebiscite on the *Anschluss* which took place on 13 April 1938, but although this was arranged with such speed that it is difficult to see how even the Nazi propaganda machine could have been fully operational in time to control the outcome, it was designed to validate the occupation and was neither free nor fair. Moreover, the resulting 99.7 per cent in favour of the *Anschluss* is more than suspicious.[61] There is, however, other circumstantial evidence in addition to contemporary reports which indicates that many, if not the majority of Austrians, did welcome the swift and apparently peaceful unification of their country with Germany. In the first place, the *Anschluss* was quickly endorsed by some very distinguished Austrians who represented different types of institutions and organisations. For instance, both the Protestant Church and the far more influential Catholic Church issued pastoral letters on the weekend of 12–13 March instructing their followers to 'thank God in their prayers on Sunday for the bloodless course taken by the great upheaval and to pray for a happy future for Austria'.[62] The Roman Catholic Church had considerable influence over the Austrian population, over 90 per cent of whom were classified as Roman Catholic, and it had also furnished as the spiritual ethos of the Corporate State. Nevertheless, church leaders did not openly oppose the *Anschluss*. They were not alone in this. Some former leaders of the Social Democratic Party appeared to concur. In a newspaper interview printed on 3 April one of them, Karl Renner, defended the unification of Germany and Austria, thereby rejecting the concept of a Danubian federation which he had supported hitherto. He referred throughout the interview to his position as a Social Democrat, as a defender of the right to national self-determination, as first Chancellor of the 1918 German Austrian Republic (the original title of the Austrian First Republic) and as the leader in 1918 of the Austrian peace delegation to St Germain, and concluded by saying that he would vote 'yes' in the coming plebiscite.[63] Renner's stance was to become highly significant in 1945 when he became the first Chancellor of the Austrian Second Republic, but in 1938 his political influence over his former comrades was probably limited. This was not the case with Otto Bauer, the popular intellectual leader of the party, who was then in exile. When SDAP members asked him after the event how they should have responded to the *Anschluss*, he replied ambiguously that 'our response to foreign rule over Austria by the satraps of the Reich cannot be the reactionary call for the restoration of Austria's independence, but can only be the revolutionary call for pan-German revolution'.[64] Although, as Foreign Minister in 1919, he had only reluctantly abandoned his dream of a united and Socialist Germany including Austria, his return to it twenty years later lacked much conviction. The Austrian Corporate State, he implied, had not been worth defending. Nevertheless, as Bruno Kreisky later commented, 'this amounted, in effect, to a sanctioning of *Anschluss*'.[65]

It is possible to interpret both the absence of protest and the utterances of leaders expressing fear or stoicism to mean that people chose to accept the inevitable and sought to minimise the danger of casualties. However, there is also convincing statistical evidence which suggests that many ordinary Austrians, and the young in particular, may have greeted the *Anschluss* with a greater sense of both optimism and confidence than they had felt for several years. This evidence comes from the registrations of marriages and births which show that between March 1938 and the early years of the Second World War the marriage rate and subsequent birth rate for Austrians soared.[66] The explanation given at the time was that people were responding to the *Führer's* call to produce soldiers for the Reich, yet this was not the response of a people cowed by fear of an occupying power, but, rather, a strong indication that many who had delayed starting a family under the Corporate State felt able to do so very soon after they had become part of the Third Reich. This, coupled with the eyewitness accounts, the film footage and the lack of open opposition, suggests that there was a great deal of relief consequent upon, and support within Austria for, the absorption of the country into the German Reich.

The scene that opened this chapter, the orgy of violence which broke out on the streets of Vienna on the evening of 11 March, relates to the most unedifying response to the 1938 Nazi take-over in Austria, namely a popular, aggressive and spontaneous anti-Semitism which anticipated *Kristallnacht*, the orchestrated pogrom against Jews and their property which was unleashed across the Third Reich the following September. Within hours of the capitulation of the Austrian government, thousands of Viennese men and women took to the streets, attacking Jews, their homes, businesses and places of worship. Storm troopers and ordinary citizens swarmed through the inner city and the Jewish districts, dragging suspected Jewish passengers from taxis and families from their homes and beating them, looting shops and flats in a frenzied outburst of brutality. That night a torchlit procession marched through the second district, Leopoldstadt, the centre of Jewish life in the city, and drew in a braying mob of 80,000 to 100,000 people.[67] Over the course of the next few days entire department stores were looted and synagogues were desecrated, their sacred Torah scrolls defiled and burned. Men wearing makeshift Nazi armbands entered Jewish flats, demanding anything of value, including money, jewellery, and even furniture. But the outburst was not confined to inanimate objects. Men were dragged out of their flats, some never to return. Jews who tried to flee were not spared: the overnight train to Prague, which seemed to offer the last hope of safety, was prevented from leaving the eastern railway terminus. Some passengers were taken away and those who were spared were robbed before the train finally departed. A short time later the train was stopped and a fresh contingent of Nazis repeated the onslaught. When the train finally reached the Czech border, those on board were told that all Austrian passport holders were to be sent back to Vienna: the border was closed, and so too were all the other borders with neighbouring countries. The next day the brutality became more ritualised as Jewish men, women and children were seized from their homes and forced to scrub the streets with acid-based solutions to remove painted slogans proclaiming Austrian independence, or made to clean toilets, sometimes using the armstraps of their phylacteries as cloths.[68]

The Austrian pogrom of March 1938 was not confined to Vienna, although, with 92 per cent of Austrian Jews living in the capital, this was where the greatest violence occurred. Nor was it co-ordinated or pre-planned. The attacks were spontaneous and their perpetrators were indigenous – Austrians not Germans; it is said that the ferocity of the Viennese mob offended even the sensitivities of the newly appointed Nazi Reich Commissioner, Joseph Bürckel.[69] But Bürckel had other reasons to be concerned, for the outburst of anti-Semitism was accompanied by a dangerous outbreak of 'wild Aryanisation', with unauthorised, self-appointed 'commissars' seizing Jewish property in the name of the Aryan race. This threatened to undermine the Nazi regime's own plans to confiscate Jewish assets, a step which it had not yet taken in Germany proper. In the face of these random expropriations, which he had earlier called 'theft', and in order to bring further 'Aryanisation' under the control of the Reich, Bürckel had no choice but to endorse the seizures by the 'wild Commissars'. The only other alternative, to demand that all appropriated Jewish property be handed over to the state, would have been impractical and highly unpopular. Gerhard Botz, Hans Safrian and Hans Witek argue that the events in Vienna in March 1938 established an 'Austrian model' for the Aryanisation of property and accelerated its introduction throughout the Reich.[70] Botz also insists that Viennese popular anti-Semitism, which has a long history, was not just racially or ideologically based. It also, he asserts, had social and economic roots which fed on envy of the size and relative wealth of Viennese Jewry and, in particular, its members' success in bourgeois occupations and professions. As a consequence, Viennese anti-Semites 'were of the opinion, and not without justification, that harassing the Jews would bring them collective benefits'.[71] The *Anschluss* gave those who held such views the opportunity to put them into action. The events of 11 March 1938 showed that anti-Semitism was a popular policy in Vienna and one which fuelled support for the Nazi regime.

As will be shown in later chapters, the 'victim thesis' was to become one of the central tenets of post-war Austrian ideology. The new principles of consensus and harmony promoted a strong and sustained sense of national identity in the post-war years in a country which had been deeply divided in the inter-war years. But the 'victim thesis' rests on a myth that Austria was occupied in 1938 against the wishes of its inhabitants, that its people opposed the incorporation of their country into the Third Reich, and that they were therefore the 'first victims of Hitlerite aggression'. This argument is irreconcilable with the response of large numbers of Austrians to the *Anschluss* as well as the absence of resistance for much of the war years and the role which Austrians were to play in the Nazi war machine. There is strong evidence from March 1938 to show that many Austrians endorsed at least some of the more rabid aspects of Nazism. Some were so opposed that they saw no point in living: the suicide rate among the Jewish intelligentsia soared in the first year of the *Anschluss*.[72] The attitude of non-Jewish workers is far more difficult to assess. Workers were not totally immune to anti-Semitism and, although Gedye stressed the petty-bourgeois character of the mob, there must also have been some workers in its midst.[73] Even the leaders of the clandestine Socialist workers' movement, the Revolutionary Socialists and the Illegal Free Trade Unions, hesitated, refusing to support the existing Austrian government unequivocally. Their reasons were clear – they were deeply suspicious of a regime which had attacked their movement and persecuted its members. But the political rift was a deep one for both sides – it was only at the midnight hour that Schuschnigg relented and agreed to meet the delegation of shop stewards which he knew would include Socialists. By the time the two sides had come to a qualified agreement, it was too late and the Nazis had taken over Austria. The lack of unity in 1938, indeed throughout the preceding two decades, would haunt political leaders after the war and convince them of the need to maintain consensus in the face of occupation.

Notes

1 G.E.R. Gedye, *Fallen Bastions: The Central European Tragedy* (London: Victor Gollancz, 1939), 295.

2 'An diesem Abend brach die Hölle los. Die Unterwelt hatte ihre Pforten aufgetan und ihre niedrigsten, scheusslichsten, unreinsten Geister losgelassen'. 'Hans Safrian and Hans Witek (eds), *Und keiner war dabei: Dokumente des alltäglichen Antisemitismus in Wien 1938* (Vienna: Picus Verlag, 1988), 19.

3 Military order, *Aufmarschanweisung für die 8. Armee, 10.3.1938*, reprinted in Heinz Arnberger, Winfried Garscha and Christa Mitterrutzner (eds), *'Anschluss' 1938: Eine Dokumentation* (Vienna: Österreichischer Bundesverlag, 1988), 302–4.

4 Evan Burr Bukey, *Hitler's Austria: Popular Sentiment in the Nazi Era, 1938–1945* (Chapel Hill, NC: University of North Carolina Press, 2000), 28–9.

5 'Es liegt in unserem Interesse, daß das ganze Unternehmen ohne Anwendung von Gewalt in Form eines von der Bevölkerung begrüßten friedlichen Einmarsches vor sich geht.' Arnberger *et al.*, *'Anschluss' 1938*, 309.

6 'so ist er mit größter Rücksichtslosigkeit durch Waffengewalt zu brechen', Befehl Hitlers für den bewaffneten Einmarsch in Österreich *(Weisung Nr.1), 11.3.1938*. Arnberger *et al.*, *'Anschluss' 1938*, 310.

7 Evan Burr Bukey, *Hitler's Home Town: Linz, Austria* (Bloomington, IN: Indiana University Press 1986), 167–70; www.linz.at/archiv/nationalsoz/ekapitel3.htm; *Ansprache Adolf Hitlers in Linz, 12.3.1938* reprinted in Arnberger *et al.*, *'Anschluss' 1938*, 329–30.

8 Bukey, *Hitler's Austria*, 29; George Clare, *Last Waltz in Vienna: The Destruction of a Family, 1842–1942* (London: Macmillan, 1981), 189.

9 *Hitler's Mein Kampf*, with an introduction by D. C.Watts (London: Hutchinson, 1969), 63–115.

10 Gedye, *Fallen Bastions*, 314–18.

11 Gedye, *Fallen Bastions*, 314; Bukey, *Hitler's Austria*, 30.

12 Clare, *Last Waltz in Vienna*, 195–6.

13 Bukey, *Hitler's Austria*, 31.

14 *Documents on German Foreign Policy 1918–1945*, Series D (1937–1945), vol. I (London: HMSO, 1949), 513. Protocol of the Conference of 12 February 1938.

15 Gulick reported rumours that Hitler had pulled off a 'masterly touch' by extending his demands for amnesty to cover the Austrian Socialists, but could find no evidence of this. Charles A. Gulick, *Austria from Habsburg to Hitler*, vol. 2, *Fascism's subversion of democracy* (Berkeley, CA: University of California Press, 1948), 1789.

16   Gedye, *Fallen Bastions*, 242. Hitler was referring to Austrians and to the German minority in Czechoslovakia, the Sudeten Germans. He described both as having formed part of the German state before 1867. In reality there had been no German state before 1867, when both peoples were part of the Habsburg Empire.
17   Gedye, *Fallen Bastions*, 250. Gedye was in the press gallery when Schuschnigg made this speech. 'Red-White-Red' are the national colours of Austria; Arnberger *et al.*, *'Anschluss' 1938*, 194.
18   Otto Leichter, *Österreichs Freie Gewerkschaften im Untergrund* (Vienna: Europa Verlag, 1963), 121.
19   Gedye, *Fallen Bastions*, 277; Kurt Schuschnigg, *Austrian Requiem* (London: Victor Gollancz, 1947).
20   Gulick, *Austria from Habsburg to Hitler*, 1585; Fritz Klenner, *Die Österreichischen Gewerkschaften von 1928 bis 1953*, vol. 2 (Vienna: Verlag des Österreichischen Gewerkschaftsbundes, 1953), 1163.
21   The Revolutionary Socialist party was originally just one of several Socialist groups to emerge after the Austrian Social Democratic Party was banned in 1934. By the end of 1934 it had incorporated all those which had not gone over to the Communists. Gulick, *Austria from Habsburg to Hitler*, 1577.
22   Gulick, *Austria from Habsburg to Hitler*, 1811; Joseph Buttinger, *In the Twilight of Socialism: A History of Revolutionary Socialists in Austria* (London: Weidenfeld and Nicolson, 1953), 458.
23   Gulick, *Austria from Habsburg to Hitler*, 1812.
24   Hillegeist was the main intermediary between the IFG and the EG. Buttinger, *In the Twilight of Socialism*, 449; Leichter, *Österreichs Freie Gewerkschaften im Untergrund*, 122.
25   Schuschnigg, *Austrian Requiem*, 295.
26   Leichter, *Österreichs Freie Gewerkschaften*, 122; Gedye, *Fallen Bastions*, 262.
27   Gedye, *Fallen Bastions*, 265–8. Gedye was present at this meeting.
28   Karl Stadler, *Austria* (London: E. Benn, 1982), 110.
29   Gulick, *Austria from Habsburg to Hitler*, 1427.
30   Timothy Kirk, *Nazism and the Working Class in Austria* (Cambridge: Cambridge University Press, 1996), 31.
31   As it was, unemployment in the *Ostmark* fell from 401,001 in January 1938 to 99,865 in September 1938. Gerhard Botz, *Der Nationalsozialismus in Wien. Machtübernahme und Herrschaftssicherung 1938/39* (3rd edn, Vienna: Buchloe, 1988), 301.
32   In 1934 the population of Graz was 152,841, Linz 108,970, Innsbruck 61,005 and Salzburg 40,232. *Die Ergebnisse der österreichischen Volkszählung vom 22. März 1934* (Vienna: verlag der osterreichischen Staatsdruckerei, 1935), 32.
33   Jill Lewis, 'Red Vienna: Socialism in one city, 1918–1927', *European Studies Review* (1983), 335–55.
34   Gedye, *Fallen Bastions*, 26–38. Gedye was an eyewitness to these events.
35   Jill Lewis, *Fascism and the Working Class in Austria* (Oxford: Berg, 1991), 122–46.
36   *Ibid.*, ch. 9; Kirk, *Nazism and the Working Class in Austria*, 31.
37   Gulick, *Austria from Habsburg to Hitler*, 978.

38 *Ibid.*, 1016–26.
39 Schuschnigg wrote in 1947 that 'Throughout 1933 the fight in Austria was directed exclusively against the nazis.' 'Austrian Apologia', published in *The Commonwealth*, vol. XLV (4 April 1947), 608, reprinted in Gulick, *Austria from Habsburg to Hitler*, 1857, fn. 276.
40 Lewis, *Fascism and the Working Class in Austria*, 189.
41 In the elections of April 1932 the Nazis won 210,365 votes and 15 seats on the Viennese provincial assembly, the SDAP won 682,323 votes and 66 seats, and the Christian Social Party won 233,622 votes and 19 seats. In Salzburg the NSDAP won 6 seats, the SDAP won 8 seats and the Christian Social Party won 12 seats. In Lower Austria the NSDAP won 8 seats, the SDAP won 8 seats and the Christian Social Party won 20 seats. The government banned all local and provincial elections in May 1933. Christine Klusacek and Kurt Stimmer (eds), *Dokumentation zur österreichischen Zeitgeschichte 1928–1933* (Vienna: Jugend und Volk, 1982), 203–5.
42 Gulick, *Austria from Habsburg to Hitler*, 1026.
43 Klusacek and Stimmer, *Dokumentation zur österreichischen Zeitgeschichte*, 263–9; Gulick, *Austria from Habsburg to Hitler*, 1082.
44 Jill Lewis, 'Conservatives and Fascists in Austria', in Martin Blinkhorn (ed.), *Fascists and Conservatives: The Radical Right and the Establishment in Twentieth Century Europe* (London: Unwin Hyman, 1990); Tim Kirk, 'Fascism and Austrofascism', in Günther Bischof, Anton Pelinka and Alexander Lassner (eds), *The Dollfuss/Schuschnigg Era in Austria: A Reassessment* (New Brunswick, NJ: Transaction, 2003), 22–4.
45 Gedye, *Fallen Bastions*, 121–6. Jürgen Gehl, *Austria, Germany and the Anschluss, 1931–38* (Oxford: Oxford University Press, 1963), 97.
46 Mussolini had instigated negotiations to establish an Italian–Hungarian–Austrian customs union in March 1934, which were scuppered by the German government which made a pre-emptive agreement with Hungary. Gehl, *Austria, Germany and the Anschluss*, 84–7. Dollfuss's family was staying with Mussolini at the time of the assassination.
47 Gehl, *Austria, Germany and the Anschluss*, 100.
48 According to Gehl, Hitler had not been fully informed about the putsch and threatened to arrest those involved if they tried to cross into Germany. He reacted in fury to news that Rieth had agreed to witness the negotiations between the Nazi putschists and the Austrian government, recalling him immediately and appointing von Papen as ambassador to Vienna on 26 July. Gehl, *Austria, Germany and the Anschluss*, 9.
49 Gedye, *Fallen Bastions*, 135.
50 *Documents on German Foreign Policy, 1918–1945*, Series C, vol. IV (London: HMSO, 1962), document 485; Series C, vol. V (London: HMSO, 1966), 755–60; Series D, vol. I, documents 160 and 168.
51 Gulick, *Austria from Habsburg to Hitler*, 1806–8.
52 Hella Pick, *Guilty Victim: Austria from the Holocaust to Haider* (London: I. B. Taurus, 2000).
53 See Introduction to this volume, 1–7.

54 *Rot-Weiss-Rot-Buch*, 70.
55 The American government argued that it had accepted the annexation of Austria *de facto*, but not *de jure*. Robert H. Keyserlingk, *Austria in World War II* (Montreal: McGill-Queens University Press, 1988), 16.
56 *Rot-Weiss-Rot-Buch*, 69–72.
57 Gottfried Karl Kindermann, *Hitler's Defeat in Austria. Europe's first Containment of Nazi Expansionism* (London: Hurst, 1988).
58 Matthew Paul Berg, Jill Lewis and Oliver Rathkollo (eds), *The Struggle for a Democratic Austria. Bruno Kreisky on Peace and Social Justice* (New York and Oxford: Berghahn, 2000), 161.
59 Otto Leichter, *Zwischen zwei Diktaturen* (Vienna: Europa Verlag, 1968), 397.
60 Clare, *Last Waltz in Vienna*, 173.
61 Bukey, *Hitler's Austria*, 33.
62 Bukey, *Hitler's Austria*, 29.
63 *Neues Wiener Tagblatt* (3 April 1938). It is reprinted in Arnberger *et al.*, '*Anschluss' 1938. Eine Dokumentation*, 467. There has never been an adequate explanation of Renner's interview, although after the war SPÖ politicians let it be known that he had been trying to negotiate the release of Robert Danneberg, the former director of finance for Red Vienna. Gerhard Botz, *Wien vom Anschluß zum Krieg* (Vienna: Jugend und Volk, 1978), 139–45. The *Auslandsbüro österreichischer Sozialdemokraten* (Brünn) issued a statement in 1938 suggesting that Renner and his family had been threatened. Josef Buttinger, the leader of the Revolutionary Socialists, believed that Renner endorsed the *Anschluss* in order to retain his freedom. Renner lived 'in retirement' in Lower Austria throughout the war. Buttinger, *In the Twilight of Socialism*, 487.
64 Buttinger, who met Bauer in Brünn on 11 March, says that Bauer was insisting then that 'nothing but strong, heroic resistance by the Austrian people themselves can arouse public opinion all over the world and thus compel the democratic nations to help'. Buttinger, *In the Twilight of Socialism*, 442.
65 Berg *et al.*, *The Struggle for a Democratic Austria*, 20.
66 Franz Mathis, 'The Austrian Economy: Basic Features and Trends', in Rolf Steininger, Günter Bischof and Michael Gehler (eds), *Austria in the Twentieth Century* (New Brunswick/London: Transaction, 2002), 228; *ÖGB Tätigkeitsbericht 1951*, 61. *Bericht des Jugendreferates KONIR:* '1938 plus 14 ist 1952. 1938 ist auf Befehl des grossen Führers die Schaffung der neuen Armeen angegangen worden. 1938, 1939 und in den folgenden Jahren haben wir doppelt so viele Kinder geboren als sonst. Diese Jahrgänge kommen jetzt aus den Schulen.' This youth delegate to the 1951 trade union conference argued that the rise in the Austrian birth rate was in response to Hitler's command to produce children for the army. The birth rate fell in the spring of 1943, following the German defeat at Stalingrad. Kirk, *Nazism and the Working Class in Austria*, 169, fn. 93.
67 Gedye, *Fallen Bastions*, 296. This account of the night of 11 March remains one of the most harrowing and detailed.
68 Safrian and Witek, *Und keiner war dabei. Dokumente des alltäglichen Anti-Semitismus in Wien 1938*, 19–38; Clare, *Last Waltz in Vienna*, 190–2; Gedye, *Fallen Bastions*, 300–11.

69 Jonny Moser, 'Österreichs Juden unter der NS-Herrschaft', in Emmerich Tálos, Ernst Hanisch and Wolfgang Neugebauer (eds), *NS-Herrschaft in Österreich 1938–1945* (Vienna: Verlag für Gesellschaftskritik, 1988), 187.

70 Botz, *Nationalsozialismus in Wien*, 480; Safrian and Witek, *Und keiner war dabei*, 19–38; Hans Witek, '"Arisierungen" in Wien. Aspekte national-sozialistischer Enteignungspolitik 1938–1940', in Tálos, Hanisch and Neugebauer (eds), *NS-Herrschaft in Österreich 1938–1945*, 199–216.

71 Gerhard Botz, 'The Jews of Vienna from the *Anschluss* to the Holocaust', in Ivaar Oxaal, Michael Pollak and Gerhard Botz (eds), *Jews, Anti-Semitism and Culture in Vienna* (London: Routledge and Kegan Paul, 1987), 187. Botz goes so far as to argue that anti-Semitism was used as a substitute for social policy in particular in relation to housing.

72 Moser, 'Österreichs Juden unter der NS-Herrschaft', 189; Bukey, *Hitler's Austria*, 142.

73 Gedye, *Fallen Bastions*, 318; Bukey, *Hitler's Austria*, 136–8.

2

1945: liberation

Many Austrians spent the early war years under the mistaken belief that their country would be spared the devastation of air attack by the Allies, thanks to the representations made on their behalf by the son of the last Emperor of Austria-Hungary, Otto von Habsburg, to the western leaders.[1] This romantic fiction was shattered on 15 December 1943, when American bombers began a sustained attack on Innsbruck, but it may well have lasted longer in Vienna, where the first bombs did not fall until September 1944. Towards the end of that year there were clear signs in the Alpine and Danubian *Gaue*[2] that morale was deteriorating into a general mood of gloom and despondency. Nazi Security Service (*Sicherheitsdienst* – SD) reports described a climate of scepticism and dejection, which was attributed to growing pessimism about the outcome of the war and dwindling faith in the possibility of German victory. The atmosphere of gloom intensified throughout that winter as news spread of Russian victories in Hungary and of Yugoslav partisan raids across the southern border.[3] The number of American bombing raids increased, culminating in massive attacks on central and eastern Austria at the beginning of March: on the anniversary of the *Anschluss*, 12 March 1945, exactly seven years after German troops had first marched into Austria, 1667 tons of bombs fell on Vienna, targeting working-class industrial areas and the inner city.[4] The opera, that symbol of Viennese pride and culture, took a direct hit. At the same time as the buildings were falling, SD reports indicated that these final and sustained attacks had destroyed the last remaining vestiges of support for the war in the city and that civilian morale had collapsed. Rations were dwindling and, according to the diary of Josef Schöner, a young former Austrian diplomat and son of wealthy restaurant-owners, who had spent the later war years working in Vienna in the Army Headquarters Administration (*Heeresstandortverwaltung*), political apathy and fear had taken hold.[5] Each day at noon the shrill screams of air-raid sirens began and continued almost incessantly until nightfall, jarring the already badly frayed nerves of the city's inhabitants. Official reports of a German counter-offensive against the advancing Red Army in Hungary failed to lift spirits. Almost no one believed them. Nazi officials noted mounting hostility and even outright, if limited, rebellion. 'This mood of pessimism presents fertile soil for enemy propaganda. Slogans on walls, leaflets, etc. are being used. After heavy air attacks army and party aid groups have been publicly abused and even attacked ... The antagonism and campaign of slander against *Altreichsdeutsche* [citizens of pre-1938 Germany] ... are constantly increasing.'[6] An SD report written in early March 1945 commented on the growing number of incidents in working-class districts where officers and Party officials were verbally insulted, even, it was pointed out, by women. One officer complained that he was no longer able to walk the streets of his own district without holding his pistol drawn and cocked.[7]

By the end of March there were fewer American air attacks, but more Russian bombing raids from the east. On 29 March rumours began to circulate that the Red Army's Third Ukrainian Front led by Marshal Tolbukhin had broken through the German lines in Hungary and had crossed the border, moving up from Koszeg to take Klostermarienberg in Burgenland.[8] For the first time Allied troops were reported to be on Austrian soil, just eighty kilometres east of Vienna. Martial law was declared in Vienna on 30 March. When news of the Russian advance was confirmed fear mounted, fuelled by years of propaganda about Russian Communism and more recent stories of atrocities on the Eastern Front, of convents in which all the nuns had been raped and of German soldiers who had had their tongues cut out.[9] Optimists continued to believe that the Americans were about to arrive and some people sought solace in the hope that the Soviet troops would march south to Graz to join up with Tito's army, thus sparing Vienna, but most people knew that the city was about to fall to the Russians. No one rejoiced. On 6 April, having marched north from Burgenland and taken Wiener Neustadt on 1 April, units of Tolbukhin's force reached the southern and eastern outskirts of Vienna.[10]

Even at this late stage preparations for the defence of Vienna were in chaos. The official position was that the city was to be defended to the last house. Months earlier, at the end of 1944, word had spread on the streets that the government had drawn up emergency plans for mass evacuation which were to be put into operation if it looked as though the city was about to fall. Heinrich Himmler, the head of the SS, had responded immediately by issuing orders that anyone who was heard to be even discussing such a proposition would be arrested on the grounds that the very mention of evacuation was defeatist. Rather than boosting morale and allaying fears, this move had instead reinforced the popular belief that Vienna and its people were to be sacrificed in some futile final gesture of defiance.[11] In January 1945 this apprehension was confirmed when the Berlin government issued a *Führerbefehl* (Hitler decree) designating Vienna a *Festung* (a fortress) to be defended to the very end using all means available, including the army, police, air-force, the Party defence militia (*Volkssturm*) and the civilian population. And yet, despite this apparently resolute public stance, there still existed no specific plans to defend the city; privately many Nazi officials were expressing doubts that any plan could actually succeed. In addition, there was discord in government: as late as 2 April the civilian and military authorities were still arguing about which of them was in charge of the overall defence of the city.[12] In a last-minute effort to create some form of co-ordinated defence, the *Gauleiter* of Vienna, Baldur von Schirach, finally issued orders to conscript all men between the ages of sixteen and sixty and to direct them to build improvised fortifications in the south of the city. Older schoolchildren were ordered to join trench-digging gangs in the outer districts. But when the order was issued, few turned out. Indeed, attendance at school had been slack for several weeks, with many pupils visiting their schools only briefly to pick up vitamins or homework. The response of the children was indicative of a growing attitude of non-compliance in the city. When martial law was declared and there was talk that the Hitler Youth would be called upon to fight in defence of the city, some Viennese mothers threatened to demonstrate.[13] There are also reports that, in what were now obviously the final days of the war and in the privacy of the home, one of the most common topics of conversation was what to do next – was it better to pack a few belongings and try to flee to the west before Russian troops set foot in the city, and so almost certainly lose home and property, or to risk the uncertainty of life under occupation, and pray that the lurid reports of rape and looting were just more examples of Nazi propaganda?[14] These were clear signs that Nazi control of Vienna had finally broken.

In the event, there was no civilian defence of Vienna. Instead, confusion reigned. On 30 March, the same day that he declared martial law, Schirach also ordered the evacuation of women and children from the southern and eastern working-class districts of Favoriten and Simmering, which lay directly in the path of the Soviet advance to other parts of the city. All private transport was confined within the city limits.[15] On 2 April, as fighting between Russian and German troops was raging beyond the city boundaries and the situation had become yet more dire, posters suddenly appeared ordering all women and children to leave the area immediately. The order was issued without prior planning, and it was, to all intents and purposes, meaningless, for there was no mention of where these evacuees were to go, nor, indeed, how they were to get there. When a crowd of people attempted to leave by train from the western railway terminus, they found that orders had been given to allow only women with children and those with official written authorisation to get on the few trains which were still running.[16]

On 5 April Schirach left Vienna, having first ordered the 6th SS *Panzerarmee* (tank corps) and the 17th Infantry Division to defend the city. The following day the Third Ukrainian Front, led by Marshal Tolbukhin, attacked Vienna from the south, and the Second Ukrainian Front under the command of Marshal Malinovsky moved up from Hungary in the east to the northern bank of the Danube.[17] They encountered fierce German military resistance on the outskirts of the city: one estimate suggests that 38,661 Red Army soldiers and 19,000 German soldiers were killed in the battle for Vienna.[18] As fighting continued in the outer districts, life in the city centre became unpredictable and frenzied. Goods which had been in short supply for weeks suddenly reappeared on the streets. Wine and meat were once again on sale, as farmers slaughtered cattle and wine growers emptied their cellars before the Russians arrived. Shoes could be bought without coupons and often without money, for what use would *Reichsmarks* be under the occupation? In fact, barter became the preferred system of exchange as most street sellers sought to swap their wares for other usable goods.[19] Some goods came free. Crowds flocked to the Stift barracks in the centre of the city when news broke that its stores of food, blankets and soap were being thrown open to all comers. No one asked whether or not this had been authorised because by this time there did not appear to be any form of authority in the city. German soldiers had disappeared and Nazi officials were burning their papers and their party uniforms. Communications with the outlying districts had broken down and there was no awareness of the ferocity of the battles that were taking place there. Writing his diary in the centre of Vienna, Schöner made little reference to the fighting in the suburbs and even recorded that, despite the certainty of imminent defeat, or perhaps because of it, the mood of the people seemed to improve when it became obvious that there would be no large-scale defence of the city. On the other hand, there was no spirit of solidarity either – fierce arguments broke out in the cellar-cum-air raid shelters over who was entitled to what space. Newcomers were unwelcome and ran the risk of forcible eviction.[20]

In contrast to the fifty-one-day siege of Budapest, the battle for Vienna lasted for only eight days, with the main fighting taking place along the banks of the Danube, north of the city centre.[21] The last clashes occurred on 14 April. Opinions vary as to why Vienna fell so rapidly. One explanation, which is to be found in the popular history of the Second Republic by Portisch and Riff, is that the Austrian resistance eased the entrance of the Soviets into Vienna. According to this account, Carl Szokoll, a major in the German Army and a member of the Austrian resistance group O5, made contact with the Soviet military commanders as they were camped in the small village of Hochwolkersdorf, near Semmering, on 2 April and offered to help capture Vienna with minimum resistance.[22] His envoy, Ferdinand Käs, urged the Russian command to lift their bombardment of Vienna and protect the city's water supply system, in order to ensure that the return to normal life would be as swift as possible after the fall of the city.[23] The story, which featured prominently in the Austrian government's *Red-White-Red-Book*, emphasizes the role which Austrians themselves were said to have played in their own liberation. But the O5 group, an alliance of diverse local resistance units which included Communists, had only existed for four months and its resources were limited. Although it was later to become a focal point in the Austrian memory of the liberation, it is difficult to see it playing more than a peripheral role in April 1945, and reports of the early relations between the local resistance and the Soviet authorities support this view.[24]

On the morning of 10 April, Red Army troops appeared on the streets of Vienna's First District, the inner city, where they were met by wary onlookers who were crammed into the doorways of buildings, unsure of what to expect. Most accounts of these early encounters between the Viennese and the Russian enemy emphasize the relief which was felt, at least by the Viennese. The first Soviet soldiers to enter the city were unkempt and seemed to lack even a basic uniform, but, although their officers were reserved, the soldiers were visibly friendly and made efforts to communicate with people on the street. Initially there was no violence and each side viewed the other with curiosity.[25] That same day Russian soldiers went from house to house asking if there were German soldiers in hiding, but without bothering to search. The distinction that was apparently being made between Germans and Austrians was not lost on many Viennese – the value of a specifically Austrian identity had never been as high and its significance was to grow over the following months and years.

There was widespread anxiety that the arrival of the Russians would be followed by violence and theft, but in these first hours of Allied occupation such fears seemed to be unfounded. The relief was short-lived. Vienna was still on the front line and had been occupied by enemy troops whose own territory had been invaded and whose people had been subjected to appalling violence by the German *Wehrmacht*. But when looting did break out, it was civilians, both local people and foreign workers, who initially took advantage of the situation when all vestiges of Nazi authority had disappeared and the occupiers had not yet had time to establish their own form of order. In the chaos of that first day, shops on the Mariahilferstrasse, one of Vienna's main shopping streets, were ransacked and general pillaging began. To his disgust, the first incident which Schöner witnessed was an attack on Herzmanzky's, Vienna's largest department store, which was carried out by ordinary Viennese men and women, who clambered through the broken windows and grabbed suits and dresses before breaking into clothing and shoe shops nearby. He commented wryly that a bolt of satin was left lying in the gutter – presumably no one had any use for it.[26] During that day more stores were ransacked and food shops were emptied. Six years of rationing had ended in a frenzy of looting. As Evan Bukey observes, there was something familiar about this behaviour – it mirrored events which had followed the arrival of German troops in March 1938, when Herzmanzky's had also been one of the first targets: 'In Vienna Anschluss ended as it had begun: in an orgy of spontaneous looting and random theft.'[27]

That night and the following day it became clear that the first impressions given by the Russians were misleading. Red Army soldiers began to stop people on the streets and demand any valuables. Watches were a prized trophy, seized from passers-by who were foolish enough to wear them: the Viennese soon dubbed their liberators 'Uris', after the German word for watch. More seriously, Soviet house-to-house searches degenerated into drunken looting forays, this time carried out by the occupying troops. Flats were searched and ransacked and valuables removed, along with any food and alcohol which had not been cleverly enough hidden. But value is relative: anything which was of use was taken – in Schöner's own case his wife's linen was later stolen, while her silver was left behind. Like the bolt of satin, it was of no practical use.[28] The Russians were sometimes guided towards their booty by local people or foreign workers who knew where best to look and who would then attempt to grab a share of the loot.[29] Schöner recounts returning to his family's main restaurant that day to find that soldiers had turned up in a lorry and driven away with the store of schnapps and sparkling wine. Two Viennese men stood in the street and watched. They had come to the restaurant earlier to demand wine,

had been refused and had then led the Russians to the site.[30] There
were also signs that local vendettas played a role when the Russians
turned their attention to the identification of Nazi Party members: those
Nazis who did not have a history of antagonising their neighbours
were, for the time being, left alone, while the first homes to be targeted
belonged to unpopular Nazis who were often denounced by their
neighbours.[31] It was on the second day of the Russian occupation that
Schöner first heard stories of rapes from one of the restaurant's cooks,
who had managed to walk into the city from the outlying district of
Oberlaa. 'The subject of rape', he wrote, 'which before and right at the
beginning of the occupation we simply dismissed as German propaganda, is looming in real earnest', particularly in the suburbs and in
homes in which soldiers were billeted.[32] Soviet officers were said to have
laughed off complaints about attacks on Austrian women, blaming
them on the long sexual abstinence their troops had endured on the
front line. But, as we see shall later, rape, looting and hunger were to
become the enduring central images in the Viennese memory of the first
four months of liberation and also of the Russian occupation in general,
and this would have a profound and long-lasting influence on Austrian
politics.

The attitude of the Soviet 'liberators' was in fact becoming increasingly contradictory. While Red Army troops had begun to behave like
a conquering army, it seemed that the policy of the Soviet military
authorities and therefore of the Kremlin itself was to treat Austrians
with relative leniency. The earliest sign of this has already been mentioned: during house-to-house searches on the first day of the liberation
Soviet soldiers had distinguished between German and Austrian soldiers.
It soon became evident that this was the official Soviet position. Within
hours posters had been plastered to walls and leaflets were being handed
out, all bearing a proclamation signed by the Soviet commanders. This
declared that the Red Army had come to Austria as a liberator, not as
a conqueror.[33] Its fight was with the German-fascist occupiers, not the
Austrian people:

> The Red Army bases itself upon the Allied Powers' Moscow Declaration
> of October 1943 concerning the independence of Austria. The Red Army
> will contribute to the restoration of the state of affairs which obtained
> in Austria prior to the year 1938.
>   The Moscow Declaration, issued by the governments of the Soviet
> Union, Great Britain and the USA, declared these countries' desire 'to see
> a free and independent Austria restored, thus enabling the Austrian people
> themselves to achieve that political and economic security which is the
> sole foundation of enduring peace'. The Declaration adds: 'Austria is

reminded, however, that she has a responsibility which she cannot evade for participation in the war on the side of Hitlerite Germany, and that in the final settlement account will inevitably be taken of her own contribution to her liberation.'

In accordance with the terms of this Declaration, the Red Army is in conflict with the German occupiers, but not with the population of Austria. The Red Army entered Austria not as an army of conquest, but as one of liberation.[34]

It is interesting to note that one year later, when the Austrian government published its own version of this proclamation, the reference to Austrian responsibility was omitted.[35] The original proclamation went on to order all civilians to return to their normal work and to co-operate fully with the Soviet troops in establishing law and order, and in the search for Nazi spies and agents. It ended with the assurance that the civil and property rights of Austrian citizens, private companies and associations would be respected.[36]

If the Soviet proclamation was greeted with disbelief by many who looked around and saw the increasingly rapacious looting of the city and its surrounding countryside, the reference to the eighteen-month-old Moscow Declaration was nevertheless reassuring to those Viennese, particularly former politicians and civil servants of the First Republic and Corporate State, who already knew of its existence and its possible significance for the future of Austria. The Moscow Declaration would quickly acquire major importance for the position of Austria in the immediate post-war years, and would underpin much of the political culture of the Second Republic, as will be shown. And yet it is doubtful that anyone involved in its drafting considered it to be more than a propaganda weapon in the war against Nazi Germany.[37] For this reason it is necessary to make a short detour back to 1943 to explain the origins of this, the first Allied statement on a post-war Austria.

The Allies had paid little attention to the question of Austria since the *Anschluss* in 1938. There were two basic reasons for this. The first was that, having accepted the incorporation of Austria into the Third Reich in 1938, they had little reason to develop a separate policy towards what had become a German region. As the British were to stress in January 1944, Austria had ceased to exist as a legal entity in 1938.[38] Second, the Austrian exile communities in the respective Allied states had failed to develop a united and effective voice. They remained deeply divided and fraught by schisms throughout the war years. The oldest groups consisted of Communists and Socialists who had fled from Austria in 1933 and 1934 in order to avoid persecution by the Christian Social government and the Corporate State. Some Communists made

their way to Russia, where they encountered the Stalinist purges.
Following the conclusion of the Molotov–Ribbentrop Pact of 1939,
Austrians were forced to register as either 'German citizens' or as
'stateless' – a distinct Austrian identity was not recognised until 1943.[39]
The Socialists, on the other hand, initially found refuge mainly in
Czechoslovakia and France, but when these countries were overrun by
the German army, many moved on to Britain and America where they
were joined by some of their own persecutors, as Austrian patriots, conservatives, and monarchists left after the *Anschluss* to avoid imprisonment or death under the Third Reich. In addition to their antipathy to
those exiles who were on the political Right, the Socialists were also
wary of any Communists who had chosen to live in the West rather
than the Soviet Union.[40] There was deep suspicion that these people
had been ordered to infiltrate and dominate refugee groups. As a result,
the Socialists refused to work with any other political group. In 1941,
an attempt to set up an all-party 'Council of Austrians' to present a
united front in negotiations with the British Government was scuppered
when the London Bureau of Austrian Socialists refused to take part. In
the United States co-operation was hampered by the presence and
influence of the heir to the Habsburg throne, Otto von Habsburg, who
did wield some influence in American governing circles, but was
completely unacceptable to the Socialists in particular. But even after
the former archduke's departure from America, there was no co-
operation between the exile groups, in particular the Austrian National
Committee established by Hans Roth, a Minister without Portfolio in
the last Schuschnigg government, and the Austrian Labor Committee
which was controlled by SDAP luminaries such as Julius Deutsch,
Friedrich Adler, the son of the Party's founder, and Karl-Hans Sailer.[41]
The consequence of this deep-seated animosity was that no Austrian
government-in-exile emerged at any time during the Second World War.

Nevertheless, Allied policy towards Austria did change in 1943 as
the tide of war turned. Following the German defeat at Stalingrad that
February and the surrender of Italy the following October, British and
American officials became convinced, mistakenly as it turned out, that
there was significant domestic opposition to Nazi rule in Austria which
could be galvanised into open resistance.[42] On 23 October 1943, the
three Allied Foreign Ministers met in Moscow to discuss 'measures to
shorten the war' and plans for post-war initiatives.[43] A declaration was
issued on 30 October which also contained two short resolutions on
the post-war status of Italy and Austria respectively. Austria was
described as the 'first free country to fall victim to Hitlerite aggression',
and the Allies, as we have seen, announced their intention of establishing

a free and independent Austrian state after the war. But the document was vague. It contained no detailed proposals for the structure of the post-war state and the concluding paragraph included the 'guilt clause' warning that Austria would be held responsible for her participation in the war and that account would be taken of her 'own contribution to her liberation'. Moreover, whereas the original draft had referred to the 'Austrian people' in the guilt clause, this had been changed to 'Austria' in the final document at the insistence of the Soviet delegation, opening up the question of legal liability and possible war reparations.[44] Within one short paragraph the Allies addressed Austria as both a victim who was to be liberated and an aggressor who was to be judged. This inconsistency arose from the goals which the Allied leaders had set for the Moscow Conference, as well as those same leaders' shared desire to avoid contentious issues during the war-time conferences, a position which would become yet more clearly apparent at the subsequent summits at Tehran and Yalta. The Moscow Conference was primarily concerned with the conduct of the war and not with post-war political strategy, as Robert H. Keyserlingk has shown.[45] A separate body, the European Advisory Commission (EAC), was set up to deal with the post-war situation, but despite many meetings and lengthy negotiations, its members failed to reach agreement on the future of Austria. At that time, the American government had no intention of sending more than a token military force into the country and resisted all suggestions that it should take responsibility for a zone of occupation.[46]

The Moscow Declaration, which was based on a document drawn up in London by a propaganda unit in the Foreign Office, did not, therefore, amount to a concrete statement of Allied policy, but was part of a propaganda campaign designed to encourage internal resistance within the Third Reich and so to speed up the Allied victory. Austria appeared to represent a soft target within Nazi Germany. There is no evidence to support the contention that the Allies were fully committed to the concept of Austrian 'victimhood' in 1943, but what does appear to be the case is that the Western Allies, in particular, had mixed feelings about the future status of Austria. Indeed, the official British view at the time, which was spelled out in a separate Foreign Office document entitled 'The Future of Austria', rejected the notion of an independent post-war Austria in favour of a Danubian Federation, a proposal which was championed by Winston Churchill. This document had been communicated to the American government before the Moscow summit, but had been withheld from the Russians, who would have opposed it.[47] Following the Moscow Conference, the British did attempt to clarify the legal position of a post-war Austria in January 1944, when they issued the aforementioned Political Warfare Executive directive which stated that:

> Because the Anschluss had integrated completely the Austrian political structure into the Third Reich, Austria had ceased to exist as a legal and administrative unit in February 1938 [*sic*], a fact acknowledged by the foreign powers. There exists therefore no legal continuity between the old Austrian Republic and the new state to be established.[48]

Nevertheless, Churchill was still pressing for a Danubian Federation as late as October 1944, when he broached the subject during discussions with Stalin, afterwards informing President Roosevelt that he had made some progress. He was mistaken. Stalin's suspicions were aroused and, within days of these talks, he ordered his generals to step up the Soviet attack on Hungary and to move on to Vienna.[49] The American government also remained uncommitted. As late as January 1945 the President approved the following memo:

> Independence alone, however, would not be an adequate basis for Austria's future. The continuation of the revived state will depend on a solution of its political and economic relations with its neighbours. [This may consist of special economic relations, political federation] or even a merger of sovereignties, provided that such an arrangement is approved by the parties concerned and is acceptable to the international organization.[50]

It is evident, therefore, that even during the closing stages of the war there was no single, clear Allied policy towards Austria. At the Moscow Conference that country's future was one issue that the Allies shelved for the time being, employing instead a classic 'carrot and stick' strategy: the promise of a 'free and independent Austria' was designed to fuel internal resistance, while the 'guilt clause' was a warning of the consequences which would arise from a failure to act. As a result, the final Declaration was ambiguous about the precise status and borders of a post-war Austria and, more importantly, about plans for the transition to democracy. This would have serious repercussions in the summer of 1945, as we shall see.

Despite Allied hopes, the Moscow Declaration did little to strengthen armed resistance on the ground: although Allied aircraft dropped thousands of copies of it over Austrian territory during the winter of 1943–44, these had little or no immediate impact. The fact that the statement had been drawn up in Moscow and bore the name of the Soviet capital increased suspicion that it was an Allied and, worse still, a Bolshevik trick. Still, according to Evan Bukey, the broad contents of the Declaration had become fairly well known in the Austrian *Gaue* by the end of 1944.[51] There was, however, uncertainty about whether or not the Declaration would indeed shape Allied policy once the war had ended. For this reason the appearance in April 1945, immediately after the liberation, of the posters proclaiming that it was the intention of the Soviet military authorities to abide by the wording of the Declaration certainly gave the first clear glimmer of hope that Austria and hence Austrians – the distinction was still unclear – would actually be treated as victims of Nazism rather than as its accomplices. This was not all. Within days the Soviets also announced that they intended to set up an entire political infrastructure, to be run by Austrian staff, including an administration, three political parties, trade unions, and representative bodies. On 27 April, two weeks after the liberation, and without consulting the other Allies, they took the remarkable step of recognising a coalition government comprising members of the three political parties which they had chosen to recognise, namely the Social Democratic and Revolutionary Party (later to become the *Sozialistische Partei Österreichs*/SPÖ), the Austrian People's Party (*Österreichische Volkspartei*/ÖVP) and the Communist Party (*Kommunistische Partei Österreichs*/KPÖ). Whereas the German people were to be subjected to years of political re-education before they could prove to the Allies that they were fit to govern themselves, the Soviets recognised a provisional government in Austria within two weeks of their arrival and before American, British or French troops had set foot on Austrian soil.[52] This decision, which in theory gave the new government extensive powers, including control of both the administration and the executive, also triggered the first major open disagreement between the Allies over Austria and set the climate of suspicion which would dominate the politics of the occupation for the next ten years.[53]

The first indication that the Russians intended to act unilaterally in establishing an Austrian government came at the beginning of April 1945, when Tolbukhin and Malinovsky received orders from Moscow that they should seek out the elderly Austrian Socialist leader, Karl Renner, and instruct him to set up an Austrian administration.[54] Renner, who was discovered in his home town of Gloggnitz some thirty-two kilometres south-west of Wiener Neustadt on 3 April, was a curious choice for Stalin to make. Although, as we have seen, he had extensive experience in government, having been the first Chancellor of the interwar republic in 1919, and president (speaker) of the National Assembly from 1931 to 1933, both his past history and his age (he was seventy-five) might have been thought to count against him. In addition, before the First World War Renner had been part of the Austro-Marxist group of thinkers and had known Lenin, Trotsky and Stalin, but his writings on nationalism had been decried by Stalin and he had been identified with the right wing of the Austrian Social Democratic Party during the First Republic. More importantly, his public statement in support of the *Anschluss* in 1938 would also have been well known.[55] In other days, Renner had typified what in Soviet eyes constituted a Social Fascist.

The reasons behind Stalin's decision to entrust this particular man with the task of building a new administration are still open to conjecture. Renner himself maintained that his role in the establishment of the First Republic had made him the obvious choice for the Russians in 1945, but this seems unlikely, as in neither of his previous official roles had he been particularly successful.[56] Manfried Rauchensteiner's point, that Renner was almost the only man whom Stalin actually knew in the area at the time, may seem trivial, but it does highlight one important Soviet imperative – to establish a government with Soviet backing quickly, before the arrival of the Western Allies in Austria.[57] As it was, US troops attempted to enter Austria from the north on 26 April, one day before the official announcement of the Renner government, but they were held back. They finally entered Braunau, Hitler's birthplace, on 2 May and took Innsbruck on 3 May.[58] By this time the Renner Cabinet had already been announced.

In these circumstances, where speed was crucial, the Soviets had few options other than to use Renner. There was no government-in-exile waiting in the wings, as we have seen. One other alternative, to establish a government based on the Austrian resistance movement, was theoretically conceivable, but highly unlikely and completely unacceptable to the Soviets for a number of reasons. The first of these was the small dimensions and sporadic nature of resistance to Nazism in Austria. As we saw in Chapter 1, there had been little support for the independent Austrian state which the *Anschluss* destroyed. Unlike its neighbours in Central Europe, Austria had not been conquered by force in 1938, even though the annexation had been heralded by the arrival of *Wehrmacht* troops and *Luftwaffe* planes. Employment had increased after 1938. Relatively few people were persecuted by the Nazi regime and those who were, in particular the Jews, either went into exile, or were removed, incarcerated, or killed. The remaining inhabitants of the *Ostmark* were not subject to the Nazi Race Laws, for they were classified as Reich Germans. Indeed, there is every indication that the denizens of the *Ostmark* were as loyal to the regime as the populations of many other German regions. In all, 1,286,000 Austrians were conscripted into the German *Wehrmacht*, where they had a low rate of desertion despite a high level of casualties: approximately 250,000 Austrians or 3.5 per cent of the entire population were killed in combat during the war.[59] Considering this level of commitment, it is unsurprising that Austrian opposition to the Nazi regime had been very slow to emerge and had remained 'small, atomized and highly incoherent' throughout the seven years since the *Anschluss*, notwithstanding the Moscow Declaration.[60]

Political resentments also contributed to the weakness of Austrian opposition to the Nazi regime. The Social Democrats played only a minor role in clandestine resistance. As we have already seen, when many of the SDAP leaders fled the country in 1934, following the civil war and the establishment of the Corporate State, some young party activists set up the Revolutionary Socialists, who vied with the Communists for leadership of the fight against Austro-fascism.[61] But, disillusioned after years of fighting and with the new leadership decimated by a wave of arrests in March 1938, this movement withdrew from clandestine operations soon after the *Anschluss*. Although some cells continued to carry out propaganda work, there was no central organisation, and once again some individual Socialists turned to the Communists, at least briefly: there is no known information about the impact of the Soviet-German Pact on Communist resistance in Austria. Nevertheless, the Communist Party, which had failed to win enough votes in the First Republic to gain even a single mandate, became the most significant force in the Austrian resistance.[62] This did not mean that the Soviets could rely on a large Communist movement in 1945. The relative strength of the Communists vis-à-vis the other resistance groups meant little in terms of actual numbers, for, as Luža has estimated, only some 100,000 Austrians in total were involved in one or other form of active resistance during the entire war, roughly 40 per cent of whom were linked to the Communists.[63] Moreover, by the spring of 1945 the strongest contingent of Communist resisters, the Austrian Battalion, was no longer in the Austrian *Gaue*, its members having gone to fight alongside Tito's troops in Yugoslavia. Within the Austrian territory, resistance groups comprised mainly Austrian patriots, liberals, conservatives and monarchists who worked in isolation from each other for most of the war. They lacked any co-ordination until 1944, when an umbrella organisation known as O5 was set up, with its main areas of influence in Vienna and Tyrol. Led by the 'Committee of Seven', this body liaised between military cells and a range of political resistance groups, many of which were liberal-conservative, but it was unable to establish a strong central organisation.[64] As has been mentioned, it was said to have played a role in the battle for Vienna in April 1945, having first made contact with Tolbukhin's forces in Hochwolkersdorf on 2 April.[65] But the role of Austrian resistance to

Nazism had been limited and the Soviet authorities did not trust the leadership of O5. It seemed they had more faith in Renner.

Although the intrigues of Soviet policy towards Austria are important, they are not the subject of this book – their importance for this thesis lies in the impact they had on Austrian political culture.[66] In that context the crucial factors were the speed with which the provisional government was formed, its relations with the Russians, and the difficulties it had in gaining recognition from the American, British and French governments. These were to have both short-term and long-term consequences for Austrian politics. For instance, the government which Renner put together was, of necessity, unelected and drawn from pre-war political circles and networks. Some of its members had been involved in clandestine activities both before and during the war and this, combined with the absence of democratic politics throughout the previous eleven years, meant that they were used to working in secret. They included former political enemies, but faced with the uncertainties of the Soviet occupation and with little or no information about the attitudes of the other Allies, they quickly realised that it was imperative to maintain unity and consensus in their negotiations with the Occupying Powers. This would only be possible if they presented a united front in which common goals were identified and decisions were based on pragmatism and not ideology. As a result, the concepts of political harmony, proportionality (*Proporz* – the system of distributing ministries and jobs according to the perceived electoral strengths of the individual political parties) and consensus, which were to become characteristic of the political culture of Austria in the second half of the twentieth century, were all evident during the initial days and weeks of frantic political discussion which followed the end of the war.[67] So too was the 'victimhood' thesis.

Renner's task of forming a new government within days of his arrival in Vienna was fraught with difficulties. Despite his previous periods in office, he had been politically inactive for more than eleven years, and had spent the war 'in retirement' in Gloggnitz. Moreover, the absence of a government-in-waiting and the weak and fragmented character of the Austrian resistance, the factors which had led the Soviets to turn to him in the first place, also raised the question of who would be suitable to serve as ministers in his new government. There were very few obvious candidates and, as Nazi officials were most certainly unacceptable, none with recent experience in government or administration. Those who, like Renner, had held office during the First Republic were now elderly and represented the political divisions which had devastated the country in that period; indeed the pattern of inter-war party politics in Austria offered little hope for the future.

The official version of the birth of the Second Republic is that it had been conceived during the war, the product of repression.[68] Opposition to the Nazi regime and the shared experience of imprisonment and incarceration in concentration camps were said to have destroyed the deep-rooted political enmities which had disfigured the First Republic, and to have convinced political leaders to bury their differences and work together for common goals. Although the images of resistance and imprisonment were to become as important to the legitimisation of post-war Austria as they were to other states which emerged from Nazi oppression, they both raised serious problems in Austria.[69] The exaggeration of the scale of resistance has already been discussed, but, in addition, the picture of the Founding Fathers spending the war years in concentration camps was also exaggerated after the war. While several post-war leaders had indeed endured long years of imprisonment during the Nazi regime, many more had been locked up for short periods and then released, or, like Renner, had remained at large throughout the war. There were some resistance leaders and concentration-camp survivors among the Founding Fathers, but their numbers were small.[70]

In reality, the foundations of the Second Republic were laid in the first weeks of liberation, when few of the camps had been opened and as Renner put together his first Cabinet. His choice of ministers was limited. The instructions he had been given by the Russian authorities, to establish an administration as quickly as possible, and the circumstances in which this was to be done both necessitated improvisation rather than careful planning. In the turmoil of April 1945, when travel meant walking, unless it was undertaken on Russian orders or, at the very least, with official Russian approval, when telephones were not working and there was seldom any electricity, Renner had to rely on personal acquaintances and a relatively small political network to establish a government. This inevitably meant that, in the earliest days of the liberation, the possession of political influence under Soviet occupation depended on two basic factors; knowing the right people and being in the right place at the right time. Renner himself was an example of this. He was appointed Chancellor by the Russians because they knew who he was, and, as he was living in the first area they moved into, he was also accessible to them. His case was not unique – the composition of the first Austrian Cabinet relied heavily upon who was in Vienna in April 1945 and whom they in turn knew. The choice was in many ways pragmatic.

Renner's task was eased by the fact that before 1945 political contacts had survived, after a fashion. Despite the limited nature of resistance, political life on an informal basis had not completely ceased during the war, but, as all organisations which were not controlled by the state were illegal, it was inevitably dangerous and therefore clandestine. Nevertheless, not even the Nazis could control social gatherings, particularly in an environment like Vienna, a compact, even dense city, in which, traditionally, public and private spheres overlapped in coffee houses and restaurants.[71] Friends and relatives still met in flats and cafes, and, not withstanding the constant fear of spies and informers, there were opportunities for former colleagues and party workers to talk informally.[72] The memoirs of Adolf Schärf, the future leader of the SPÖ, record visits from erstwhile comrades which, according to him, helped to keep the spirit of the SDAP alive during the war years. Josef Schöner also wrote of meetings with intimates, particularly during the last nine months of the war when there was open discussion about defeat and the possibilities which the political future might hold.[73] These impromptu meetings became more regular and the discussions grew more earnest after the defeat of the German army at Stalingrad in 1943, when the level of popular cynicism intensified and there were strong rumours that the *Wehrmacht* casualties included a disproportionate number of Austrians. These reports fuelled suspicion and anti-German resentment.[74] It has been argued by Karl Stadler and Felix Kreissler that Nazism's hold over Austria was broken after Stalingrad, laying the basis for modern Austrian national consciousness.[75] According to Evan Bukey, there was an increase in popular discontent in the Austrian *Gaue* at the time, but this was also seen in the rest of the Reich and there is little evidence to support the argument that Stalingrad marked anything as specific as the birth of a distinct and new Austrian identity.[76] Still, the defeat at Stalingrad did lead to growing disenchantment with the war and an increase in Gestapo raids on dissenters and resistance groups. There was also an increase in covert political activities. Spurred on by shock at the outcome of the battle and by the increase in Allied bombing raids on Austrian towns and cities, a small number of clandestine political groups began to draw up plans for life after a Nazi defeat. One example is the circle of former Christian Social leaders which at the end of 1943 began meeting regularly in the Viennese flat of Leopold Figl. Figl, who had been the administrative director of the Austrian Peasant Union in the Corporate State, was the model of the post-war leader whose political ideas had been affected by long years in prison, having spent the first four years of the war in concentration camps.[77] Two other central figures in this group had also been leading officials in the Corporate State: Julius Raab had been Minister of Trade in the last Schuschnigg government, and Lois Weinberger had been one of the leaders of the Corporate State's Unified Trade Union Federation until 1938 and later leader of the underground Christian Workers' Trade Union. In April 1944, shortly before Figl was arrested once again by the Gestapo, these three agreed to set up a new party after the war which would succeed the Christian Social Party and include representatives of its three most important wings – the peasants, Catholic workers, and trade and industry. The Catholic Church was to be precluded from exerting any direct political influence.[78]

Before Renner arrived in Vienna on 20 April, indeed even before the fighting there was completely over, political groups were breaking cover and rushing to set up new parties. The Socialists were the first to make a public announcement. On 12 April, officials of the inter-war SDAP led by Adolf Schärf, and representatives of the party's small and radical Revolutionary Socialists met in the town hall, and two days later the new Socialist Party was founded. Its cumbersome original title was the Socialist Party of Austria (Social Democrats and Revolutionary Socialists), reflecting the two main factions which had developed in the underground movement before 1938.[79] Five days later the new conservative party, the Austrian People's Party (ÖVP) was officially announced by Leopold Kunschak, the elderly former leader of the Christian Workers' Union, alongside Figl, Raab and Weinberger.[80]

Figl was not only the model of the post-war politician who emerged from the concentration camps to become one of the Founding Fathers of the Second Republic. His story is also another example of the importance of being in the right place at the right time, though his case was very different from Renner's. Having been rearrested by the Gestapo in July 1944 in the wake of the most serious assassination attempt on Hitler, he had spent months in Mauthausen concentration camp, before being transferred to Vienna in January 1945 to be tried by the People's Court (*Volksgerichtshof*). He had only been released from prison on 6 April as the Russians entered Vienna. When Leopold Kunschak, the seventy-four-year-old Christian Social trade union leader, turned down the position of leader of the newly formed ÖVP because of his age, Figl was eventually chosen instead. He was not particularly well known at the time, but unlike possible rivals for the position, such as the Tyrolean politician and resistance leader Karl Gruber, he was in Vienna. Another case which proves the importance of presence, but conversely, because of his absence at the key moment, is that of Karl Seitz, the charismatic mayor of Red Vienna and chairman of the SDAP in the First Republic. The Russians had wanted to reappoint Seitz as mayor of Vienna, but he could not be found. Like Figl, he had been arrested in the wake of the July 1944 attempt on Hitler's life, but he had been sent to Ravensbrück concentration camp and had then been released, or so it is said, in Plau at the request of Himmler's masseur.[81] As a result, although Ravensbrück was liberated by the Russians on 30 April, Seitz was not found until June 1945, when he was picked up by US troops. By this time the Russians had appointed a new mayor in the person of General Theodor Körner, a retired officer from both the Imperial and Republican armies, as well as one-time leader of the Socialist paramilitary, the *Schutzbund*, and a fluent Russian speaker.[82] Körner set up a Viennese administration on 18 April and immediately issued instructions for the removal of all Nazi signs and street names in the city.[83]

The Communist Party did not announce its rebirth. Presumably it argued that it had never gone away. Within hours of the sightings of the first Soviet tanks, men appeared on the streets wearing armbands in the red and white of Austria, embellished with the hammer and sickle. On 14 April, four days after Johann Koplenig, the chairman of the Austrian Communist Party, and Ernst Fischer, a member of the Austrian Politburo, flew back from exile in Moscow, the first meeting of Communist shop-stewards took place in Vienna.[84]

This swift reaction to the liberation of Vienna was not restricted to party politicians. An appeal went out to civil servants from the Corporate State, many of whom had worked in subordinate positions in the Nazi administration or in private firms, to attend a meeting in the Chancellery on 15 April, when the first steps were taken to rebuild the civil service, starting with clearing the rubble and attempting to recover official papers from the debris left by the Nazis. Here too, personal contacts were important.[85] The call was issued by word of mouth, the only means possible in the circumstances. Josef Schöner, himself a former civil servant, recorded in his diary how he went on foot to the resistance headquarters in the Auersperg Palace, and then to the Chancellery, in a determined bid to play a role in rebuilding the administrative structure.

Trade union leaders were also busy. But if political parties and the civil service appeared to have been resurrected from the ashes of the First Republic and Corporate State, the structure of the new trade union organisation which emerged in the first week of liberation was the earliest real indication of the new oligarchic political culture which would come to dominate all spheres of political life. Six Socialist trade union officials from the First Republic, among them Josef Battisti and Johann Böhm, the former secretary and chairman of the Building-Workers' Union in the First Republic, met at Battisti's flat on 13 April to finalise their plans for forming a new trade union federation.[86] Böhm, who had been a fierce advocate of industrial unions in the 1920s and early thirties, now went one step further, and he and his friends agreed that the revival of a freely organised labour movement should avoid the pattern of political sectarianism of the First Republic by including Socialists, Communists and members of the former Catholic Trade Unions.[87] Nazi Party officials were the only employees who were specifically excluded from membership. A ruling committee of eleven was set up, which was to include at least two Communists and two Catholic trade unionists, and it and a federal structure of sixteen industrial unions were both endorsed at a meeting of Viennese Socialist trade unionists on 15 April.[88] The Russians gave their approval on 30 April, the official date of the foundation of the Austrian Trade Union Federation (*Österreichischer Gewerkschaftsbund* – ÖGB).[89]

As soon as he set foot in the city, Renner began talks on forming a provisional government with the leaders of the factions that had been endorsed by the Soviets. The key to this was to establish a coalition of the three political parties which, it was hoped, would be acceptable to the occupying powers and which would forget or put aside past conflicts. A list of Cabinet members was published on 24 April and approved by the Russian authorities on 28 April. Renner's initial and indeed only Cabinet included eleven Socialists, nine representatives of the ÖVP and seven Communists, including Helene Postranecky, the first woman to be included in an Austrian government.[90] Johann Böhm was appointed Minister of Social Affairs.[91] Two important posts, those of Minister of the Interior, which controlled the police, and of Minister for Popular Enlightenment and Education, were given to Communists, namely Franz Honner and Ernst Fischer. Ministerial portfolios were allocated according to the relative strengths of the parties, or at least the estimation of their strengths made at the time. Two under-secretaries were appointed to each ministry, selected from one of the other parties. This established the precedent of proportionality which after 1947 was to lead to two-party domination of Austrian politics for over twenty years. In 1945 it also created one very strange anomaly: the portfolio of the Ministry for Popular Enlightenment and Education, which was allocated to the Communist Ernst Fischer, included responsibility for 'Religious Affairs'. A later American report suggested that 'the Socialists and the *Volkspartei* people held opinions which if pushed to extremes might raise religious issues at moments when it was desirable to avoid all conflict over the question . . . Since the position of the Communists in these matters was mediatorial [*sic*], their possession of this state office would avoid conflict between church and state.'[92]

After eleven years of authoritarian government, including seven years of Nazi rule, it had taken less than two weeks to rebuild the basic framework of political life. Three of the four political parties which were to dominate Austrian domestic politics for the next four decades had been established, along with the trade union federation.[93] The fact that there had been no time and little desire to start by building grass-roots support gave enormous powers to those who later became known as the Founding Fathers of the Second Republic. Their first task was not to impress voters, but to induce the Soviet authorities, and later the other Allied Powers, to recognise them as the political leaders of the new state. The speed of the operation also influenced the character both of the new parties and of the government. The fact that the field was restricted to those people who found themselves in Vienna and its surrounding districts in April 1945, or who had contacts in the city, was to have a profound influence on one party in particular, namely the Socialist Party. The core of its pre-war left-wing intellectual leadership was either dead, in exile or in concentration camps. The party was therefore re-established by men, like Renner and his former secretary, Adolf Schärf, and some women, who had represented its 'moderate' right wing in the First Republic; many of these had been party bureaucrats and were largely unknown to the wider public. The new party leadership had sat out the war within the Third Reich and it represented a different style of socialism from the intellectually based idealism of the SDAP in the inter-war years. Having gained control of the party, these new leaders became intent on maintaining their position and were deeply wary of the influence of dissenting voices, particularly those of 'returnees' who had spent the war in exile and who, in the words of Josef Schöner, could 'neither understand nor learn anything'.[94] As a result, there was no left-wing philosophy in the post-war party, which became the domain of right-wing pragmatists.

The political system which developed in Austria after 1945 was necessary in the circumstances of occupation by potentially hostile and conflicting forces, but it laid the foundation for a political culture in which, officially, political harmony and consensus would dominate. There was to be no public dissent and no open debate. But such a culture could not be introduced overnight: it had to be cultivated, for in 1945 there were still issues which deeply divided even the leadership. The most contentious of these was the attitude of the Socialist leaders, in particular Karl Renner, to the Corporate State. In a series of speeches, letters, papers and pamphlets which he produced in the first month of liberation, Renner displayed a marked inability to 'forget the past'.[95] In a speech to the civil servants of the State Chancellery on 30 April, he lamented the passing of the concept of the *Anschluss*, and Hitler's distortion of it. He went on to argue that there had been two types of fascism, both foreign, but that Dollfuss had played the role of Mussolini's representative in Austria, splitting the country and thus destroying any possible resistance to Nazi occupation. He went on to announce that no one who had played a leading role in either 'Mussolini-Fascism' or 'Hitler-fascism' would find a place in public service in the new Austria.[96] This was an astonishing speech to make to an audience of civil servants, many of whom had served in the Corporate State. Speaking later in Cabinet, he announced that he would not allow the injustices of the civil war of 1934 to be forgotten. As Josef Schöner commented, Renner, in an attempt to justify his own position, delivered a highly partisan account of the 1930s in which he seemed to condemn the 'Austro-fascists' of 1934 with greater force than he condemned the Nazis.[97] His attitude was less than helpful to the search for 'consensus' between the Socialists and the People's Party. In addition, in his early encounters with the Allied Powers, Renner took pains to acknowledge Austrian war 'guilt', when his government had already adopted the strategy of war 'victim'. In time Renner would learn to temper his language, but his early outbursts illustrate the difficulties which could arise for those who had elected to 'forget the past'.

Nevertheless, before the war had even ended, Austria had its own provisional government.

Notes

1 Bukey, *Hitler's Austria*, 92, 199.
2 In 1942 the *Ostmark* had become the *Alpen- und Donaugaue* – the Alpine and Danube Provinces.
3 Bukey, *Hitler's Austria*, 219–21.
4 Manfried Rauchensteiner, *Der Krieg in Österreich 1945* (Vienna: Österreichischer Bundesverlag, 1984), 64.
5 Josef Schöner, *Wiener Tagebuch 1944/1945* (Vienna: Böhlau, 1992), 112–14.
6 Radomir Luža, *Austro-German Relations in the Anschluss Era* (Princeton, NJ: Princeton University Press, 1975), 344.
7 *Ibid.*
8 Rauchensteiner, *Der Krieg in Österreich 1945*, 63. Bukey says the Russians crossed the border on 20 March at Koszeg; Bukey, *Hitler's Austria*, 223.
9 Margarete Hannl, 'Mit den Russen Leben. Ein Beitrag zur Geschichte der Besatzungszeit im Mühlviertel' (Diplomarbeit, University of Salzburg, 1988), 46.
10 Rauchensteiner, *Der Krieg in Österreich 1945*, 153–60; John Erickson, *The Road to Berlin, Stalin's War with Germany*, vol. 2 (New Haven, CT: Yale University Press, 1999), 550.

11 *Rot-Weiss-Rot-Buch*, 151.
12 Rauchensteiner, *Der Krieg in Österreich 1945*, 151–5.
13 Schöner, *Wiener Tagebuch*, 103; Rauchensteiner, *Der Krieg in Österreich 1945*, 155–7, 159. In January part of the Hitler Youth Battalion, the *Werwolf*, had joined the *Volkssturm*.
14 Schöner, *Wiener Tagebuch*, 101.
15 *Ibid.*, 116.
16 *Ibid.*, 123; Hugo Portisch and Sepp Riff, *Österreich II. Der Wiedergeburt unseres Staates* (Vienna: Kremayr and Scherlau, 1985), 79.
17 Soviet plans to encircle Vienna from the south and east were delayed for several days by fierce fighting by the 2nd and 3rd SS Panzer Corps. Rauchensteiner, *Der Krieg in Österreich 1945*, 160–5; Erickson, *The Road to Berlin*, 550, 765. Soviet armies were known as 'fronts'.
18 Peter Gosztony, 'Planung, Stellenwert und Ablauf der "Wiener Angriffsoperation" der Roten Armee 1945', in Manfried Rauchensteiner and Wolfgang Etschmann (eds), *Österreich 1945: Ein Ende und viele Anfänge* (Graz: Verlag Styria, 1997), 142.
19 Schöner, *Wiener Tagebuch*, 126–7.
20 *Ibid.*, 134–5.
21 The battle for Budapest lasted 102 days from the appearance of the first Soviet tanks on the outskirts of the city, but the siege itself lasted for 51 days. Approximately 160,000 people died in the fighting. Kristián Ungváry, *The Battle for Budapest: 100 Days in World War II* (London: I.B. Taurus, 2003), xi. Official figures for those who died in the battle for Vienna were 37,000 – 19,000 Germans and 18,000 Russians. Rauchensteiner, *Der Krieg in Österreich 1945*, 191; Adolf Schärf estimated that the German losses were lower at 12,000. Adolf Schärf, *April 1945 in Wien* (Vienna: Verlag der Volksbuchhandlung, 1948), 26.
22 Portisch and Riff discuss the role of Szokoll in the plot of 20 July 1944 to kill Hitler, stating that the Austrian soldiers were more successful than their German colleagues during the attempt to bring down the Third Reich. Portisch and Riff, *Österreich II*, 85. Luža agrees that the coup 'got off to a successful start' in Vienna. Luža, *The Resistance in Austria*, 340.
23 Portisch and Riff, *Österreich II*, 84–9.
24 Schöner wrote on 12 April that negotiations between the Russian city commander and the ÖFB (*Österreichische Freiheitsbewegung*) on the role of the resistance in the new regime had stalled. Schöner, *Wiener Tagebuch*, 155.
25 *Ibid.*, 136–41; Johann Böhm, *Erinnerungen aus meinem Leben* (Vienna: Europa Verlag, 1964), 193.
26 Schöner, *Wiener Tagebuch*, 138.
27 Bukey, *Hitler's Austria*, 224.
28 Schöner, *Wiener Tagebuch*, 349. His wife's flat was ransacked in August 1945.
29 Bukey, *Hitler's Austria*, 218. Prisoners of war, foreign labourers and concentration camp inmates had been brought into Austria to alleviate the shortage of labour which arose after 1939. Bukey estimates that there were 320,000 foreign workers in Vienna in April 1945.
30 Schöner, *Wiener Tagebuch*, 147.
31 *Ibid.*, 141.
32 *Ibid.*, 148.

33 Manfried Rauchensteiner, *Der Sonderfall: Die Besatzungszeit in Österreich 1945 bis 1955* (Graz: Verlag Styria, 1995), 66; *Rot-Weiss-Rot-Buch*, 191–2, *Erklärung der Sowjetregierung über Österreich*.

34 Portisch and Riff, *Österreich II*, 161; Keyserlingk, *Austria in World War II*, 148.

35 *Rot-Weiss-Rot-Buch*, 191. It was also omitted from the wording of the State Treaty in 1955.

36 'Alle persönlichen Rechte und Eigentumsrechte österreichischer Staatsbürger, privater Gesellschaften und Vereine und das ihnen zugehörige Privateigentum bleiben unangetastet', Stefan Karner, Barbara Stelz-Marx and Alexander Tschubarjan (eds), *Die Rote Armee in Österreich. Sowjetische Besatzung 1945–1955. Dokumente* (Graz: Oldenbourg, 2005), 93.

37 Günter Bischof, 'Die Instrumentalisierung der Moskauer Erklärung nach dem Zweiten Weltkrieg', *Zeitgeschichte*, Jahr 20, Heft 11/12, 1993, 345–66.

38 British Political Warfare Executive (PWE) report 'Opinion and Morale in Austria', 6 January 1944, reprinted in Keyserlingk, *Austria in World War II*, 210. The USSR (along with Mexico) had actually protested formally against the *Anschluss* in 1938.

39 Rauchensteiner, *Der Sonderfall*, 53.

40 Helene Maimann, *Politik im Wartesaal. Österreichische Exilpolitik in Großbritannien 1938–1945* (Vienna: Böhlau, 1975), 217.

41 Peter Schwarz, 'Österreichische politische Exilorganisationen', in Claus Dieter Krohn and Patrik von zur Mühlen (eds), *Handbuch der deutschsprachigen Emigration 1933–1945* (Darmstadt: Primus Verlag, 1998), 519–42.

42 Bukey, *Hitler's Austria*, 207–9.

43 Keyserlingk, *Austria in World War II*, 123–56. Anthony Eden, *The Eden Memoirs*, vol. 3, *The Reckoning* (London: Cassell, 1965), 410–18. Eden attended the meeting as the British Foreign Secretary. The Moscow Conference was attended by representatives from the USA, UK and the USSR. China was invited to append her signature to the Declaration as the US government sought to consolidate a Four-Power declaration on war aims and strengthen the Pacific Alliance.

44 www.yale.edu/lawweb/Avalon.wwii/Moscow.htm; Keyserlingk, *Austria in World War II*, 152.

45 Keyserlingk, *Austria in World War II*, 123–56.

46 Bischof, *Austria in the First Cold War*, 28.

47 Keyserlingk, *Austria in World War II*, 140–1.

48 PWE report, Opinion and Morale in Austria, 6 January 1945, reprinted in Keyserlingk, *Austria in World War II*, 210. This was later interpreted by the Austrian Government to mean that, as no Austrian state existed during the war, Austria was not liable for any reparations. This is the reason for the Soviet ploy of seizing 'German property' as reparations.

49 Ungváry, *Battle for Budapest*, 4.

50 Reprinted in Keyserlingk, *Austria in World War II*, 212.

51 Bukey, *Hitler's Austria*, 208.

52 The French Provisional Government had been invited to join the EAC in October 1944. In January 1945 it was allocated zones in both Germany and Austria. Michael Balfour and John Mair, *Four-Power Control in Germany and Austria, 1945–1946* (London: Oxford University Press, 1956), 287–9.

53 Bischof, *Austria in the First cold war*, 36.
54 Rauchensteiner, *Der Sonderfall*, 66–8: the story of the search for Renner was confirmed in 1972 in the memoirs of the Russian General Shtemenko. S.M. Shtemenko, *The Soviet General Staff at War, 1941–1945* (Moscow: Progress Publishers, 1970).
55 Renner's resignation from the Presidency of the National Assembly in March 1933 triggered events which led to the destruction of the First Republic. Lewis, *Fascism and the Working Class in Austria*, 191–4. For details of Renner's life and controversies see Karl Renner, *An der Wende zweier Zeiten* (Vienna: Donubia Verlag, 1946); Jacques Hannak, *Karl Renner und seine Zeit* (Vienna: Europa Verlag, 1965); Anton Pelinka, *Karl Renner zur Einführung* (Hamburg: Junius, 1989); Walter Rauscher, *Karl Renner. Ein österreichischer Mythos* (Vienna: Ueberreuter, 1995).
56 Karl Renner, *Denkschrift über die Geschichte der Unabhängigkeitserklärung Österreichs und die Einsetzung der Provisorischen Regierung der Republik* (Vienna: Österreichische Staatsdruckerei, 1946).
57 Rauchensteiner, *Der Sonderfall*, 67. In autumn 1944 the Allies had agreed to a tripartite division of Austria. Churchill had expected British troops to advance on Austria from Italy and reach Vienna before the Russians. At the beginning of March, having been informed that the British and Americans were negotiating the German surrender in Switzerland, Stalin ordered Tolbukhin and Malinovsky to speed up the assault on Vienna in order to extend Soviet penetration of Austria. Rauchensteiner, *Der Krieg in Österreich 1945*, 20–1.
58 *Ibid.*, 346–50.
59 Walter Manoschek and Hans Safrian, 'Österreicher in der Wehrmacht', in Tálos *et al.* (eds), *NS-Herrschaft in Österreich 1938–1945*, 350; Peter Thaler, '"Germans" and "Austrians" in WW2: Military History and National Identity', *Center for Austrian Studies Occasional Paper*, September 1999. www.cas.umn.edu/wp991.pdf. The Austrian population was 6,999,284 in 1938.
60 Bischof, *Austria in the First Cold War*, 19.
61 Buttinger, *In the Twilight of Socialism*, 59–123.
62 Kirk, *Nazism and the Working Class in Austria*, 102–8. Kirk identifies acts of industrial sabotage and resistance among Austrian workers, but concludes that 'this national element in the resistance to Nazism, widespread also in the attitudes of foreign workers in Austria, was not generally to be found among the native Austrian population', 140; Luža, *The Resistance in Austria*, 278. Luža does not mention the 1939 Soviet-German Pact at all, but jumps from spring 1939 to late 1940 in his discussion of the KPÖ.
63 Luža divides the resistance into nine broad categories – the Communists, the Social Democrats, industrial workers, Monarchists/Legitimists, Christian Socials, non-party patriots, members of the military, former *Heimwehr* members, and Jehovah's Witnesses. *Ibid.*, 278–82.
64 *Ibid.*, 160–4, 216–8; 'O5' represented the first letter of the word 'Österreich', 'Ö' where the Umlaut is replaced by an 'e', the fifth letter of the alphabet. Schärf, *April 1945 in Wien*, 54.
65 Rauchensteiner, *Der Krieg in Österreich 1945*, 147–8. See also *Rot-Weiss-Rot-Buch*, 141, 195–7.
66 There are still few detailed accounts of Russian policy on Austria in the early post-war years.

67 The first official mention of *Proporz* occurred during the cabinet meeting of 5 May 1945. *Protokolle des Kabinettsrates der Provisorischen Regierung Karl Renner* (hereafter *Protokolle des Kabinettsrates*), vol. 1, 29. *April 1945 bis 10. Juli 1945* (Vienna, Verlag Österreich, 1995).

68 *Rot-Weiss-Rot-Buch*.

69 Judt, 'The Past is another Country', 296–7.

70 Leopold Figl is one example of the former – he was interned in concentration camps for four years after the *Anschluss* and rearrested in the wake of the assassination attempt on Hitler in 1944. More conservatives than Socialists experienced long-term incarceration. However, Franz Olah, the Socialist trade union leader, was held in Dachau for seven years, and met Figl there. He returned to Vienna on 1 July 1945. Franz Olah, *Die Erinnerungen* (Vienna: Amalthea, 1995), 70–107, 114.

71 One explanation for the cultural intensity of *fin-de-siècle* Vienna was the overlapping circles of intellectuals, artists and politicians who met in various coffee-houses. Another was the role of the Jews of Vienna. While the coffee-houses survived the war, the Jews did not, and Viennese high culture never did regain the vitality it had had at the beginning of the twentieth century. See Edward Timms, *Karl Kraus: Apocalyptic Satirist. Culture and Catastrophe in Habsburg Vienna* (New Haven, CT: Yale University Press, 1986), 8.

72 Adolf Schärf, *Österreichs Erneuerung 1945–1955* (Vienna: Verlag der Wienervolksbuchhandlung, 1955), 19.

73 Schöner, *Wiener Tagebuch*, 31, 40–1, 44–6.

74 Bukey, *Hitler's Austria*, 186–8. There were reports of open criticism of the Nazi leadership. One mother, on being informed of the death of her son, struck the SS officer who had brought the news.

75 Felix Kreissler, *Der Österreicher und seine Nation* (Vienna: Böhlau, 1984), 286–99; Karl Stadler, *Österreich 1938–1945* (Vienna: Herold, 1966), 14, 293–303.

76 Bukey, *Hitler's Austria*, 186–9.

77 Luža, *The Resistance in Austria*, 184–5.

78 Nevertheless, Cardinal Innitzer's blessing was sought before the launch of the ÖVP. Luža, *The Resistance in Austria*, 185–6. Fritz Weber, *Der Kalte Krieg in der SPÖ. Koalitionswächter, Pragmatiker und Revolutionäre Sozialisten 1945–1950* (Vienna: Verlag für Gesellschaftskritik, 1986), 10. In the 1950s the Roman Catholic Church succeeded in claiming compensation from the state as a 'victim of Nazism' for property which had been confiscated during the war. Irene Bandhauer-Schöffmann, 'Restitution Laws for the Austrian Catholic Church (1945–1960). Dealing with an Ambiguous Past', unpublished conference paper, Vienna, May 2005.

79 Schärf had been private secretary to the last Socialist presidents/speakers of parliament, Karl Seitz and Karl Renner. Schärf, *April 1945 in Wien*, 66–68; Oskar Helmer, *50 Jahre Erlebte Geschichte* (Vienna: Verlag der Wiener Volksbuchhandlung, 1957), 212. The party had originally been called the *Sozialdemokratische Arbeiterpartei (SDAP)* and after the war it was known as the Socialist Party of Austria (Social Democrats and Revolutionary Socialists). Its final change of name to the *Sozialistische Partei Österreichs* (SPÖ) was announced in the *Arbeiter-Zeitung* by its editor in September 1945. There had been no discussion or consultation with the party membership, but nor was

there any protest. Kurt Shell, *The Transformation of Austrian Socialism* (Albany, NY: State University of New York Press, 1962), 29–36; *Arbeiter-Zeitung* (30 September 1945).

80 Weber, *Der Kalte Krieg in der SPÖ*, 10.

81 Rudolf Spitzer, *Karl Seitz. Waisenknabe – Staatspräsident – Bürgermeister von Wien* (Vienna: Franz Deuticke, 1994), 145. Seitz had been mayor of Vienna from 1923 to 1934 and chairman of the SDAP from 1920 to 1934.

82 Körner had been replaced as leader of the *Schutzbund* in 1931 for advocating guerrilla warfare. Lewis, *Fascism and the Working Class in Austria*, 187–8.

83 Wien im Rückblick. 30.4.1945, www.wien.gv.at/ma53/45jahre/inhalt.html.

84 Ernst Fischer (translated by Peter and Betty Ross), *An Opposing Man* (London: Allen Lane, 1974), 405; Ernst Fischer, *Das Ende einer Illusion. Erinnerungen 1945–1955* (Vienna: Molden, 1973), 19–23, 38–50.

85 Schöner, *Wiener Tagebuch*, 163.

86 Böhm and Battisti had also been leaders of the illegal trade union movement from 1934–8. Klenner, *Die österreichischen Gewerkschaften*, vol. 2, 1302, 1599.

87 There had been a number of trade union federations in the First Republic, each allied with a political party or group. The largest was the Socialist Free Trade Union Federation. Gulick, *Austria from Habsburg to Hitler*, ch. 9; Lewis, *Fascism and the Working Class in Austria*, 212.

88 Klenner, *Die österreichischen Gewerkschaften*, vol. 2, 1600.

89 *Ibid.*, 913.

90 Ernst Hanisch, *Der lange Schatten des Staates. Österreichische Gesell-schaftsgeschichte im 20. Jahrhundert* (Vienna: Ueberreuter, 1994), 402.

91 Until December 1945, Ministers were called 'Secretaries of State' in deference to the provisional status of the government. To avoid confusion, they will be referred to as 'Ministers' throughout.

92 Report by Edgar N. Johnson and Paul R. Sweet (OSS), 14 September 1945, reprinted in Oliver Rathkolb, *Gesellschaft und Politik am Beginn der Zweiten Republik* (Vienna: Böhlau, 1985), 176.

93 The fourth party was the *Verein der Unabhängigen* (VdU), the forerunner of the *Freiheitliche Partei Österreichs*, which was founded in 1948 once the 'lesser' Nazis were re-enfranchised.

94 Schöner, *Wiener Tagebuch*, 388. Schöner was writing on 23 September about Oskar Pollak, the editor of the *Arbeiter-Zeitung*, who had written an editorial on Otto Bauer which attacked everyone who had played a role in the Corporate State. Schöner considered this to be a direct attack on Figl. 'Die "AZ" wird immer mehr zum typischen Emigrantenblatt – nichts verstehend und nichts lernend.'

95 Schöner, *Wiener Tagebuch*, 55–8; Renner, *Denkschrift über die Geschichte der Unabhängigkeitserklärung Österreichs und die Einsetzung der Provisorischen Regierung der Republik.*

96 *Protokolle des Kabinettsrates*, vol. 1, sitting 10 May 1945, appendix 10, 54–8.

97 *Ibid.*, 236–8, 253–8, 289.

3

Hunger, rape and
recognition

The Western Allies' reaction to the news from Vienna was swift. On 1 May the BBC announced that both the United States and the United Kingdom had refused to recognise the Renner government.[1] Their main objection was that the Soviet decision to establish an Austrian administration had been taken unilaterally. The American and British governments referred to the Yalta Agreement which stated that the Allied goal in liberated Europe was to establish:

> the right of all peoples to choose the form of government under which they will live – the restoration of sovereign rights and self-government to those peoples who have been forcibly deprived of them by the aggressor Nations.
>
> To foster the conditions in which the liberated peoples may exercise these rights, the three Governments will jointly assist the people in any European liberated state or former Axis satellite state in Europe where in their judgment conditions require (a) to establish conditions of internal peace; (b) to carry out emergency measures for the relief of distressed peoples; (c) to form interim governmental authorities broadly representative of all democratic elements in the population and pledged to the earliest possible establishment through free elections of governments responsive to the will of the people; and (d) to facilitate where necessary the holding of such elections.
>
> The three Governments will consult the other United Nations and provisional authorities or other Governments in Europe when matters of direct interest to them are under consideration.
>
> When, in the opinion of the three Governments, conditions in any European liberated state or any former Axis satellite state in Europe make such action necessary, they will immediately consult together on the measures necessary to discharge the joint responsibilities set forth in this declaration.[2]

They also quoted the Memorandum by the Committee on Post-War Programs of 8 June 1944, which stated that 'unless a provisional

Austrian government emerges at the time of surrender, with which the three powers might agree to deal, direct military government should be installed in Austria supplanting the German political authorities'.[3]

The appointment of Renner and his cabinet did not comply with the wording of the Agreement, they argued, because there had been no consultation between the Soviets and the other Allies. The British, in particular, also raised a number of objections to the composition of the new government. It had been imposed centrally from above, rather than having been nurtured from the grass roots, as the British had proposed, and was, they pointed out, unrepresentative of the Austrian people as a whole as its members were drawn exclusively from eastern Austria and, more specifically, from Vienna. The western provinces had not yet been liberated and their politicians were therefore excluded. Moreover, there was as yet no agreement between the Allies on the division of the country into zones of occupation: the legacy of the ambiguity of the Moscow Declaration was very apparent. But the British also had grave reservations about Karl Renner himself, whom they judged to be an unreliable political maverick with a dubious history. Last, but by no means least, the British were deeply suspicious of what they considered to be the excessive presence of Communists in the new government, and in particular that of the two ministers, Franz Honner and Ernst Fischer, both of whom were believed to have spent the war years in Moscow.[4] Although some of these objections arose from the specific situation in Austria, there were also wider considerations which related to the entire question of post-war Allied policy in central and eastern Europe. During its drive westwards, the Soviet Union had employed a popular-front policy under which it established anti-fascist coalitions in eastern Europe, except in Albania and Yugoslavia, where the Communists had come to power through military victory. By May 1945 the Communist parties in Bulgaria and Rumania were beginning to dominate the new governments, gaining control of internal security by securing their grip on the respective Ministries of the Interior and on the police, and through the use of newly created 'people's courts'.[5] In addition, the inter-Allied dispute over the government in Poland was continuing. In January 1945 Stalin had recognised the provisional government formed by the Polish Committee for National Liberation at Lublin, which was dominated by pro-Soviet Communists and Socialists. The Western Allies supported the London-based Polish government-in-exile and refused to endorse the Soviet-backed provisional government. The issue was raised at the Yalta Conference in February, when a compromise was reached under which the provisional government was to be broadened to include other domestic and émigré groups, but in

March Soviet forces in Poland arrested representatives of the western-backed government-in-exile and by April a civil war had broken out. In May and June pitched battles raged between members of the Polish Home Army and the Polish security forces.[6] What was happening in Austria appeared to resemble certain aspects of developments in Poland, and even in Bulgaria and Rumania, and this served to reinforce western suspicions about Soviet motives concerning not only the decision to install the Renner government, but to an even greater extent the appointment of a Communist as Austrian Minister for Internal Affairs.

The result was stalemate. A provisional government had been recognised by one Allied Power, but rejected by the other three, and although it purported to represent the whole of Austria its jurisdiction was unclear. Nor did it extend beyond the area of Soviet occupation – at this time Vienna, Lower Austria, Styria and Burgenland. Although the war in Europe ended officially on 8 May and all four Allied powers were now on Austrian soil, it was another four weeks before the Allies met in Vienna to discuss the demarcation of zones of occupation and four months before the first meeting of the Allied Control Council and the recognition of the Renner government by all four Allied Powers.

In Vienna, the first month of liberation was therefore beset by contradiction and confusion. Nevertheless, the Soviet authorities did endeavour to create some semblance of normality by reactivating the city's cultural life, beginning with an apparent tribute to Vienna's reputation as a leading centre of classical music. On 27 April, while American, British and French troops were still fighting in the west of the country and Soviet troops themselves continued to encounter fierce resistance to the north of Vienna in Klosterneuburg and Mistelbach, the first public concert of the Vienna Philharmonic Orchestra was held in the Konzerthaus, with a repeat performance the next day. Despite unseasonably cold weather, with temperatures barely reaching six degrees centigrade, people queued in the street for tickets. Inside, according to Schöner, who was present, only three-quarters of the seats were occupied and most of those present came from the newly formed ministries, parties and administration, with a particularly strong contingent from the Communist Party. About one hundred Soviet officers were also in the audience.[7] The choice of conductor was contentious. Clemens Krauss, an Austrian, had been director of the Vienna State Opera under the First Republic, but had disagreed with the Austrian cultural authorities in 1934 and had accepted the post of Director of the Prussian State Opera that same year, rising to the position of *Generalmusikdirektor* in Germany in 1936. Although Krauss fell out of favour with Hitler during the course of the war, he had been one of the most influential musical figures in the Third Reich. His appearance at the first concert after the liberation was greeted by the audience with loud applause and a few hisses. The hisses were a response, not to his career under Nazism, but to his behaviour in 1934. Not only had his decision to move to Berlin come shortly after the assassination of Engelbert Dollfuss by the Nazis, but it had also involved an injury to the Viennese opera-going public which some of the audience considered to be unforgivable: he had persuaded a number of the company's leading soloists to desert their country and go with him to Berlin.[8] The concert programme itself was less problematic: Schubert's Unfinished Symphony, Beethoven's Leonore Overture No. 3, Tchaikovsky's Symphony No. 5, thus a mixture of Russian and Viennese music, on the general theme of liberation, which Schöner described as a homage to the immortal spirit of Vienna.[9] But the Leonore Overture No. 3 did also have other connotations. It was the original revision to the overture to Beethoven's only opera, *Fidelio*. The opera itself had first been performed in the Theater an der Wien in Vienna in November 1805, seven days after the last occupation of the city, by Napoleon's troops.[10] This point was obviously lost on the Communist Deputy Mayor, Steinhardt, who took to the stage during the interval to reflect that despite the food problems the Viennese love of culture was still alive and well. He went on to say that the Russians had not only freed the audience from the Brown Plague (in other words, the Nazis), but had also made the concert possible, and concluded his speech by saying that the war had been won by Athens rather than Sparta (i.e., by cultural rather than militaristic values). Schöner's response was to wonder how many people in the audience had, like himself, fallen victim to Soviet looting.

Within days Vienna's prestigious companies had returned to the stage, albeit in alternative venues where necessary: the Burgtheater, which had been bombed, opened in the Ronacher theatre with Grillparzer's *Sappho*, the tragic love story of the Greek poetess of ancient times, the entire company at the Staatsoper moved across to the Volksoper to perform Mozart's *The Marriage of Figaro*, and the Akademietheater staged a romantic satire, *Das Mädl aus der Vorstadt*, by the quintessentially Viennese playwright Johann Nestroy. The lead role in this last production was played by Paul Hörbinger, a renowned film and stage actor who had been imprisoned by the Nazis. On 24 April the first cinema opened with a showing of the Russian film *Ivan the Terrible*, but the programmers soon switched to old German-language films; by July 1945 there were sixty-two cinemas operating in the city.[11] Their main problem was the erratic electricity supply.

The real situation, however, for most Viennese was far removed from the distractions of high culture or even cinemas. By May 1945 the most crucial issue facing the population had become a critical lack of food and fuel. In early April many people were living in cellars and air-raid shelters, relying on their dwindling stores of food and what they could steal or scavenge. As soon as fighting in the city ended, the Soviet military authorities appointed mayors in each of the districts, who then became responsible for requisitioning and distributing food stocks on the basis of the last Nazi ration card to have been issued (No. 74). On 27 April the provisional government set up the State Office for Public Nutrition (*Staatsamt für Volksernährung*) and attempted to take over control.[12]

But by May the supply of food from the surrounding countryside had broken down, and looting by locals, foreign workers and Russian troops was taking its toll; one account suggests that during the last two weeks of April alone two million kilos of flour was stolen from the largest bakery in the city, the central Anker bakery.[13] The supply of flour was already too small and the official bread ration at the beginning of May was a mere 500 grams per week. There was also a shortage of bakers: the Anker bakery placed an urgent advertisement for skilled workers in the only newspaper, *Neues Österreich*, on 2 May.[14] At the beginning of May the Red Army, which had problems of its own in providing food for its troops, announced that it would distribute a 'May donation' to the population of Vienna, amounting to 200 grams of dried beans, 200 grams of dried peas, 50 grams of cooking oil, 150 grams of meat and 125 grams of sugar per person per week.[15] Although the nominal daily ration at the beginning of May was just 350 calories, roughly one third of the level needed to sustain life and less than one quarter of what was necessary for basic healthy living, even this was not always available. During those early weeks many people staved off hunger on a frugal diet of dried peas, dried milk and tinned food, augmented by barter, looting and foraging. Meat was a luxury and long hours were spent trekking into the suburbs to search for wild plants and other kinds of food. Powerful images from this time survive in the historical memory. In its attempt to control the food supply, the provisional government initially banned all private food transactions and attempted to prevent civilians from venturing into the countryside to gather food or to barter with farmers. The trams had stopped running, all motor vehicles had been requisitioned by the Red Army and petrol was in any case unobtainable, so such journeys were carried out on foot. Women with rucksacks on their backs walking to the city's out-skirts in order to exchange household goods and valuables for food were soon associated with hoarding and the black market. Warnings were issued about the damage which such 'selfish' *hamstern* (hoarding) could do to the population as a whole. But, as it was impossible to survive on the official rations, such journeys were a matter of life and death for many families and there was little the authorities could do to prevent them.[16] Fuel was also a major problem. The electricity supply, which was cut off on 7 April, had been only partially restored by the end of the month and remained erratic until the beginning of June.[17] Gas was only available on the northern bank of the Danube, as the gas pipeline into the rest of the city had been destroyed. Solid fuel could not be bought, but wood to heat food was gathered from parks and woods, or salvaged from the ruins of bombed-out buildings. Suddenly access to wood-burning stoves became crucial: one woman recalled her family's good fortune in owning a stove which they 'loaned' to neighbours in exchange for fuel, thus freeing themselves from the task of gathering their own wood.[18]

However, the most enduring image for those who experienced those days became the dried peas which were handed out by the Red Army from its own supplies and which the local population has ever since associated with the Soviet occupation. The peas were old and worm-eaten, requiring long soaking before they were cooked. In interviews given forty years after the end of the war, many women recalled the monotonous task of removing the worms, or hoping they would fall to the bottom of the pot.[19] Some wits dubbed the hated pulses 'peas with added meat' (*Erbsen mit Fleischbeilage*).[20] A year later, when the government organised a competition to choose a new national anthem, people sent in poems about the dried peas and later reworded the successful lyric, changing it from 'Land of mountains, land on the river, land of fields, land of cathedrals' to 'Land of peas, land of beans, land of the four occupied zones'.[21] Although by this time there had been some improvement in the allocation of rations compared with the first weeks of liberation, the average person in Vienna in 1946 was consuming approximately 25 per cent of the fats and meat, and less than 75 per cent of the bread that was the average in 1937, while the consumption of peas rose threefold.[22]

The dried peas, transformed into processed peas, flour, soups and even sausages, became the staple food of the hungry Viennese in May 1945 and, despite later resentment, it prevented wider famine. But it was still not enough. On 16 May Renner addressed a letter to Stalin in which he blamed the Nazi regime and the Allied bombing for the critical food situation in the city, which he described as 'alarming'. It had been impossible to plant summer crops and the autumn harvest was just ten weeks away. In the meantime there was only three weeks' supply of food in the city. The letter was ostensibly a report on conditions and Renner refrained from asking for aid directly, but on 25 May he received a reply from Stalin agreeing to supply sufficient food to raise rations by 50 to 100 per cent from the beginning of June until the harvest had been gathered in. The relief consisted of 45,000 tons of grain, 4,000 tons of meat, 1,000 tons of fats, 2,700 tons of sugar, 225 tons of coffee substitute and 1,800 tons of salt. But there was a sting in the tail. In return, the Austrian government had to agree to supply 'industrial goods insofar as we are able'.[23]

The Russians' demand for payment for food supplies was understandable considering the plight of their own population, but it was also indicative of the long-term strategy which the Soviet administration was to adopt towards Austria and its economy. At the same time as they were supplying food, the Soviets were also dismantling and removing essential plant, machinery, tools and transport, much of which was essential for local food production and distribution. A report produced in June by the British delegation to the Allied 'Vienna Mission' estimated that, of the four thousand vehicles in the city at the beginning of April 1945, only forty still remained under Austrian control.[24] Soviet requisitioning of lorries prevented the Viennese authorities from transporting either food or fuel into the city. In addition, the removal of bridging equipment delayed the reconstruction of the bridges across the Danube; by June only one bridge had been brought back into use. Engineering works and factories were stripped of machinery, which was shipped back to the USSR. Bank safes were opened and their contents removed. In September 1945 Austrian officials estimated that the replacement value of assets requisitioned by the Russians during the first five months of the occupation was one billion Reichsmarks.[25] When Theodor Körner, the Soviet-appointed mayor of Vienna, complained in early May that the removal of plant would lead to critical unemployment problems, he was informed that all equipment which had been installed after March 1938 was to be confiscated.[26] This was one of the earliest references to Russian claims for reparations at the expense of Austrian companies. At the Potsdam conference in July and August 1945 the Russians were to insist on their right to seize 'German foreign assets' in the territories they had occupied in eastern Europe, naming eastern Austria specifically.[27] The definition of what should be deemed to be 'German foreign assets' was to be given a very wide interpretation by the Russians, and this had a serious impact on the economic reconstruction of Austria. But in the first weeks of the occupation, the chief effects of the unauthorised looting by Soviet troops and the official requisitioning of goods were to be seen in the hindrances caused to the supply and distribution of food and mounting local antipathy to the Russian 'liberators'.

The dearth of food and the breakdown of the city's infrastructure inevitably affected the health of the population. Dust, flies and filth predominated among the rubble of the bombsites. Rubbish lay in the streets for weeks until a rudimentary system of refuse collection was set up at the beginning of June. One piece of good fortune was that the water supply did not break down completely, but, as sewage and water mains had been damaged, it was reduced by 70 per cent for more than a month and consumers were instructed to boil all drinking water, a task which was made more difficult by the lack of fuel.[28] Cases of dysentery, typhoid and typhoid fever and diphtheria all increased in May, although extensive epidemics were avoided. There was a shortage of medical supplies and also of doctors, the latter partially as a result of early de-Nazification. Three of the main hospitals had been bombed out and there were only three ambulances working in the entire city area.[29] One growing problem was the escalation in the number of people infected with venereal diseases. In the eyes of most Viennese, the question of sexually transmitted disease was irrevocably tied to another deeply imprinted image of the Soviet occupation – that of rape.

Although the precise number of rapes committed by Soviet soldiers will never be known and even approximations are difficult to calculate, there is no doubt that in the months from April to September 1945 thousands of Austrian women were raped by Soviet soldiers and many more lived in constant fear of being raped. One estimate based on contemporary accounts is that the number of cases in 1945 in Vienna alone was 70,000 to 100,000.[30] However, it is impossible to corroborate such figures, both because of the nature of rape itself and because the contemporary accounts are themselves speculative. Nevertheless, the existence of the problem, particularly during the first five months of the occupation, is beyond dispute and most contemporary accounts of the period refer to the fear which the attacks instilled in the women of the city and the surrounding area.[31] Apart from this, much of the evidence which has survived comes from local health office (*Sanitätsdepartement*) reports on the treatment of venereal diseases (VD), and material concerning abortions. In relation to rape, these provide only fragments of the overall picture and the evidence they do provide remains circumstantial: for instance, although there are obvious links between rape and the spread of venereal disease, these are not conclusive. Sexual diseases were also transmitted by consensual sex, whether with Soviet soldiers or local men, some of whom had returned from the Eastern Front. However, some medical reports do give a clearer picture. For instance, reports from the department of health in the Soviet-occupied district of Melk in Lower Austria show that the incidence of sexually transmitted diseases rose sharply in the spring of 1945, with a second wave in September. Between May and December, the number of infected women who reported that they had contracted VD as a result of rape was 1,300, or 5.8 per cent of all women in the area between the ages of fifteen and sixty.[32] These figures relate to the number of women who said they had been raped, not to the number of rapes, for many had been subjected to multiple attacks. In addition, the outbreak of rapes led to a temporary change in the practice of abortion: by the summer of 1945 Austrian doctors were carrying out abortions on women with 'war-related pregnancies', which meant pregnancies resulting from rape, although the legal basis for this was unclear.[33] In May 1945 the provisional provincial authority in Styria, which was under Soviet control at the time, issued directions to local health officials restoring the inter-war regulations which prohibited abortions in all cases except where the health of the mother was at risk, but adding one further exception: 'the termination of a pregnancy may be permissible on ethical grounds in proven cases of rape'. In such cases the women were required to prove 'with certainty or a high degree of probability' that a rape had taken place, and they would then be examined by a doctor to confirm that the timing of the conception coincided with the date of the alleged rape.[34] Recent research indicates that in eastern Austria as a whole most abortions were performed in an ad hoc manner up to the middle of 1946, without a clear legal basis but 'with the consent of an influential though very small political, legal, medical – and, as some evidence shows, also clerical – elite. It is very unlikely that these procedures were made public.'[35]

The medical evidence, combined with contemporary accounts, leaves no doubt that there was a high level of rape in eastern Austria in 1945. And yet, despite the importance which this form of assault was to assume in the popular memory of the Soviet occupation, detailed research on it was not undertaken until the 1980s, when oral history projects tried to piece together the surviving evidence.[36] The women who were interviewed for these projects were, by definition, young in 1945. They gave very similar accounts of their attempts to avoid contact with the Russians, of disguising their age by their dress, and of smearing their faces with dark, thick plum jam to make them look as though they were suffering from disease or infection. Many said they rarely slept at home, but took refuge at night in fields, barns and haystacks, or with friends and relatives. There was also mention of women who deliberately established sexual friendships with Russian soldiers in the hope that this would provide them with some form of protection from violent attack by other members of the Red Army. Even forty years after the event, few of the women interviewed would admit that they themselves had been raped, recounting instead the fate of friends, relatives or neighbours, or describing their own experiences of narrow escapes.[37]

While the scale of rape in Austria was horrific and represented a very real threat to women during the early months of the occupation, the figures which are available 'clearly contradict the popular version, still reflected even in academic texts, which has 10 per cent of women being raped in some villages', as Maria Mesner has pointed out.[38] The conclusion reached by Günter Bischof, that 'undoubtedly the crime of violence against women was as common in Austria as in Germany', is also open to question.[39] There were strong similarities in the early weeks and months of the liberation: Norman Naimark observes that, as the Red Army advanced across central Europe in 1944 and 1945, it was the units under the command of Marshal Malinovsky which had the worst reputation for committing crimes against the local populations; this army 'was reputed to include large numbers of released criminals who left a trail of rape and murder from Budapest to Pilsen'.[40] Malinovsky's soldiers were among the first Soviet troops to enter Vienna in April 1945. Nevertheless, there are also indications that by the autumn of 1945 the Soviet authorities in Austria were taking a sterner view of the behaviour of their troops than they did in Germany and that the number of rapes was declining.[41] An American report on the Russian occupation of Austria, written in July 1945, recounted an interview with a Socialist informant who said that looting and rape by Soviet soldiers was still taking place in rural towns and villages, but had ceased in Vienna. Officially, the punishment for such crimes was death, but there had been no attempt to enforce this in the early stages of the occupation. More recently, the informant said, a number of soldiers and some officers had been executed, indicating that the Soviet military commanders were actually taking steps to curb the excesses of their troops.[42] The report concluded that 'there is no evidence or reason to believe that the undisciplined conduct of individual Red Army men in Austria was part of a plan or a phase of Russia's policy in Austria', and went on to point out that the Soviet military commander in Austria, Marshal Tolbukhin, had been replaced shortly before the arrival of the Western Allies in Vienna in July. The Soviet authorities in Moscow were said to have taken this decision in reaction to his inability to control the behaviour of his troops.[43] In contrast, Naimark has argued that the

Soviet authorities in Germany failed to deal effectively with the issue of rape until the summer of 1947, although some attempts to tighten discipline were introduced in June 1945.[44] Tolbukhin's failure reflected differences between the official Soviet policy on Austria and the attitude of many soldiers who had spent five years fighting the German enemy and whose own women had been subjected to assault, rape and enforced prostitution by the German army.[45] One former Soviet soldier described his view of the Austrians as 'split' (*gespaltet*): on the one hand, Austria had been occupied by the German Reich, as had Czechoslovakia and Poland, but on the other hand, Austrians had been unwilling or unable to build a resistance against the Germans. Despite official edicts, apparently many ordinary Russian soldiers saw no difference between Austria and Germany, or between Austrians and Germans.[46]

The behaviour of Soviet troops in the early phase of the occupation in general and the sexual attacks on Austrian women in particular were to have long-term political as well as social consequences. The misogynistic approach to rape, where the victims are considered to be at least partially to blame for their fate, is largely, though not entirely, missing from contemporary Austrian accounts.[47] Indeed, the violated women came to symbolise the fate of the occupied country itself, both being victims of atrocities by the 'Mongol hordes', a connection which was not lost on the first contingents of American personnel who arrived in eastern Austria that summer: they were greeted with lurid tales of Russian outrages, which they initially dismissed as exaggerations designed 'to drive a wedge between the American and Russian occupying forces'.[48] But the most important consequence was that many Austrians developed a deep-seated and permanent hatred of the Soviet Union and all it stood for, including its Communist ideology. The Austrian Communist Party, in turn, became tainted by its association with the Red Army, and its hopes of gaining a strong and increasing influence in the country's political process were significantly damaged as a result. Moreover, much of eastern Austria, namely, Vienna, Lower Austria and Styria, which the Russians occupied first and where the worst violence occurred, also contained much of the country's industry and a large proportion of its industrial working class. These were the very constituencies where the Communists might have expected to win support in any future national elections. When the first elections were held in November 1945, far sooner than the KPÖ had wanted, the damage became patently clear, as we shall see.

The confusion and trauma of life under Soviet occupation in eastern Austria were compounded by uncertainty about the future of the country, which continued throughout the summer of 1945. Despite the stalemate over recognition of the Renner government, the Allies did begin to make progress over the 'Austrian Question', but the negotiations were protracted and fraught with mutual suspicion. By the end of the war in Europe, the Western Allies had occupied southern and western Austria, with French troops in Vorarlberg, the Americans in Salzburg, Tyrol and sections of Upper Austria, and the British in Carinthia.[49] Each imposed separate and differing regulations: initially the American and British authorities both issued a ban on fraternisation with the local population, particularly Austrian women, while the Americans also forbade all local political organisation and the display of the Austrian flag.[50] By June there was still no agreement about the exact demarcation of the respective zones of occupation or the future political structure of the country. On 18 May, Stalin invited 'missions' from the other Allied Powers to meet in Vienna for preliminary discussions on the Austrian Question. The three western delegations to what became known as the 'Vienna Mission' were placed in a difficult position, as they had still not recognised the Renner government and avoided all meetings with its members during their ten-day stay. No detailed decisions were made at this time about the zones, as these matters were left to the European Advisory Commission. As a result, it was not until 4 July that the first Inter-Allied Control Agreement setting up the organisational structures for the occupation of Austria was signed. The Zones Agreement establishing the areas of occupation followed five days later.[51] The final demarcations involved the transfer of military authority in several provinces and thus the movement of Allied troops. Tyrol came under French control, the section of the Mühlviertel in Upper Austria which had been occupied by the Americans was transferred to the Russians, and Styria came under British control. Vienna was divided into five zones, one for each of the four Allied Powers while the fifth, the central district, was placed under Four-Power administration: the latter arrangement resulted in one of the most enduring and strange images of Austria during the early Cold War years – the sight, even in 1955, of the 'international military police patrol consisting of four military policemen in a jeep, each drawn from one of the four occupying Powers, and each in his national uniform'.[52] The relocation of personnel took time. At the beginning of July the Americans withdrew from Tyrol. Later that month British troops entered Graz and the first western 'reconnaissance parties' took up residence in Vienna to prepare for the arrival of the Western High Commissioners and their military contingents at the end of August. But the Allied Control Council, headed by the four Commanders-in-Chief, which had been invested with 'supreme authority' by the EAC, did not meet officially until 11 September, when its members gathered in Vienna's Imperial Hotel. A statement issued the following day reaffirmed the Allies' commitment to the wording of the Moscow Declaration and to the establishment of a free, democratic and independent Austria. In preparation for future elections, the restrictions on political activity which had been imposed by the American and British authorities in their respective zones were lifted, and the three political parties which had been sanctioned by the Russians were finally allowed to pursue their activities throughout the country. Allied policy in Austria was not going to follow the German model, although no date for the elections was announced and the Renner government was not mentioned.[53]

The delay in completing and implementing the Allied Control Agreement added to the existing tension in Vienna. As the summer wore on the food situation deteriorated yet again, and the Allies could not agree on who should provide food supplies for the city. In the second week of August even the nominal ration of 850 calories failed to be met.[54] Towns and villages to the north of the city were faced with additional problems when the number of refugees fleeing into the country escalated following the Czech expulsion of the Sudeten Germans. There were stories of violence breaking out when locals tried to prevent refugees from entering their villages.[55] Former members of the Nazi Party had more to fear when in May the provisional government passed the de-Nazification Law requiring them to register with the police, but distinguishing between 'illegal' Nazis who had joined the party between 1933 and 1938, and those who had joined after the *Anschluss*.[56] In the first case to be tried by the 'people's court', guilty verdicts were returned on 17 August on four SA men accused of murdering Jews in Engerlau concentration camp and on the death march to Deutsch-Altenburg, three being sentenced to death and one to eight years' hard labour.[57] The accused all claimed that they had merely been following orders.

Throughout this period it was difficult for the local population to obtain reliable information on the state of the inter-Allied negotiations; until the beginning of August only two newspapers appeared in the city – *Neues Österreich*, whose editor-in-chief was the Communist Minister, Ernst Fischer, and the Soviet authorities' own *Österreichische Zeitung*.[58] There were frequent rumours in May and June that the Americans were about to arrive, but even after the announcement of the Allied Control Agreement and the first sighting of American jeeps in early July, there was no clear picture as to what type of administration would be set up in Austria, and there were fears that it would follow the German pattern, where German personnel acted as advisers to the military authorities.[59] In August the flow of information improved when the three permitted parties were given authorisation to print limited runs of their respective newspapers – the *Arbeiter-Zeitung* (Socialist), *Kleines Volksblatt* (ÖVP) and *Österreichische Volksstimme* (KPÖ). On 12 September the *Arbeiter-Zeitung* published details of the Allied Control Council's meeting on its front page, including a promise to raise the level of rations in the city by an unspecified amount. The increase, which was introduced on 23 September, was from 800 to 1,550 calories per day.[60]

The arrival of the Western Allies in Vienna brought hope and the prospect of more food, but it did not result in an immediate solution to the question of the status of the Renner government. The British refused to change their minds and continued to oppose its recognition as long as Honner remained Minister of the Interior and the provinces were not represented.[61] Renner succeeded in breaking the deadlock on 14 September by announcing a conference of delegates from the provinces (*Länderkonferenz*) which would take place at the end of the month and would discuss political, economic and cultural reconstruction and plans to expand the government to include representatives from the western zones. He also stated that the provisional government would seek Allied permission to hold elections at the earliest possible moment.[62] The announcement of the *Länderkonferenz* removed at least one of the British objections and at the same time led to the beginning of national party politics in Austria. In preparation for the conference, Socialists from the western provinces met in Salzburg on 13 September and members of the People's Party arrived in the same city five days later, intending to travel en masse to Vienna by air on 23 September, the day the conference was scheduled to start. As it happened, torrential storms grounded their plane and they were forced to travel by road, thus delaying the start of the conference by a day. The British were still sceptical and their representative on the Allied Control Council refused to forward the government's invitation to the Styrians and Carinthians on the grounds that it had been issued by an unrecognised body (*nicht zur Kenntnis genommene Körperschaft*) – namely, the provisional government.[63] Nevertheless, representatives from Austrian administrations and parties in all of the zones attended the two-day session in the building of the Lower Austrian provincial assembly on the Herrengasse, in the very heart of Vienna, and a series of unanimous resolutions was passed, including one setting the election date for 25 November. This display of unity followed the pattern already established in Cabinet: disputes could take place behind closed doors, but they were not to be aired in public nor in the hearing of the Allied Powers. But there had in fact been major differences of opinion during the debates. Two members of the ÖVP, its co-founder, Julius Raab, who was

Minister for Reconstruction in the Renner government, and Karl Gruber, who had been appointed provincial governor of Tyrol, attempted to remove Honner from the Interior Ministry, which had been given responsibility for arranging the elections. Renner refused to budge on this issue even though Honner's removal would clearly have been welcomed by the Western Allies, and despite Gruber's threat to withdraw the ÖVP's western delegates from the conference. His overriding concern was that the Russians might well respond to the dismissal of the most important Communist minister by vetoing the entire election process.[64] The Communist Party had strenuously opposed holding the elections so soon, ostensibly on the grounds that it would take longer than two months to organise a free and fair vote, but there was speculation that in reality they believed that they needed more time to convince voters to support them in the aftermath of the Soviet outrages. In the end a compromise was reached: the Communists agreed to the election date and Honner remained at the Interior Ministry, but a new commission, comprising two members of the People's Party, two Socialists and one Communist, was given the task of preparing for the elections. Seven new members, most of them from the People's Party, joined the government, including Gruber, who was appointed Under-Secretary of State in the Foreign Office.[65] Proportionality was again in operation.

The September conference removed the last obstacle to the resolution of this particular problem. On 1 October the Allied Control Council's members agreed to recommend to their respective governments both the recognition of the Renner government and the extension of its jurisdiction throughout Austria.[66] The Council also agreed that elections should be held no later than 31 December. In the event, the elections were held on 25 November as proposed, leaving less than two months for preparations. The task was enormous. The most recent electoral list had been drawn up in 1930, since when the population had altered greatly. As all adult Austrian citizens over the age of twenty-one were eligible to vote, there were by now thousands of new voters. On the other hand, many who had been registered in 1930 had since fled or had died in the war, while thousands of soldiers were still in prisoner-of-war camps, or on their way home. The de-Nazification laws had also disfranchised all former members of the Nazi Party, said at the time to number 428,249, or 10 per cent of the adult population; electoral registration forms, issued on 22 October, contained seven questions about membership of the NSDAP.[67] By the day of the election 3,449,605 people had registered to vote, 64 per cent of whom were women.

The election campaign began in earnest at the end of October, when the KPÖ and the Socialists published their programmes. The People's

Party followed suit four days later.[68] The programmes contained little of substance, for the three parties were all part of the same coalition government and that government had, as yet, little room to manoeuvre. As a consequence, the campaign became a battle of slogans and accusations. All three parties targeted women in particular, for obvious reasons, calling on them as wives and mothers to vote for peace and reconstruction. Much of the campaigning took place in the party newspapers, as the chronic lack of paper limited the number of posters which could be printed. This worked to the advantage of the Communists, who were able to produce more designs and copies than their rivals, using supplies provided by the Soviets. One result was that rivalry broke out as each party tried to maximise the effectiveness of its own publicity; the *Arbeiter-Zeitung* published strict instructions for Socialist workers about where and how to stick up placards: only one per site, but in the best location. It pointed out that even the most striking poster was useless if it was left in someone's desk drawer, and urged its readers to send any which were surplus to requirements to the provinces, where supplies were even tighter.[69] But the Socialists did outperform the other two parties on the streets, holding 635 election meetings in Vienna, as opposed to 286 Communist meetings and 167 for the People's Party.[70] The election campaign, however, unveiled deep-rooted hostilities between the parties, and it was clear that the pledge to forget the past and concentrate on the future was a hollow one. This was most obvious in the campaign mounted by the Socialists. Their primary target at this time was the People's Party and its links to the Corporate State, Austro-fascism and the civil war. Socialist posters carried frequent references to the squalor, scandals and unemployment of the First Republic, as well as lurid depictions of the devastation caused by Nazism and war. Several drew a direct connection between the two, pointing out that the destruction of democracy had started in February 1934, not March 1938. In contrast, the glories of Red Vienna were once again extolled; the slogan 'We built Red Vienna, our next task is to build Red Austria' was painted across the wall of one block of flats, and the *Arbeiter-Zeitung* ran stories reminding readers of the benefits which socialism had brought to the city.[71] Some posters combined the two themes – one bore a picture of the Karl-Marx-Hof housing estate, the symbol of Viennese municipal socialism, after it had been subjected to mortar attack by government forces during the civil war. But references to the past could be dangerous, as the Socialists discovered when the People's Party produced a poster displaying quotes by both Otto Bauer and Karl Renner in support of the *Anschluss*.[72] The Socialist leaders were treading a difficult path, for their campaign was essentially negative, invoking a past in which many of them found little comfort; the radicalism of Red Vienna was a dangerous legacy for men such as Adolf Schärf and Oskar Helmer, as well as for Renner, for it represented the very type of ideological socialism which they opposed. As a result, an article in the *Arbeiter-Zeitung* in which Paul Speiser promised a programme of house-building based on the model of Red Vienna was one of the few to actually mention Hugo Breitner, Julius Tandler and Otto Glöckl, the men who had been behind the SDAP's experiment in municipal socialism.[73] At the same time, the party leaders also found themselves confronting a growing danger on their left wing, where members of the Revolutionary Socialists led by Erwin Scharf were advocating closer co-operation with the Communist Party. A second goal of the Socialist election campaign was therefore to rein in the left and to counter Communist attempts to don the mantle of working-class solidarity and anti-fascism. Renner seized upon this issue during a gruelling election tour through the western provinces, when he stressed the Socialists' tradition of unity above all else, quoting the founder of the party, Victor Adler.[74] But the main attack on the Revolutionary Socialist group within the party came before the election campaign had officially begun, in an editorial in the *Arbeiter-Zeitung* written by Oskar Pollak, the news-paper's editor. Pollak had only recently returned to his old job after years of exile in London, where he had developed close links with the British Labour Party. During the election campaign the *Arbeiter-Zeitung* carried several front-page stories on Labour's victory in the 1945 elections in Britain, heralding this as a good omen for Socialist success in Austria. However, on 30 September the paper published an editorial in which Pollak mounted a full-scale attack on the Revolutionary Socialists, accusing them of weakening the party by sowing confusion among its supporters, a confusion which was compounded by the party's cumbersome name, the *Sozialistische Partei Österreichs (Sozialdemo-kraten und Revolutionäre Sozialisten)*. His argument had a distinct air of generational as well as ideological conflict which was reflected in frequent references to 'us' and 'them'. 'We', he asserted, were old party comrades and functionaries steeped in the traditions and discipline of the pre-war party, the first 'Revolutionary Socialists' who had fought fascism. 'They', on the other hand, were young and had grown up in an eleven-year political vacuum, knowing little about the history of the party and lacking political experience. 'They' failed to understand that it was impossible for the party to begin again where it had left off in 1934. Revolutionary socialism belonged to the era of illegality and had no role in the present day.[75] Pollak's words were significant, for not only did they indicate serious tensions within the party executive, but they also succeeded in changing the party's name. From October onwards, without further discussion or debate, the party dropped the words in brackets and became the *Sozialistische Partei Österreichs* (SPÖ).[76]

The KPÖ's election campaign also concentrated on the past, with many of its posters carrying caricatures of Nazi and *Heimwehr* figures and demands for swift and effective de-Nazification. A series of three posters bore the names of victims of Nazi terror, while others suggested that the Communists alone were intent on purging Austria of fascists. Another theme was the need for unity between farmers and workers, as, in a bid to win votes from the SPÖ, the party portrayed itself as the true representative of the working class as a whole. It also attacked the ÖVP, targeting in particular three of its leading members, Julius Raab, Vinzenz Schumy and Eugen Margaretha, for their earlier activities in the *Heimwehr*.[77] But the KPÖ was also forced to defend itself against allegations that it presented a threat to private property and over its association with the Red Army; one punning ÖVP slogan, which loses much in translation, played on the similarity between the German word for a watch, *Uhr*, and the prefix *Ur*, meaning 'original'.[78] Communist leaders were clearly aware of the enormous damage which the behaviour of Soviet troops had inflicted on the party and took steps to distance themselves by stressing their Austrian patriotism and excluding the symbol of the hammer and sickle from their election propaganda. But during the campaign it became increasingly obvious that these tactics were not working, and a few days before the election the Communist newspaper, the *Volksstimme*, printed a full-page article accusing both the ÖVP and the SPÖ of engaging in smear campaigns and spreading lies about the conduct of the Red Army and the Soviet Union in Austria in order to undermine support for the KPÖ.[79]

The one campaign which did not dwell on the mistakes of the past was that run by the ÖVP. It promoted itself as 'the party of the people' and 'the party of the centre', and its slogans concentrated on the concepts of work, bread, freedom, equality, property, and faith in the future of Austria. The starting-point for Austria should be not 1918/19, nor 1934 or 1938, but 1945.[80] The party also used wit and exploited its own lack of resources with the slogan, 'some parties have more paper and more posters, others have a better programme and more votes'.[81] But the most important theme of its campaign was the threat of Communism both to the future of the country and to the fortunes of its people. ÖVP posters warned voters of the danger which a Socialist victory would bring not only to property through socialisation, but also to the individual in terms of loss of liberty. Electors were told that a vote for the SPÖ was in fact a vote for Communism, since a victory for the left would result in the unification of the SPÖ and the KPÖ and the establishment of a dictatorship of the proletariat.[82] The spectre of a surrender to Soviet domination loomed large and forced the SPÖ to respond swiftly, producing a new poster rebutting the accusation.

The Allied Powers did not interfere in the election to any great extent; aside from supplying paper to the KPÖ, the Soviets reopened the bridge over the Danube at Krems and pledged a million Schillings to help rebuild the Vienna opera; the Americans returned paintings which had been removed by the Nazis from the Viennese Museum of Cultural History during the war; and the British delivered one thousand lorries to the capital. The first Austrian prisoners-of-war returning from Soviet captivity arrived at the railway station in Wiener Neustadt shortly before the start of the election campaign, to be greeted by Ernst Fischer.[83]

The weather on Sunday 25 November, the election-day itself, was dismal and wet. Nevertheless, the turnout was high, with a national average of 94 per cent of electors casting their votes. The earliest unofficial results for St Pölten and Wiener Neustadt were broadcast by loudspeaker in the election commission in the early hours of the following morning.[84] Later that afternoon the final results were declared. The ÖVP won just under half of the national vote and 85 of the 165 seats in parliament (the *Nationalrat*), as well as a majority in 7 of the 9 provincial assemblies, the exceptions being Vienna and Carinthia. The SPÖ gained 76 seats nationally and 57 per cent of the votes in Vienna. The Communists sustained a devastating blow. Having predicted before the elections that they would win over 20 per cent of the national vote, their final count was just 174,257, or 5.4 per cent. The results were dramatic. The ÖVP had an overall majority and was therefore entitled to form a single-party government. This would have altered the course of Austrian political history and destroyed the embryonic culture of consensus which had already been largely ignored over the previous weeks. The calamitous performance of the KPÖ negated its claims for a share of power and threw the whole question of its role in government into doubt. Martin Herz later recalled that the Americans were worried about how the Russians would react to the exclusion of the Communists, and, equally important, what tactics the KPÖ itself might adopt if it was relegated to the political wilderness. He was sent to discuss the matter with Leopold Figl, the ÖVP leader and future Chancellor, but was agreeably surprised to find that Figl had already decided to retain an all-party government, albeit with a much reduced Communist presence.[85] Figl's proposed list of ministers, comprising eight members of the ÖVP, six Socialists, two candidates who were unaffiliated to any political party and one Communist, was handed to the Allied Control Council for ratification on 8 December. The Russians rejected four names on the list, including Julius Raab, who was ruled out on account of his activities in the *Heimwehr*.[86] A revised list was then submitted by Figl which was passed by the Allied Control Council on 18 December. Two days later the two parliamentary chambers met in joint session and elected Karl Renner as President of the Republic.[87]

By the end of 1945 the most pressing political dilemma facing Austria had been resolved. There were still controls at the border crossings between Allied zones, but the country was unified, with a newly elected government that was recognised by the Four Powers (although official notification of the British recognition did not arrive until 5 January). The system of coalition government which was to dominate Austrian politics for decades was in place. In addition, the elections showed very clearly that there was no popular support for Communism in Austria. The reasons for this are not difficult to deduce. Historically, the Communists had never managed to challenge the Socialists' support within the working class and had failed to win a single parliamentary seat during the First Republic. The KPÖ's leaders had hoped to capitalise upon the role of party members in the resistance against both Austro-fascism and Nazism, but this hope had been thwarted by the rapes and looting by Red Army soldiers as well as the Soviet policy of dismantling and removing essential industrial plant. Moreover, as has already been pointed out, the regions which came under early Soviet occupation included key industrial areas where the bulk of the Austrian industrial labour force lived and worked. Although the Communists had performed relatively well in two provincial areas, Carinthia and northern Styria, and had won over 10 per cent of the votes in Vienna North-East and Vienna South-East, this did not make up for the disastrous results elsewhere. When Communist delegates met in conference two weeks after the election, several speakers, including some leading members, supported calls for the party to spurn Figl's offer of one ministry which was then on the negotiating table and to concentrate on building the movement on the streets.[88] This proposal was rejected. However, the most crucial consequence of the 1945 election for the KPÖ was that it strengthened Soviet scepticism about the party's leadership and the prospects for Communism in Austria, for without at least some basis of popular support a Communist takeover would be impossible.

Figl's cabinet, which finally met at the end of December, included seven ministers from the ÖVP, five from the SPÖ and one Communist, Karl Altmann, who was appointed Minister for Energy and Electrification. Adolf Schärf became Vice-Chancellor and his fellow Socialist,

Oskar Helmer, replaced Honner at the Ministry of the Interior. Karl Gruber became Minister of Foreign Affairs. The most pressing domestic problems for the new government over the following years were to be food, economic reconstruction, the containment of inflation and reining in growing popular discontent, all set against the backdrop of mounting hostility between the USSR and the Western Allied Powers and the protracted and frequently interrupted negotiations for an Austrian State Treaty.[89]

Notes

1   Schöner, *Wiener Tagebuch*, 208. The news was broadcast by the BBC.
2   Yalta Agreement. www.yale.edu/lawweb/Avalon/wwii/yalta.html.
3   *Foreign Relations of the United States, Diplomatic Papers (FRUS)*, 1944, vol. I, *General* (Washington: Government Printing Office, 1966), 443.
4   Siegfried Beer, 'Die Besatzungsmacht Großbritannien in Österreich', in Alfred Ableitinger, Siegfried Beer and Eduard G. Staudinger (eds), *Österreich unter alliierter Besatzung 1945–1955* (Vienna: Böhlau, 1998), 59. Ernst Fischer escaped to Moscow in April 1934 and broadcast from there to the Austrian people throughout the war. Fischer, *An Opposing Man*, 252–405. Franz Honner spent two periods in Moscow, returning to Yugoslavia in 1944, where he organised armed resistance on the Styrian border and set up an Austrian battalion under Tito.
5   *FRUS, 1944*, vol. I, 467. The Chargé d'Affaires in the Soviet Union (George Kennan) to the Secretary of State, Moscow, 3 November 1944; *FRUS, 1945*, vol. III, *European Advisory Commission; Austria; Germany* (Washington: Government Printing Office, 1968), 98–106; Mark Pittaway, *Eastern Europe 1939–2000* (London: Arnold, 2004), 36–40.
6   R.J.Crampton, *Eastern Europe in the Twentieth Century – and after* (2nd edn, London: Routledge, 1997), 198–9, 217–19; Geoffrey Swain and Nigel Swain, *Eastern Europe since 1945* (3rd edn, London: Macmillan, 2003), 38–44.
7   Schöner, *Wiener Tagebuch*, 191–3.
8   Michael Kater, *The Twisted Muse: Musicians and their Music in the Third Reich* (London/New York: Oxford University Press, 1997), 46–56.
9   Schöner, *Wiener Tagebuch*, 191.
10 The Leonore Overture No. 3 had been added four months later. It was replaced by the final version of the overture in 1814.
11 Wien im Rückblick. www.wien.gv.at/ma53/45jahre/inhalt, 24, 27, 30 April 1945; Rathkolb, *Gesellschaft und Politik am Beginn der Zweiten Republik*, 281.
12 SPÖ Bericht an den Parteitag, 18 November 1949, Volksernährung 1945–1949. Schärf Papers (*Nachlass*), Verein der Geschichte der Arbeiterbewegung, Box 44, 4/294.
13 Irene Bandhauer-Schöffmann, 'Women's Fight for Food in Post-War Vienna', in Claire Duchen and Irene Bandhauer-Schöffmann (eds), *When the War was over: Women, War and Peace in Europe, 1945–1956* (Leicester: Leicester University Press, 2000), 71.

14 Wien im Rückblick, 2 May 1945.
15 Bandhauer-Schöffmann, 'Women's Fight for Food', 72. Figl told Herz in September 1945 that roughly 100,000 Russians were living off the land in Lower Austria. Reinhold Wagnleitner (ed.), *Understanding Austria: The political reports and analyses of Martin F. Herz, Political Officer of the US Legation in Vienna 1945–1948* (Salzburg: Neugebauer, 1984) (henceforth Herz, *Understanding Austria*), 41.
16 Herz, *Understanding Austria*, 24.
17 Letter from the Chief Magistrate of the City of Vienna to Vice-Chancellor Adolf Schärf, 2 January 1948. Schärf's notes for his book, including dozens of letters he received in reply to his request for information on the situation in Vienna during that month, are held in the Schärf Papers, Verein der Geschichte der Arbeiterbewegung, Box 6.
18 Oral interview tape-recording at the exhibition *Die Sinalco Epoche: Essen, Trinken, Konsumieren nach 1945*, Museum of Vienna, May 2005.
19 UNRRA officially took over control of food supplies in Vienna in June 1946.
20 Suzanne Breuss (ed.), *Die Sinalco Epoche. Essen, Trinken, Konsumieren nach 1945* (Vienna: Czernin Verlag/Wien Museum, 2005), 136.
21 Bandhauer-Schöffmann, 'Women's Fight for Food', 80; Breuss (ed.), *Die Sinalco Epoche*, 136. This is better in the original German where '*Land der Berge, Land am Strome, Land der Äcker, Land der Dome*' becomes '*Land der Erbsen, Land der Bohnen, Land der vier Besatzungszonen*'.
22 Irene Bandhauer-Schöffmann and Ela Hornung, 'Geschlechtsspezifische Auswirkungen von Hungerkrise und "Freßwelle"', 15–19, in Thomas Albrich, Klaus Eisterer, Michael Gehler and Rolf Steininger (eds), *Österreich in den Fünfzigern* (Innsbruck: Österreichischer Studienverlag, 1995). Bandhauer-Schöffmann, 'Women's Fight for Food', 80. She points out that UNRRA shipped in even greater quantities of dried peas as these provided a high level of calories. Rauchensteiner states that during negotiations over the State Treaty, the Russians demanded payment for the gift of peas. Rauchensteiner, *Der Sonderfall*, 79.
23 *Protokolle des Kabinettsrates*, vol. 1, 148–50, sitting 25 May 1945. During the course of this cabinet meeting, ministers argued at length over whether the food relief was intended for Vienna only or for the Soviet-occupied territory as a whole.
24 'Report on the British Mission to Vienna, 3–13 June 1945', by Major-General T.J.W. Winterton, to Sir Richard L. McCreery, TNA/PRO/FO 1020. F.28, reprinted in Siegfried Beer and Eduard G. Staudinger, 'Die "Vienna Mission" der Westallizerten im Juni 1945', *Studien zur Wiener Geschichte, Jahrbuch des Vereins für Geschichte der Stadt Wien*, vol. 50 (Vienna, 1994), 373, 379, 404. See also Bischof, *Austria in the First Cold War*, 36–43.
25 Rathkolb, *Gesellschaft und Politik*, 338. An American official was sceptical about the reliability of this figure.
26 Rathkolb, *Gesellschaft und Politik*, 274.
27 Potsdam Agreement, Section III, para. 9. www.yale.edu./lawweb/Avalon/wwii/potsdam.html See also Rathkolb, *Gesellschaft und Politik*, 337.
28 Letter from the Chief Magistrate of the City of Vienna to Vice-Chancellor Adolf Schärf, 2 January 1948.

29 'Report on the British Mission to Vienna, 3–13 June 1945', 388–94.
30 Bischof, *Austria in the First Cold War*, 33. In a footnote, Bischof states that two million women were raped in Germany, citing Norman Naimark. But Naimark is far more circumspect about the numbers involved, and the figure of two million is mentioned only as a possibility. Bischof, 172, ftn. 26; Norman Naimark, *The Russians in Germany: A History of the Soviet Zone of Occupation, 1945–1947* (Cambridge, MA: Yale University Press, 1995), 133. One contemporary source for Vienna which Bischof cites is a British Foreign Office document dated July 1945. However, Allied reports at this time contained conflicting statistical information. For instance, the British delegation to the Vienna Mission of June 1945 reported that 65,000 women had been treated for venereal diseases in the city, while 6,000 cases of gonorrhea had been notified in 1944. Beer and Staudinger, 'Die "Vienna Mission" der Westalliierten im Juni 1945', 390, 392. An American Intelligence Summary dated 15 October 1945 stated that the incidence of VD had increased tenfold between July 1944 and July 1945. It also stated that the number of recorded cases of gonorrhea in the city between April and August 1944 had been 502, rising to 6,000 in 1945. Rathkolb, *Gesellschaft und Politik*, 326. For a discussion of the difficulties in calculating the statistics, see Marianne Baumgartner, 'Vergewaltigungen zwischen Mythos und Realität: Wien und Niederösterreich im Jahr 1945', in *Frauenleben 1945. Kriegsende in Wien. Sonderausstellung des Historischen Museums der Stadt Wien* (Vienna: Eigenverlag der Museen der Stadt Wien, 1995), 59–71.
31 Schöner, *Wiener Tagebuch*, 148, 149, 153, 161, 166, 174, 180, 200; Schärf, *April 1945 in Wien*, 28; Rathkolb, *Gesellschaft und Politik*, 298–301.
32 Marianne Baumgartner, '*Jo, des waren halt schlechte Zeiten …*'. *Das Kriegsende und die unmittelbare Nachkriegszeit in den lebensgeschichtlichen Erzählungen von Frauen aus dem Mostviertel* (Frankfurt am Main: Peter Lang, 1994), 96, 99.
33 Maria Mesner, 'Gender and Abortion after the Second World War: the Austrian Case in a Comparative Perspective', in Eleonore Breuning, Jill Lewis and Gareth Pritchard (eds), *Power and the People: A Social History of Central European Politics* (Manchester: Manchester University Press, 2005), 255–60.
34 Rundschreiben der Provisorischen Steiermärkischen Landesregierung an alle Gesundheitsämter betreffend Schwangerschaftsunterbrechungen aus gesundheitlichen oder anderen Gründen, 26 May 1945, reprinted in Karner, Stelzl-Marx and Tschubarjan (eds), *Die Rote Armee in Österreich. Sowjetische Besatzung 1945–1955. Dokumente*, 607–8.
35 Mesner, 'Gender and Abortion after the Second World War', 257.
36 Baumgartner, 'Vergewaltigungen zwischen Mythos und Realität. Wien und Niederösterreich im Jahr 1945'; Baumgartner, '*Jo, des waren halt schlechte Zeiten …*'; Hannl, *Mit den Russen leben. Ein Beitrag zur Geschichte der Besatzungszeit im Mühlviertel*; Irene Bandhauer-Schöffmann and Ela Hornung, 'Der Topos des sowjetischen Soldaten in lebensgeschichtlichen Interviews mit Frauen', in *DÖW Jahrbuch 1995*. Maria Mesner has recently pointed out that there is still no comprehensive study of rape by Allied soldiers in Austria: 'Gender and Abortion after the Second World War', 254.

37 Hannl, *Mit den Russen leben*, 62–9; Baumgartner, 'Vergewaltigungen zwischen Mythos und Realität', 61. Rapes took place in all occupation zones, but in Austrian popular memory they are usually associated with the Russians. Ingrid Bauer, ' "Ami-Bräute" – und die österreichische Nachkriegszeit', in *Frauenleben 1945*, 78.

38 Mesner, 'Gender and Abortion after the Second World War', 254. See also Baumgartner, '*Jo, des waren halt schlechte Zeiten. . .*', 93, ftn. 154. There were reports in Lower Austria that 20 to 60 per cent of women had been raped and in one district, Pfaffstätten, all the women were said to have been raped.

39 Bischof, *Austria in the First Cold War*, 33. Mesner's view differs from this: 'In terms of bare numbers, there is evidence that rape was less frequent here than, for example, in Eastern Germany.' Mesner, 'Gender and Abortion after the Second World War', 254.

40 Naimark, *The Russians in Germany*, 71.

41 Baumgartner shows that the greatest numbers of rapes reported in Melk were in early June 1945 and that they sank notably after October 1945. Baumgartner, '*Jo, des waren halt schlechte Zeiten. . .*', 98. Hannl gives the figures for Freistadt as 861 from May to December 1945 and 8 for the first three months of 1946. Hannl, *Mit den Russen leben*, 87.

42 Martin F. Herz, 'Allied Occupation of Austria: The Early Years', in Robert Bauer (ed.), *The Austrian Solution* (Charlottesville, VA: University Press of Virginia, 1982); Peter Hart, Report on Russian occupied Austria, 10 July 1945. National Archive (NA), RG 260 (Austria), Box 38. Reprinted in Rathkolb, *Gesellschaft und Politik*, 278.

43 Leonard J. Hankin, 'Soviet policy in Austria', 23 November 1945. NA, RG 59, 740.00119 Cont. (Aust.)/11–2345. Rathkolb, *Gesellschaft und Politik*, 342.

44 Naimark, *The Russians in Germany*, 79, 90, 96.

45 Baumgartner, '*Jo, des waren halt schlechte Zeiten. . .*', 127.

46 Interview with Georgi Leskis published in Erich Klein (ed.), *Die Russen in Wien: Die Befreiung Österreichs, Wien, 1945: Augenzeugenberichte und über 400 unpublizierte Fotos aus Russland* (Vienna: Falter Verlag, 1995), 172.

47 Mesner, 'Gender and Abortion after the Second World War', 259. There were exceptions. In June 1945 the British delegation to the Vienna Mission was told by Dr Lande of the Vienna Public Health Service that 'the accusations of extensive and uncontrolled raping of Austrian women were untrue. He stated that if it is borne in mind that the Russian is a "simple soldier" and should misconstrue the welcome of the female population as an invitation, it cannot be classed as rape. Further, a number of cases were stated to be rape which were in fact not technically so.' The report added, in brackets, 'in this, as in other statements, his evidence was distinctly biased'. Reprinted in Beer and Staudinger, 'Die "Vienna Mission" der Westalliierten im Juni 1945', 391.

48 Herz, 'Allied Occupation of Austria', 19; private letters from Paul R. Sweet to his wife, 17 and 18 September 1945, Rathkolb, *Gesellschaft und Politik*, 302–3.

49 Rauchensteiner, *Der Sonderfall*, 64.

50 Josef Leidenfrost, 'Die Nationalratswahlen 1945 und 1949: Innenpolitik zwischen den Besatzungsmächten', in Günter Bischof and Josef Leidenfrost, *Die Bevormundete Nation* (Vienna: Haymon, 1988), 129; Balfour and Mair, *Four-Power Control in Germany and Austria*, 317. The ban on fraternisation

was lifted at the beginning of September 1945 despite demonstrations by soldiers' wives in the USA who demanded its retention. Rauchensteiner, *Der Sonderfall*, 121.

51 Eric Erickson, 'The Zoning of Austria', *Annals of the American Academy of Political and Social Science* (January 1950), 113. The zonal boundaries were defined by the European Advisory Commission.

52 Balfour and Mair, *Four-Power Control in Germany and Austria*, 314.

53 *Ibid.*, 312–13. Until 1949 the Western Allies restricted political parties in their German zones to organising on a regional basis.

54 Schöner, *Wiener Tagebuch*, 347; Bischof, *Austria in the First Cold War*, 49.

55 Eva Hahn and Hans Henning Hahn, 'Between "*Heimat*" and "expulsion": the construction of the Sudeten German "Volksgruppe" in post-war Germany', in Breuning *et al.*, *Power and the People*, 82; Schöner, *Wiener Tagebuch*, 290.

56 *Protokolle des Kabinettsrates*, vol. 1, 30–34, sitting 8 May 1945.

57 Schöner, *Wiener Tagebuch*, 346, 349.

58 Although a leading Communist who had spent ten years in Moscow, Fischer was a political intellectual who was mistrusted by the Russian authorities. A secret Soviet report, dated 12 September 1947 and entitled 'Concerning Certain Erroneous Utterances by Member of the Politburo of the Austrian Communist Party Ernst Fischer', described *Neues Österreich* as 'the organ of the in reality non-existent democratic unity', in which there is 'no clear-cut political line to be found'. Russian State Archive of Socio-Political History (RGASPI), Fond 575, Op.1, Delo 8.

59 Schöner, *Wiener Tagebuch*, 302.

60 Balfour and Mair, *Four-Power Control in Germany and Austria*, 313.

61 Rauchensteiner, *Der Sonderfall*, 118.

62 *Arbeiter-Zeitung* (14 September 1945), 1.

63 Rauchensteiner, *Der Sonderfall*, 120–4.

64 Herz, *Understanding Austria*, 50–1. Gruber and two other members of the People's Party spent the late evening of 24 September in Herz's flat, where they seemed 'singularly uninterested in compromise', to Herz's obvious dismay.

65 Bischof, *Austria in the First Cold War*, 51.

66 The last Allied government to recognise the Austrian government was the British, on 16 October. Official collective Allied recognition came on 20 October.

67 *Arbeiter-Zeitung* (21 October 1945); Anton Pelinka, *Austria. Out of the Shadow of the Past* (Boulder, CO: Westview Press, 1998), 30; the registration form is reproduced in Portisch and Riff, *Österreich II*, 486.

68 Two other political parties were permitted to take part in Carinthia – the Osvobodilna Fronta za Slovensko Koroško/the Liberation Front for Slovene Carinthia (OF) and the Demokratische Partei Österreichs (DPÖ). The OF withdrew shortly before the elections and urged its supporters to vote for the KPÖ. Robert Knight, 'The Carinthian Slovenes', in Breuning *et al.*, *Power and the People*, 111. The DPÖ was banned in December.

69 *Arbeiter-Zeitung* (10 November 1945).

70 Bernhard Denscher, 'Die Werbungen in Wien für die Nationalratswahl am 25. November 1945', *Studien zur Wiener Geschichte, Jahrbuch des Vereins für Geschichte der Stadt Wien*, 42 (1986), 132.

71 Denscher, 'Die Werbungen in Wien für die Nationalratswahl', 130.
72 Portisch and Riff, *Österreich II*, 482–3.
73 Lewis, 'Red Vienna: Socialism in One City, 1918–1927', 335–54.
74 Leidenfrost, 'Die Nationalratswahlen 1945 und 1949', 135. Erwin Scharf should not be confused with Adolf Schärf.
75 *Arbeiter-Zeitung* (30 September 1945).
76 Kurt Shell, *The Transformation of Austrian Socialism*, 36; Julius Deutsch, *Ein Weiter Weg* (Vienna: Amalthea Verlag, 1960), 378.
77 Denscher, 'Die Werbungen in Wien für die Nationalratswahl', 125–9.
78 '*Urwiener und Wiener ohne Uhr wählen ÖVP*' (native Viennese and Viennese without watches vote ÖVP), Portisch and Riff, *Österreich II*, 474. A similar slogan was used by the Styrian ÖVP. Portisch and Riff cite a second ÖVP poster which declared that '*Wer die Russen liebt, wählt kommunistisch*' (whoever loves the Russians votes Communist), but this story is probably apocryphal. Denscher, 'Die Werbungen in Wien für die Nationalratswahl', 128.
79 *Volksstimme* (22 November 1945).
80 There were exceptions: an ÖVP poster issued in the Tyrol demanded strong government, citing putsch 'attempts' in 1927, 1932 and 1934 as evidence. Portisch and Riff, *Österreich II*, 482.
81 '*Die einen haben mehr Papier und mehr Plakaten, die anderen ein besseres Programm und mehr Stimmen*', Denscher, 'Die Werbungen in Wien für die Nationalratswahl', 134.
82 Portisch and Riff, *Österreich II*, 484.
83 *Ibid.*, 476–81.
84 Schöner, *Wiener Tagebuch*, 426–9.
85 Herz, 'Allied Occupation of Austria: the Early Years', 30.
86 Rathkolb, *Gesellschaft und Politik*, 211. Raab became the director of the Federal Chamber of Business (*Bundeswirtschaftskammer*) and succeeded Figl as Chancellor of Austria in 1953.
87 The second chamber, the *Bundesrat*, was elected by the provincial assemblies.
88 Herz, *Understanding Austria*, 70.
89 The treaty to end the occupation was known throughout the negotiations and thereafter as the Austrian State Treaty, despite the fact that, as Günter Bischof has insisted, this was a misnomer, for the Austrian State already existed. Bischof, *Austria in the First Cold War*, 105.

4

Supervised independence

By the beginning of 1946 the most critical period of political insecurity had passed, but resolving the problem of Allied recognition of the Austrian government did not lead to independence. The country's 'ambiguous' status, as it had been outlined in the Moscow Declaration, remained. Austria was both 'victim' and 'perpetrator', 'liberated' but occupied and, under what has been termed Allied 'tutelage', her politicians were forced to prove their democratic credentials before being granted full independence.[1] The 1945 Allied Control Agreement had granted supreme authority over the country to the Allied Commission for Austria, while the four Allied Military Commissioners (Commanders-in-Chief) enjoyed similar powers in their respective zones. In practice, the military commanders also exercised real power nationally, for they comprised the Allied Control Council, the principal body of the Allied Commission, which met every ten days to vet proposed new laws submitted to them by the Austrian government. Under Article 6a of the original Allied Control Agreement, all decisions by the Allied Council had to be issued unanimously and those matters on which agreement could not be reached were withheld from public scrutiny. As a consequence, Allied members each had the power of veto over all Austrian legislation. It was a confusing and contradictory situation which effectively demoted the role of the democratically elected government to that of adviser to the Allied Council. This problem was obvious to the British, who, as soon as the elections were over, insisted on fresh discussions to revise the Control Agreement. They submitted draft proposals to the Allied Council in March 1946, suggesting the abolition of border controls for the zones as well as changes to the veto. The Russians rejected these proposals. The major stumbling-block was the proposal to revise Article 6a by replacing the simple veto with a 'reverse veto'. This would remove the power of an individual Council member to block legislation in the absence of the agreement of the other three. The Russians refused to give up their veto and for several months they appeared to be obdurate. Then in May 1946, to the astonishment of the British and Americans, they relented, accepting a compromise solution which restricted the individual veto to changes to constitutional law.[2] The Second Control Agreement was finally passed by the Allied Council and came into force on 28 June, to the relief of the Austrian government and its citizens – Karl Renner was applauded by the audience at the Volkstheater when he attended a performance the evening after the Agreement had been made public, and the *Arbeiter-Zeitung* devoted most of its front page to the economic benefits which would result from lifting the trade barriers between the zones.[3] Nevertheless, little attention was paid locally to the reverse veto, despite the fact that this gave a far greater degree of independence to the Figl government. Under the new version of Article 6a, all legislation submitted to the Allied Council by the Austrian government was automatically passed providing that no objections were forthcoming from the Council within thirty-one days. The fact that all such objections now had to be unanimous meant that the acquiescence of just one Allied member could overturn the ruling of the other three. This was to have enormous significance as the Cold War intensified and the respective goals of the Western Powers and the Russians in Austria began increasingly to diverge. Indeed, it is unclear why the Russians conceded the point and there is every indication that they quickly regretted their decision, for in August they made two attempts to reinterpret Article 6a, both of which were rejected by the other Powers.[4]

The first crucial test case involving the revised Control Agreement arose in June 1946 when the Allies clashed over the question of reparations. Along with many others, this was one issue on which the EAC had failed to reach a decision by the end of the war.[5] Nevertheless, as has already been mentioned, Soviet forces had begun to remove plant and machinery from Austrian territory in May 1945, requisitioning what they deemed to be 'war-booty' and targeting primarily heavy industry and engineering. Austrian officials later estimated that the replacement value of the requisitioned industrial equipment, raw materials, and finished and semi-finished products which were removed in the first five months of the occupation was over a billion Reichsmark.[6] The issue had been raised at the Potsdam Conference (17 July to 2 August 1945), when agreement had been reached that the Soviet Union could remove 'German assets' from those countries which the Red Army had 'liberated', including Bulgaria, Finland, Hungary, Rumania and Eastern Austria. The definition of 'German assets', however, remained vague.[7] Shortly after the Potsdam Conference, the Russians approached the Renner government with proposals to set up

Soviet-Austrian joint-stock companies to take over the Zistersdorf oilfields and the Danube Shipping Company. Renner refused, not least because the oilfields had been partly owned by American companies before the war and he had been warned by the United States that any agreement along these lines could jeopardise American aid to Austria.[8] In early spring 1946, after the Communist Party's defeat in the Austrian elections the previous November, the Soviet authorities began to evaluate and confiscate 'German assets' in their zone. They produced a new definition of the term 'German assets' and laid claim to all property which had been in German ownership before 1938, as well as that which had been acquired after the *Anschluss*, including Jewish property which had been 'aryanised' after 1938. They also set up a central administrative trust, the Administration of Soviet Property in Austria (*Upravleniye Sovietskovo Imushchestva v Avstrii* – USIA) to oversee the running of what was now described as Soviet property, including the Soviet Petroleum Authority, which had taken control of the Zistersdorf oilfields and the Danube Shipping Company.[9]

On 27 June, the day before the signing of the Second Control Agreement, the Soviets, citing the terms of the Potsdam Agreement, announced that all German property in their zone would be transferred to Soviet ownership, formally notifying the Austrian government of this three weeks later. The American and British governments protested in vain, but the Austrian government took more decisive action, passing a Nationalisation Law on 26 July. This law brought into public owner-ship the mining, steel, machinery, chemical and electrical industries, along with three major banks, establishing them as limited com-panies. It was also intended to cover those enterprises which had been seized by the Russians. The law was laid before the Allied Council on 2 August, where the Soviet Element attempted to block it, arguing that such wide-ranging legislation constituted a change in constitutional law and was therefore subject to the simple veto. The timing was highly significant. Had the Nationalisation Law been submitted to the Allied Council before July 1945, it would have been vetoed by the Russians, but, under the Second Control Agreement, rejection now required Allied unanimity. The three Western Elements threw out the Soviet argument and approved the law, which came into force on 17 September.[10]

The pronouncement on 'German assets' reflected an important change in Soviet occupation policy. The initial policy of dismantling plant and shipping much of it back to the Soviet Union, leaving the rest to decay and thus rendering it useless to Austrian economic recovery, was literal asset-stripping, with the immediate needs of the Soviet economy taking precedence over industrial reconstruction in Austria itself. It could not long be sustained, for, at some point, the supply of useful plant would be exhausted. There are two possible explanations for its adoption: either the Russians envisaged a short occupation during which they would remove as much industrial capital as they could in the shortest period of time, or they had not yet developed a long-term policy. In 1946, the foundation of USIA and the expropriation of companies which had been either partially or solely under German ownership and their transfer to Soviet control indicated that the Russians had indeed now developed a long-term strategy. As a result, USIA companies were to remain on Austrian soil, but operating according to Soviet law and serving the Soviet economy, which had just introduced its first post-war Five Year Plan.[11] They were therefore to be exempt from Austrian taxation and legislation and their products would not contribute to Austrian export revenues. The Russians obviously intended to remain in Austria for the foreseeable future.

The expropriation of German property was a severe blow. It clearly illustrated that the Austrian government's control over the economy was still restricted. Despite the introduction of the revised Control Agreement, neither the Western Allies nor the Austrian government were able to prevent the expropriation of what in time amounted to 30 per cent of industrial production in Vienna and Lower Austria and 5 per cent of industrial production nationally. Over the following ten years, Austria was even forced to import crude oil from the West, while 63 per cent of its own crude oil production went to the USSR.[12]

The economic consequences of these losses were grave, but the crisis of 1946 also produced important political repercussions which strengthened the position of the Austrian government and reinforced the culture of elite consensus which had underpinned it since the first days of the Renner government. The year 1946 was to prove a pivotal one in post-war Austrian politics. In the first place, the failure of Soviet attempts in the Allied Council to overturn the reverse veto by widening the definition of constitutional law showed that the new Control Agreement had curbed the influence of the individual Allied Powers, and of the Soviet Union in particular, and had thus given the Austrian government greater room for manoeuvre. The Western Allies, particularly the United States and Great Britain, could, to an extent, temper Soviet interference in Austrian national politics, with France developing the role of broker between the two sides, although at the local level, within the Soviet zone, there were still problems over jurisdiction, as we shall see. Moreover, the Austrian government's response to the seizure of German assets had been both swift and innovative and had provoked its first direct confrontation with the Russian authorities.

The Nationalisation Law did not prevent the expropriation of a large sector of the economy, but it did strengthen Austria's relations with the United States and Great Britain. Any lingering fears that the Western Powers might have had about the Austrians dancing to the Soviet tune evaporated. The following October the American and British governments, the latter wrestling with its own economic problems, announced a package of grants and credits designed to alleviate the prospective Austrian trade gap, which was expected to amount to $200 million. This aid would also compensate for the loss of productive capacity following the Soviet expropriations and prevent the Austrian economy from depending on trade with the Soviet sector for goods produced in industries such as glass, chemicals and metal which were dominated by USIA.[13] The aid not only provided much-needed food and fuel, but it also proved that the Western Powers were committed to Austrian independence. On 12 March 1947, President Truman pledged that the United States would 'help free people to maintain their free institutions and their national integrity against aggressive movements that seek to impose upon them totalitarian regimes'.[14] The relevance of this was transparently clear to Austrian politicians.

At the domestic level, the Nationalisation Law also reflected the fundamental change in Austrian party politics which had occurred since 1938. In the longer term, this law, along with a second which was passed in 1947, created one of the largest public sector economies, relatively speaking, in the western world.[15] Its most unusual feature was that it was introduced by a coalition government led by conservative politicians and was endorsed by the employers' associations as well as the trade unions. The reason for this development was not elite conversion to socialism, particularly not on the part of the employers, but the recognition by all major political parties and interest groups that they were united in wishing to protect Austrian capital from Soviet reparation claims. When the first Nationalisation Law came before parliament in 1946, it was passed unanimously, even gaining the support of the four Communist deputies in the face of vociferous Soviet opposition. Austrian nationalisation was, therefore, the product of elite consensus based on political compromise, and resulted from ideological shifts which had been brought about by the Allied occupation. It was a far cry from the political intransigence of the inter-war years. Despite its scale, however, Austrian nationalisation did not result in a centralised planned economy, but in what Eduard März has described as an early 'mixed economy'.[16] The companies concerned retained managerial control and operated according to the principles of a market economy, but the political influence they had exerted before the war was reduced. The Association of Austrian Industrialists (*Vereinigung Österreichischer Industrieller –* *VÖI*), the largest employers' association, no longer represented banking and heavy industry, while the nationalisation of these industries provided the government with a lever with which to enforce price restrictions upon both the private and public sectors, as will be shown. The nationalisation policy itself also proved that, if the situation was critical, the political Right would even compromise on such crucial issues as property rights, allowing public ownership as long as this did not involve state-run management. It was a prime example of the elite consensus which was to prevail in the first decades of the Second Republic and it laid the foundation-stone of an extraordinary model of institutionalised economic decision-making, the Austrian Social Partnership.

The government's success in passing the 1946 Nationalisation Law was, however, a flawed one, for it only operated in the western zones and this remained the case until the end of the occupation. The presence of the USIA empire in eastern Austria became a continuing hindrance both to national economic reconstruction and to negotiations over the State Treaty, for there was little reason for the Russians to withdraw from Austria while they were still benefiting from the revenue and goods which flowed from their zone of occupation. But the economic division of the country also affected the political culture in general and labour politics in particular. In the first five years of the trust's existence, between 22,000 and 60,000 Austrian workers were employed in USIA concerns in Vienna, Lower Austria and Burgenland and were thus subject to Russian control. Discipline in the factories was maintained by the *Werkschutz*, an armed factory guard of Austrian Communists variously estimated to number between 1,600 and 12,000, whose official job was to 'protect' Soviet property.[17] This situation posed a potential threat to the internal security of the country. From 1947 onwards, as we shall see, the Austrian government frequently expressed fears that the Communists, backed by the Soviet Union, were planning to overthrow the existing regime by means of a putsch in which the USIA workforces would supply the shock-troops. The danger of a Communist takeover in Austria was to become a constant and effective refrain in the early years of the Cold War, strengthening the government's position in its negotiations with the Western Allies. It was also effective in containing the domestic protest which arose in the wake of the stringent economic policies of the late 1940s. Strikes and demonstrations were regularly denounced as Communist conspiracies designed to destroy democracy and draw Austria into the Soviet bloc. The impact this had on Austrian workers and on the development of industrial politics will be the subject of later chapters.

In 1946 the Austrian government and its people were faced with major economic as well as political problems. The occupation costs alone accounted for almost 35 per cent of the national budget in 1946.[18] The country had also emerged from the Second World War with a fragmented and weak economy, which lacked resources, infrastructure, raw materials, markets, power and a skilled labour force. Food supplies had to be imported and paid for and so did coal, raw materials and power. But the currency was unstable, industrial production was dangerously low, capital investment was urgently needed and real wages had fallen catastrophically.[19] There was also a constant threat of galloping inflation. Austria was dependent on foreign aid, first through the United Nations Relief and Rehabilitation Administration (UNRRA) and later through the European Recovery Programme (ERP), otherwise known as the Marshall Plan. The food situation was critical, but Marshall Aid was intended to provide industrial investment in order to increase productivity and foreign earnings, not to pay for imported foodstuffs.

Although Austria's industrial plant had suffered less war damage than that of neighbouring countries, output in the first few years remained perilously low; in 1947, when a new production index was published, it showed that combined production of investment and consumer goods had only reached 61 per cent of the level attained in 1937 (which, moreover, had been a poor year). The figures also showed a marked discrepancy between the output of investment goods and that of consumer goods: whereas the former had reached 84 per cent, the latter was only 42 per cent of the 1937 level.[20] This could have been good news, because Austria depended on foreign trade and she desperately needed to produce and export goods. But in the immediate post-war years, when her balance of payments was in chronic deficit, the few products she was exporting were raw materials and semi-manufactured goods, which had low added value. The Austrian economy derived no direct benefit from goods produced in the Soviet-controlled plants, while many of these products, including oil and semi-manufactured goods, were denied to Austria's own engineering industries, where, indirectly, they could have earned higher added value on the export market.

The country was reduced to exporting low value-added goods in return for power and raw materials. Moreover, the domestic consumer market, which, in theory, could have stimulated the economy, was, in reality too weak. Employment had risen steadily after the summer of 1945 and the official unemployment rate fell to just 2.8 per cent in 1947, denoting notional full employment.[21] Nevertheless, real wages remained low and the supply of foodstuffs was meagre. This chronically weak domestic market meant that economic revival had to be based on the export market. But which market? Before the war Austria's traditional trade links had been with the east, from where she had imported 80 per cent of her coal requirement, which was essential for the steel industry, but this trade link became increasingly tenuous after 1945. In addition, trade with the western zones of Germany was restricted under the terms of the Potsdam Agreement.[22] Austrian goods were uncompetitive in western markets, many of which were facing comparable problems. Austria also had to import consumer goods to provide essentials (chiefly foodstuffs) for the domestic market. The country therefore required a stable currency, new markets and large-scale investment in order to be able to compete on the world market. By early 1947 she had achieved none of these.

The food supply had been the most pressing domestic problem since the end of the war. Indeed, the population could not be fed without large-scale foreign aid. Domestic agricultural production, which had accounted for no more than 75 per cent of food requirements before the war, was falling yet further. The urban population, as we have seen, was on the point of starvation, relying on food relief, scavenging, the black market and barter. The situation was still critical at the end of 1946 when a report prepared by the United States Forces in Austria, Economics Division, included the comment that 'for over 18 months Austrian peoples [*sic*] have been subsisting on a near-starvation diet. Malnutrition has resulted in a serious reduction of workers' productive capacity. This too has caused a substantial delay in the previously anticipated industrial recovery.'[23] Rations remained under the 2,000 calorie level, considered at the time to be the minimum for a healthy diet, until the autumn of 1947.

The food problem had political as well as economic dimensions and illustrates the crucial dilemmas confronting the Austrian government in relation both to its own people and the Occupying Powers. The country was still haunted by two spectres from the First Republic – the threat of civil violence stemming from a politically divided populace and the fear of a non-viable economy. The long-term political solution to the first problem was to cultivate a sense of Austrian national identity, emphasizing the culture of consensus which was already being fostered by the politicians, and with it the concept of a common struggle for reconstruction.[24] A viable economy, on the other hand, required a healthy and efficient workforce, enhanced productivity and increased trade. The most urgent tasks were to improve the food supply and to contain the popular discontent over food shortages and the low standard of living which was fermenting in the towns. The immediate danger of starvation in the cities was averted by UNRRA aid, which provided 64 per cent of Austrian basic ration requirements between March 1946 and June 1947. This aid had originally been intended to stimulate industrial growth by increasing capital investment. It failed to do so because the food crisis at this time was so severe that 90 per cent of the UNRRA funding had to be diverted to provide food and support for agriculture. As a result, no new machinery was imported into Austria before 1948.[25] The government also tried to increase the food supply by introducing large-scale food subsidies in order to encourage farmers to increase their yields, but this angered the Americans, who opposed subsidies, and left domestic agricultural prices far below world market prices, thus adding to the supply problem: imported food bought on the open market was expensive. Even so, farmers complained that, despite the subsidies, their incomes were too low to cover costs; by contrast, there also were many rumours about rich farmers exploiting the plight of famished city-dwellers to line their own pockets by substituting wax for fat, and decorating their barns with the pianos and Persian carpets they had received in exchange for food.[26] The weather did not help matters either. In 1946 a drought caused serious disruption to domestic food production and to the power supplies, which relied heavily on hydro-electricity. This crisis was followed by one of the harshest winters on record. The 1947 harvest, which was the worst in living memory, brought in a mere 44 per cent of the 1937 total for wheat and rye, 30.3 per cent for potatoes and 33 per cent for coarse grains such as maize, barley and oats. Food supplies were again critical and hunger demonstrations broke out in towns in all zones. Rising prices in 1946 also led to a series of protests over wages and, by the end of that year, the wage index for Vienna showed a rise of 59 per cent over the level for April 1945.[27] There were strong indications that the increases in prices and wages were fuelling inflation. Labour productivity, which had been rising steadily in the first half of 1946, slipped again at the end of the year and there were calls for the Schilling to be stabilised.

By the beginning of 1947, therefore, the economy appeared to be spiralling out of control and street protests were increasing. The timing of these developments was unfortunate for the government: it was not the moment for civil unrest. The last shipments of UNRRA aid were due to be delivered in June, and it was unclear how the urban population would be fed once this had run out. Moreover, the diplomatic situation was tense, with negotiations over the Austrian State Treaty about to open in London.[28] In June 1947, the American Secretary of State, George Marshall, announced plans for the economic reconstruction of Europe, in the shape of the European Recovery Programme. Based on the

principle of 'self-help' rather than simple aid, the plan required prospective recipient states to submit detailed proposals for economic
reconstruction within the framework of free trade in an integrated
European market. Central to these plans was the need for stable
convertible currencies, the reduction of tariff barriers to create 'free
trade', and a commitment to invest funds in capital goods in order to
increase industrial productivity and stimulate growth. Such sustained
economic reconstruction, it was asserted, required short-term controls
on consumption, but would, in the long term, lead to prosperity. It also
required acceptance of the laws of economics as interpreted by the
United States and of the right of US agencies to oversee European
economic policy.

The Americans did not restrict applications for Marshall Aid to
Western European states, but invited representatives from 'any country
that is willing to assist in the task of recovery' to attend a meeting in
Paris on 12 July. Those invited included Russia and the Soviet-dominated
countries of Eastern Europe – Albania, Bulgaria, Czechoslovakia,
Finland, Hungary, Poland, Rumania and Yugoslavia.[29] The British
Foreign Secretary, Ernest Bevin, and his French counterpart, Georges
Bidault, also invited Vyacheslav Molotov, the Soviet Foreign Minister,
to join them in preliminary talks about the American proposals.
These began in Paris at the end of June. Molotov arrived with over
one hundred advisers on 27 June, but walked out of the talks on 2 July,
dismissing the Marshall Plan as an American device to establish a
dollar-dependent economic empire in Europe 'which would split Europe
into two groups of states and would create new difficulties in the
relations between them'.[30] Russian suspicions were fuelled by American
plans to include Germany in the ERP before the question of Soviet
demands for reparations had been resolved. On 7 July Moscow informed
the Eastern European states that it would be undesirable for them to
attend the Paris meeting on 12 July. All but the Czechs and Poles
conformed at once. The Soviet government then applied additional
pressure. The Czech Prime Minister, Klement Gottwald, and the Foreign
Minister, Jan Masaryk, who were already in Moscow, were summoned
by Stalin and ordered to recall the Czech delegation. Masaryk was
reported to have said on his return that, 'I went to Moscow as the
Foreign Minister of an independent sovereign state; I returned as a lackey
of the Soviet government.'[31] Both the Polish and Czech delegations
returned home.

One crucial question which faced the Austrian government in the
summer of 1947 was whether the Soviet Union would also attempt to
block Austrian participation in the Marshall Plan. Austria's situation

was, however, markedly different from that of her eastern neighbours, for the influence of the Soviet Union here was much weaker. The Soviet Union was only one of the four Occupying Powers and the revision of Article 6a in the Second Control Agreement had made it impossible for the Russian Element on the Allied Council to veto Austrian participation in the ERP. Moreover, the unpopularity of the KPÖ indicated that this situation was unlikely to change, at least in the foreseeable future. Nevertheless, the Soviets did protest in the Allied Council on the grounds that membership of the ERP would violate the Moscow Declaration and undermine Austria's independence by subjugating her economy to American control. It was an accusation which would loom large in Soviet and Austrian Communist Party propaganda over the following years, but the protest was immediately rejected by the other three Elements on the Allied Council.

In July 1947 Austrian delegates duly attended the first meeting in Paris of the Committee of European Economic Co-operation (CEEC), whose members included representatives of the sixteen states which were applying for Marshall Aid. Their presence thus confirmed the western focus of Austria's economic and political orientation.[32] Detailed statements of Austrian requirements were submitted to the ERP in late 1947; these were based on government predictions that the balance of payments deficit for each of the fiscal years 1948–9 and 1949–50 would exceed $650 million. As was the case for all prospective recipient states, Austrian expectations were set too high. The US government allocated $13 billion in total to finance Marshall Aid, much less than the combined sum of $30 billion which was originally requested by CEEC members. Austria was initially offered between $151 and $197 million for the first year of the Marshall Plan. The Austrian government responded by claiming that, as a result of the deepening division of Europe between East and West, Austria was a 'special case'.[33] It emphasised the country's dependence on imported food and coal and the growing difficulties in obtaining these from Czechoslovakia and Hungary, as well as the consequences of Soviet policy in regard to German assets, which had created a divided economy in which important industrial sectors in the eastern zone were under Russian rather than Austrian control. The domestic situation was also precarious for, as we shall see, food riots had broken out in several Austrian towns. The government's argument succeeded. Indeed, there were already indications that the American government had recognised the gravity of the Austrian food crisis and the potential threat it represented to politics in the region, for, in June 1947, President Truman asked Congress to authorise the granting of $90 million of aid for Austria under the Foreign Relief Program. But

Congress prevaricated for three months, only approving the aid in September and thus forcing the Austrian government to postpone until the end of the year plans it had submitted to the Allied Council in July to increase the official basic ration from 1,550 to 1,800 calories.[34] Nevertheless, three weeks after the authorisation of this emergency relief, Congress also passed the Foreign Aid Act providing Interim Aid to France, Italy and Austria, the three European governments the Americans considered to be the 'most threatened by Soviet tactics'.[35] Under this scheme, Austria received a further $57 million of Interim Aid during what was dubbed the 'Marshall gap', the three-month period from January until March 1948. After President Truman signed the Economic Co-operation Act in April 1948 setting up the administrative body of the Marshall Plan, the Economic Co-operation Administration (ECA), $280.5 million was allocated to Austria for the twelve months from 1 July 1948 to 30 June 1949 (the Marshall Plan's financial year), $70 million of which was issued in advance.[36]

According to Alan Milward, in the first year of the Marshall Plan Austria received the largest injection of ERP funding, in relative terms, of all sixteen recipients, amounting to 14 per cent of her national income.[37] The country's precarious political position had produced economic dividends. And yet, this sum was still not as much as the Austrian government had hoped for, and it continued to argue that the country should receive special consideration. In addition, Austrian politicians had not bargained for the conditions which were attached to participation in the Marshall Plan. Direct Marshall Aid did not come in the form of cash, but as plant, goods and raw materials imported from the United States for specific projects, and carried in ships, lorries and trains which were clearly marked with the slogan 'For Economic Recovery – Supplied by the United States of America': the importance of propaganda had not been forgotten. Each CEEC member prepared a prioritised list of 'requirements' for specific micro-economic investment schemes based on detailed plans drawn up by their respective industries and economic interest groups. This list was then submitted to the ERP in Paris for approval. In theory, European recovery was to be administered by Europeans, but in reality it was the Americans who were financing the aid, and from the beginning American advisers 'took an increasingly firm line in telling the CEEC delegates what their requirements and expectations of aid ought to be'.[38] Nor was American influence limited to the deliberations in the CEEC. In order to qualify for direct aid, members of the CEEC were required to sign bilateral treaties with the United States which included pledges that they would take steps to stabilise their currencies, increase productivity, co-operate with other CEEC members, submit progress reports, provide the United States with 'needed materials' and adopt policies which would result in their return to economic self-sufficiency. This gave the United States extensive influence over economic and fiscal policy in the recipient states, as a report in the *Department of State Bulletin* makes clear: 'Never before in history [. . .] has any nation undertaken by solemn international agreement [. . .] to stabilise its currency, establish or maintain internal fiscal stability'.[39] In 1948 sixteen European countries did just that.[40] Under the terms of these bilateral agreements, they were each also obliged to set up a 'Counterpart' account into which domestic companies paid funds to the value of the plant and equipment they had received from the ERP. Payments were made in the local currency equivalent of the dollar value of the imported aid, and funds from this account could be used to promote monetary stability, to defuse inflationary tendencies and to reduce short-term public debt, as well as to provide additional capital investment. These monies were not intended to be used to defray either private or public consumption. Although 95 per cent of Counterpart funds were deemed to belong to the recipient state, they could not be released without the agreement of the local ECA mission and, ultimately, the American Congress.[41]

In contrast to the way in which the matter was handled in most other countries, the Austrian decision to apply to join the ERP and to sign a bilateral agreement was not put to parliament but was taken in Cabinet, and as a result there had been little public debate about the conditions attached to membership. The presence in Vienna of an ECA mission staffed by American personnel who offered 'advice' on economic issues, but who could also recommend delaying or even withholding crucial Counterpart funds, came as a shock to many Austrian policy-makers who quickly became aware of the stringent rules about how the funds should be spent. Although half of the direct aid which Austria received in the first year of Marshall Aid came in the form of foodstuffs, with raw materials accounting for a further 25 per cent, the chief goals of the ERP planners from the outset were to stimulate industrial productivity by increasing capital investment and to foster an integrated European economic recovery by encouraging recipient nations to develop joint planning and intra-continental trade. Expenditure on consumer goods, including subsidies to domestic farmers and the purchase of imported food supplies, was not encouraged. This made sound economic sense as a long-term economic policy, for capital investment would promote increased productivity and trade and would therefore eventually result in increased prosperity and consumption. But in the short term it called for some very difficult decisions. The discrepancy between the first Austrian bid for ERP funds and the amount of aid the country actually received led to a reduction in food imports in 1948–9.[42] The Americans and Austrians, not surprisingly, had differing views on the role of the ECA which came to the fore on 27 October 1948, when the head of the ECA mission in Vienna, Westmore Willcox, wrote a letter to Chancellor Figl concerning the 1949 budget proposals. In this letter Willcox stated that 'in connection with the uses of schilling counterpart, this Mission is inevitably and deeply concerned with the broad general questions of Austrian financial and fiscal policies'. He drew the Chancellor's attention to the conversation he, Willcox, had had two months earlier with the Austrian Finance Minister, Georg Zimmermann, in which 'I specifically advised Minister Zimmermann that we wished an opportunity to consult with him well in advance of the presentation to Parliament of the 1949 budget.' No such consultation had taken place and he had now seen details of the proposed budget which were unsatisfactory:

> Not only is the ordinary budget increased by some 20% over that of 1948, but the extraordinary budget, when added to the reconstruction program of the Planning Ministry, reaches an aggregate figure far in excess of any probable resources as hastily estimated by us. . . . I feel it necessary, under the circumstances, to re-iterate that releases of ECA counterpart can be considered only against the background of over-all fiscal and financial policies and considerations. The mere desirability of a given project is not sufficient criterion to warrant the release of counterpart if, coincidently, the over-all financial situation gives cause for concern.[43]

In the first six months of the Allied occupation, the Austrian government had been accused by the Americans and the British of being a Soviet puppet. The 1945 elections had legitimised the country's political process and had eventually resulted in extended, though still limited, powers for the Austrian government under the continuing super-vision of the Allied Council. By 1948, Austrian politicians were begin-ning to display the ability to react to adverse circumstances, at times even turning these to their country's advantage. It had not been possible to resist Soviet expropriation of German assets, and so the Austrian government lost control, temporarily, of many industrial concerns in its eastern provinces, while the rest of the economy was subject to the constraints of the Marshall Plan. But the Nationalisation Laws succeeded in protecting major branches of the economy, and these laws had been introduced with the support of all political parties and of the economic elites, without rekindling the ideological battles of the inter-war years.

Thus were sown the early seeds of the Austrian 'model' of political and economic life based on formal consensus and shared elite decision-making. Moreover, despite its disappointment over the amount of ERP aid Austria received, the Austrian government had negotiated the most successful bid for Marshall Aid in 1948–9. By the middle of 1948, during the Berlin Blockade and after Soviet-style 'people's republics' had been established along Austria's borders with Yugoslavia, Hungary and Czechoslovakia, the Austrian government was being accused by the Soviet Union of being a lackey of Western imperialism. A year later, metal fences and watch-towers were in place dividing East from West along the Iron Curtain. The line bisecting Europe becomes blurred around Austria's eastern border, for between 1949, when Germany was divided, and 1955, when the Austrian State Treaty was finalised, Austria was the only state under joint four-power occupation. Her geographical position exaggerated her strategic importance: this was the region of Europe where East and West continued to confront each other eye-to-eye during the early years of the Cold War, the cross-roads between East and West, which provided the setting of intrigue and espionage for Graham Green's 'The Third Man'. In addition to the prevailing state of international tension, the Austrian government also continued to be faced by domestic problems concerning food supplies and the threat of inflation, which it was feared might destabilise the country and draw it into the Soviet bloc.

Notes

1 For a more detailed consideration of the use of the term 'tutelage' see Knight, 'Narratives in Post-war Austrian Historiography', in Bushell (ed.), *Austria 1945–1955: Studies in Political and Cultural Re-emergence*, 11–36. The term 'tutelage' (*Bevormundung*) has been adopted by many Austrian historians in preference to the German term 're-education' (*Umerziehung*).

2 Balfour and Mair, *Four-Power Control in Germany and Austria*, 324–9; in 1958 the British ambassador in Vienna communicated a translation of a British memorandum on the negotiations for the 1946 Allied Control Agreement. Schärf Papers, Box 30, 4/216.

3 Balfour and Mair, *Four-Power Control in Germany and Austria*, 327; *Arbeiter-Zeitung* (29 June 1946).

4 The most serious Russian attempt to abrogate Article 6a was in seeking to widen the definition of constitutional law.

5 Bischof, *Austria in the First Cold War*, 39.

6 Rathkolb, *Gesellschaft in der Politik*, 338.

7 *FRUS, 1945. The Conference of Berlin (The Potsdam Conference)*, vol. I, 342; Wilfried Aichinger, 'Die Sowjetunion und Österreich 1945–49', 277–8, in Bischof and Leidenfrost (eds), *Die bevormundete Nation*, 274–92. Winston

Churchill led the first British delegation to Potsdam, but flew back to London for the announcement of the British election results on 25 July. The Labour Party won the election and Clement Attlee replaced Churchill in Potsdam on 28 July. Alan Bullock, *The Life and Times of Ernest Bevin*, vol. 3, *Foreign Secretary 1949–1951* (New York/London: Norton, 1983), 23–4.

8   Herz, 'Allied Occupation of Austria', 40.

9   USIA was officially established on 27 May 1946. Österreichisches Staatsarchiv (ÖS), Archiv der Republik (AdR), Bundesministerium für Finanzen (BMfF), (06/9) Box 4.876, Staatsvertragsakte, 66/349: 'Information über USIA-Betriebe', 4.3.1948; Karner, Stelzl-Marx and Tschubarjan (eds), *Die Rote Armee in Österreich. Sowjetische Besatzung 1945–1955. Dokumente*, 431–7, 457–9.

10 Balfour and Mair, *Four-Power Control in Germany and Austria*, 352; Rauchensteiner, *Der Sonderfall*, 179–83.

11 Martin Malia, *The Soviet Tragedy: A History of Socialism in Russia, 1917–1991* (New York: Maxwell Macmillan International, 1994), 293.

12 Ingrid Fraberger and Dieter Stiefel, ' "Enemy Images": The Meaning of "Anti-Communism" and its Importance for the Political and Economic Reconstruction in Austria after 1945', in Günter Bischof, Anton Pelinka and Dieter Stiefel (eds), *The Marshall Plan in Austria* (New Brunswick, NJ: Transaction, 2000), 75–7.

13 Hans Seidel, 'Austria's Economic Policy and the Marshall Plan', in Bischof, Pelinka and Stiefel (eds), *The Marshall Plan in Austria*, 250; Fraberger and Stiefel, ' "Enemy Images" ', 79–80.

14 The Truman Doctrine. www.yale.edu/lawweb/Avalon/trudoc.htm.

15 Eduard März, 'Austria's Economic Development 1945–85', in Jim Sweeney, Josef Weidenholzer and Jeremy Leaman (eds), *Austria: A Study in Modern Achievement* (Aldershot: Avebury, 1988), 32. The power industries were nationalised in March 1947.

16 Eduard März, *Österreichs Wirtschaft zwischen Ost und West* (Vienna: Europäische Perspektiven, 1965), 19.

17 Rauchensteiner, *Der Sonderfall*, 228. Rauchensteiner dismisses the figure of 12,000 in favour of 1,500 to 2,000 members.

18 K.W. Rothschild, *The Austrian Economy since 1945* (Aberdeen: Royal Institute of International Affairs, 1950), 22, ftn. 1.

19 Rothschild, *The Austrian Economy since 1945*, 27.

20 *Ibid.*, 41.

21 *Jahrbuch der Arbeiterkammer in Wien 1948* (Vienna, 1950), 251.

22 Bischof, *Austria in the First Cold War*, 97; Rothschild, *The Austrian Economy since 1945*, 23.

23 'Austria's Import Requirements and Balance of Trade for the year 1947' (to be referred to as 'Project R'), prepared by Economics Division USACA Section, Headquarters, United States Forces Austria. AdR, BKA/AA, WPol.Wi.Eur., 1947, Box 87, Marshallplan.

24 Anthony Bushell, 'Austria's political and cultural re-emergence: The First Decade', in Bushell (ed), *Austria 1945–1955*, 4–7.

25 OEEC report, Paris, 19 July 1949. AdR, Bundesministerium für soziale Verwaltung (BMfsV), Section III, Sa 11, Box 216, 12932/III.

26 Bandhauer-Schöffmann, 'Women's Fight for Food in Post-war Vienna', 81.

27 Rothschild, *The Austrian Economy since 1945*, 29, 36.

28 Bischof, *Austria in the First Cold War*, 106–7. Schärf, *Österreichs Erneuerung 1945–1955*, 132–8. Peace treaties were signed with Italy, Hungary, Bulgaria, Rumania and Finland in February 1947, but negotiations over the German treaty had also faltered over the question of Soviet reparations.

29 Scott Parrish, 'The Marshall Plan, Soviet-American Relations and the Division of Europe', in Norman Naimark and Leonid Gibianskii (eds), *The Establishment of Communist Regimes in Eastern Europe, 1944–1949* (Boulder, CO: Westview Press, 1997), 267, 275. Parrish comments that 'most of the available evidence indicates that the Western Powers never intended to allow Moscow to participate in the aid programme', but were forced to consider this in order to attract bids from Italy and France, both of which had large and influential Communist Parties.

30 Parrish, 'The Marshall Plan, Soviet-American Relations and the Division of Europe', 284.

31 Zbynek Zeman, *The Masaryks* (London: Weidenfeld and Nicolson, 1976), 208. In September 1947, in response to the Marshall Plan, the Soviet Union set up the Cominform, the successor to the Comintern.

32 Wilfried Mähr, *Der Marshallplan in Österreich* (Graz: Verlag Styria, 1989), 74–80.

33 Seidel, 'Austria's Economic Policy and the Marshall Plan', 253, 273–5.

34 Unsigned letter to the Austrian special envoy in Washington, 19 September 1947, AdR, BKA/AA, W.Pol. Wi. Eur., Box 87; Mähr, *Der Marshallplan in Österreich*, 248.

35 Alan Milward, *The Reconstruction of Western Europe* (London: Methuen, 1984), 86.

36 Seidel, 'Austria's Economic Policy and the Marshall Plan', 253–4; Mähr, *Der Marshallplan in Österreich*, 248.

37 Milward, *The Reconstruction of Western Europe*, 96, tab. 15.

38 Anthony Carew, *Labour under the Marshall Plan* (Manchester: Manchester University Press, 1987), 11.

39 *Department of State Bulletin*, 11 July 1948, 36, quoted in Carew, *Labour under the Marshall Plan*, 11–12.

40 The American proposal that any planned currency devaluation should be first submitted to the International Monetary Fund was defeated by the united opposition of the CEEC members. In April 1948 the CEEC became the Organisation for European Economic Co-operation (OEEC).

41 Michael Hogan, *The Marshall Plan: America, Britain and the Reconstruction of Western Europe, 1947–1952* (Cambridge: Cambridge University Press, 1987), 153–5. Seidel, 'Austria's Economic Policy and the Marshall Plan', 265.

42 Seidel, 'Austria's Economic Policy and the Marshall Plan', 253–4, 273–5.

43 AdR, BKA, Verbindungsstelle zum Alliierten Rat, Box 134, 3849/VI, ECA Vienna, 27 October 1948. Westmore Willcox to Figl.

5

Labour and threats
to consensus

Although the most pressing problem facing the Austrian government in 1946 continued to be its relations with the Occupying Powers, the domestic situation in the first years of peace was also highly volatile. At the end of the First World War, hunger, economic crises and labour shortages had led to riots, rebellion and even revolution. Similar conditions prevailed in 1945. And yet the situation which developed in the wake of the Second World War was significantly different from that of 1919. Amid the confusion and lawlessness which had followed in the wake of military defeat, the arrival of the Red Army was hailed as a 'liberation', and there is little evidence of concerted popular protest of any kind in the first six months of peace. Indeed, as Chapter 3 showed, the main preoccupation for most ordinary people was with how to earn, barter or steal the basic essentials on which to live. The battle for survival left them with neither the time nor the energy for the expression of discontent. Nevertheless, there remained the possibility that civil and political disturbances might break out if and when conditions improved, for, as the election campaigns of November 1945 revealed, underlying tensions between and even within the political parties had survived the years of fascism and war. On the other hand, Figl's decision to form a coalition government following the ÖVP electoral victory and his appointment of a Communist cabinet minister did indicate that the official policy of proportionality and public consensus continued to prevail within leading political circles.

In 1946 the first significant steps were taken to extend political consultation beyond the political parties by inviting representatives of the economic sectors, leading figures in industry and business, trade union leaders, and representatives of agriculture to advise on the formation of domestic policy. The economic elites were being co-opted into political decision-making. The basis of this arrangement was that leaders of the three main economic sectors, industry, labour and agriculture, would renounce long-standing principles and recognise a set of common goals, including full employment, increased productivity, currency stability and low inflation, and would acknowledge that these could only be achieved through compromise.[1] The employers made their first concession, as we have seen, in 1946 when they agreed to the nationalisation of key economic sectors and to restrictions on their managerial autonomy. Union leaders, for their part, abandoned the creed of class conflict in return for a share in policy formation, social welfare gains and long-term economic stability. In the case of the labour leadership, this approach reflected a fundamental ideological shift from the belief in the inevitable conflict of class interests which had dominated the First Republic, to championship of social harmony and compromise. In return for this concession, these same labour leaders were invited for the first time to join the political elite and to take part in the formation of national economic and social policy. Their most difficult task would be to persuade their members to accept policies which were both crucial to economic growth and highly unpopular.

In many ways, the men who emerged in 1945 as leaders of the trade union movement had already embraced the culture of consensus before the war was over. As was shown in Chapter 2, within days of the announcement of the Second Republic, former trade union activists set up a single highly centralised umbrella federation of sixteen industrial unions (the ÖGB), which was based on the newly emerging principles of consensus and power-sharing. Although its leader, Johann Böhm, was a Socialist, his two deputies came from the other two political parties: Lois Weinberger was a member of the ÖVP and had been a leader of the Catholic labour movement, while Gottlieb Fiala had been a founding member of the KPÖ, joining its executive committee as early as 1923. The decision of these former adversaries to set up a single trade union body arose from their analysis of the failures of organised labour during the First Republic. At that time trade union membership had been high, reaching a peak of 1.2 million in 1921, though falling to just under 750,000 by the end of 1931.[2] But the power of the labour movement had been weakened by a plurality of union federations, each representing a political party or faction, as well as by the devastation caused by high structural unemployment in the 1920s, which was then compounded by the crisis unemployment of the 1930s. As a consequence, the unions had been able to protect neither the legal rights nor the jobs of their members. It became obvious as soon as the fighting ended in April 1945 that the lessons of the First Republic had been learned. The goal of the new labour leaders was to create a trade union movement based on unity and support for a return to economic stability, thus ensuring full employment for its members. By 1947 union leaders had gone one step further and had become involved in the formation of an official policy which was designed to achieve economic growth.

The framework of the new union federation was ratified at a meeting of trade unionists held at the Westbahnhof railway terminus on 15 April and was approved by the Soviet authorities on 30 April. From its birth, the ÖGB was not only unified, centralised and hierarchical, but it was also dominated by the Socialists. Its first executive committee comprised twenty-seven members, fifteen of whom were members of the SPÖ and had worked for the Free Trade Union Federation before 1934. The other seats on the committee were divided equally between the ÖVP and KPÖ.[3] In 1946, when the number of committee members was reduced to twenty-three, seventeen, including Böhm (who remained president of the ÖGB), and all sixteen leaders of the individual unions, were Socialists. According to British sources, seven of these union leaders had been elected by show of hands (although it is not clear whose hands these were) and the rest were 'self-appointed'.[4] The number of seats allocated to the other two parties was halved.

Following its recognition by the Soviet authorities, the ÖGB executive, in its capacity as the only legally recognised trade union body in Austria, controlled the reconstruction of the labour movement. New trade unions could only be set up with ÖGB approval. Moreover, the influence of the Federation soon extended beyond the field of industrial relations into politics. For instance, at the end of April 1945 the Russians invited the ÖGB executive to nominate five members of the Vienna city council (*Stadtrat*) and five members of the local councils (*Gemeinderäte*).[5] Union leaders were also integrated directly into the emergent new political system to a degree which would have been unimaginable in the First Republic, accumulating a cluster of political appointments in addition to their union work. The clearest example of this pluralism is Johann Böhm. During the seven months of the Renner government, Böhm held a staggering array of positions. Within the ÖGB, he was not only president, but until October 1945 he also acted as head of the Building Workers' Union, the post which he had occupied at the end of the First Republic. In addition, he represented the ÖGB on the executive committee of the SPÖ, having been co-opted along with the leader of the Chemical Workers' Union, Robert Pipelka. However, it was his appointment as Minister for Social Administration in the Renner government, a position which he held in tandem with the presidency of the ÖGB, which was most notable. As a result of holding both offices simultaneously, Böhm was in charge not only of the rebirth of the trade union movement but also of the re-establishment of the Ministry of Social Administration during the first crucial seven months of the post-war period. As he himself acknowledged in his autobiography, the strain of combining these two roles proved too much and he stood down as minister after the November elections.[6] But his initial appointment and the subsequent decision by Chancellor Figl to appoint Karl Maisel, the leader of the Metalworkers' and Miners' Union, as Böhm's successor in the post set a long-lasting precedent: for the following two decades the Minister of Social Administration would be a leading trade unionist.[7]

Böhm's influence on the formation of the labour movement under the Second Republic was immense. He had earlier been a strong advocate of centrally organised industrial unions, drawing on his own experience as leader of the Building Workers' Union in the early 1930s. At the 1931 Free Trade Union conference he had accused fellow Socialist union leaders of undermining the ability of his union to negotiate collective contracts with the employers from a position of strength by 'trespassing' on its membership.[8] The Building Workers' Union, he contended, should be the only union in the building industry. The historic system of skill-based trade unions had led to a proliferation of associations, all competing for members and all claiming to represent the workforce. It had encouraged factionalism and union rivalry and dissipated the power of the working class. It should be replaced by a smaller number of larger industrial unions, each recruiting all the workers within one industry, irrespective of their original trade, for the strength of the union movement lay in the size and unity of its membership. After 1945, Böhm and his colleagues in the ÖGB succeeded in extending the basic principle of industrial unionism across the entire union movement, with only one major concession to differences in status and skills: for non-manual workers, two separate unions were set up, one to represent civil servants and the second for white-collar workers employed in the private sector.

Böhm was therefore firmly committed to the use of negotiation rather than confrontation in industrial relations, but maintained that this approach could only succeed if the trade union movement presented a united and informed front. To this end, and in his role as ÖGB leader, he called on the government in May 1945 to re-establish the Chambers of Labour. These regionally based bodies had been established by law in 1920 and had been unique to Austria. Along with the Chambers of Trade, on which they had been modelled, and the Chambers of Agriculture, which had also been set up in the 1920s, the nine provincial Chambers of Labour had together comprised one of the first 'peak interest groups' in Austria; as statutory bodies they had provided the government with economic information on their respective provinces and advised on proposed legislation. Although the influence of the Chambers of Labour had declined in the 1930s, Böhm insisted that they were essential to the new Republic, for they would provide legislators with the means of identifying the opinions of workers on any impending legislation which related to them. His view prevailed and a new law based on that of 1920 was passed on 20 July 1945, re-establishing a Chamber of Labour in each province. Under the new law, the Chambers were required to draw up reports for the government on social legislation and the state of the labour market, to collect labour statistics, and to represent labour in negotiations with other organisations. All draft legislation relating to industry, commerce or labour relations was to be submitted to them for comment. They were also made responsible for educating workers in labour law and retraining the unemployed, but were specifically excluded from taking part in individual wage negotiations, which remained the province of the trade unions. Membership was compulsory for all manual and white-collar workers who were covered by sickness insurance (unlike the trade unions); representatives to the regional Chambers were elected by proportional representation. The regional structure of the system ran counter to Böhm's policy of centralisation and he attempted, unsuccessfully, to amend the 1945 law to include an overarching national Chamber.[9] However, there was one amendment to the 1920 law which was agreed: as the situation in 1945 was deemed to rule out immediate elections, the first members of the Chambers of Labour were appointed by the Minister for Social Administration – Johann Böhm.[10] As a result, by the summer of 1945 the labour movement possessed two strong representative bodies, both of which were dominated by Böhm and the Socialist trade union leaders.

The ÖGB's leadership and its institutional framework were therefore in place by the beginning of May 1945, well before there had been time for most Austrian workers to hold local meetings, let alone elections for trade union representatives, and before the western provinces had been liberated. This could have had repercussions for the new leadership, and almost did: for the first three months of the occupation the American and French authorities banned trade union activity in their respective zones. In addition, the American and British governments had already drawn up plans to rebuild the unions from the bottom up, beginning with individual factories and linking these into regional and then national bodies.[11] However, the speed with which the Austrians set about establishing their own institutions, combined with the Soviet decision to recognise the ÖGB, had effectively pre-empted the Western Allies' plans. In a letter to the British Foreign Secretary and trade unionist, Ernest Bevin, the British Political Representative in Vienna, J. W. Nicholls, later explained that 'the rapidity with which the movement organised itself, both centrally in Vienna and more or less independently in the western provinces, rendered this plan obsolete, and in October 1945 the British Element accorded de facto recognition to the Federation on the unwritten understanding that officials would be submitted to the test of election within a reasonable period of time'.[12] Nicholls described Böhm as combining 'Trade Union toughness with Austrian charm to a remarkable degree'. An earlier memorandum from the Labour Division of the British Element of the Allied Commission for Austria had emphasised that any objection to recognition of the ÖGB would be opposed by the other three Elements, adding that 'conditions and trends in Austria make temporarily desirable a more close and centralised control over union activities than would ordinarily be acceptable. If we agree, as I think we may, that the Austrian Trade Union movement as now constituted is well intentioned and democratic in principle, its greatest immediate need is unity and strength.'[13] Nevertheless, British labour leaders continued to raise objections to the ÖGB's effective monopoly on trade union activity in Austria, which they considered to be an infringement of the democratic right to freedom of association. They were suspicious that 'the leaders of the Austrian T.U.C. are anxious to prevent an open-shop in order to preserve their own personal positions'.[14]

The British government, however, was persuaded by Böhm's proposals; in contrast to their initial intransigence on the question of recognising the Renner government, all three Western Allies accepted the existence of the trade union federation as a fait accompli and the Allied Council recognised the ÖGB before the November 1945 general election. The first national conference of trade union delegates was held in Vienna at the beginning of September. Despite twelve years of repression, Austrian trade unionism was still strong; by the end of 1945 the ÖGB was able to record a membership of 298,417 and this grew to almost one million over the next twelve months, establishing it as the largest voluntary representative body in the country.[15]

The institutional strength of the trade union federation stemmed from the foresight of its founders in 1945 and the support they received from all four Occupying Powers, each of which saw advantages in a strong and united trade union movement. But the actual power of the movement domestically depended on its ability to recruit shop-floor workers and to retain their support. It soon became clear that the structural transformation envisaged by Böhm and the majority of the ÖGB executive was to be accompanied by a radical change in the traditional goals of the labour movement. The first sign that trade union leaders (with the exception of the Communists) were modifying the unions' long established objectives of protecting their members' wage rates, standards of living, and working conditions, came in the late summer of 1945, when, after some protest, the Federation eventually supported an Allied emergency measure holding wages at the level of May 1945.[16] It justified this decision by pointing to the critical economic situation and to signs that the food shortages were stimulating inflation. Grain production was hit by drought in the summer of 1945, cutting the harvest in the Soviet zone to 15 per cent of the 1944 level. The production of milk, sugar and fats was also drastically reduced. Lack of transportation was compounding an already desperate situation and it was in October that the government announced that it was unable to issue the meagre normal ration of 800 calories.[17] It was for these reasons that, for the first time, the ÖGB backed wage restraint. Its leaders were convinced that higher wages would inevitably lead to higher prices in an economy which was beset by shortages. Although their decision was sound in terms of economics, it contrasted starkly with the radical position taken by labour leaders in 1919, who had fought for and won index-linked wages.[18] The evidence that trade union priorities had indeed changed was confirmed in 1946, when, despite a deepening food crisis, rising prices and a shortage of labour, ÖGB leaders again warned their members that large wage demands would fuel inflation rather than raise living standards. Their greatest fear was of the possibility that wildcat strikes and protests would break out which would be beyond their control and would weaken their relationship with the government, the Allies and the employers; formal negotiations would, they argued, achieve far more than any unauthorised protests.[19] The question remained as to whether union leaders could convince their members that such a strategy would best defend workers' interests in the long term.

It was, indeed, soon to become apparent that some Austrian workers were deaf to the warnings of the ÖGB executive. Less than three months after the November 1945 national elections, a wave of workers' protests broke out over the supply of food, beginning on 5 February when miners at the Fohnsdorf lignite pit in British-occupied Upper Styria went on strike to demand an increase in their rations. This was the first strike in the Second Republic and it erupted in one of the country's few industrial regions, an area, moreover, where the Socialist trade unions had encountered their most significant defeat in the First Republic and where they were already experiencing difficulties in the Second Republic. Over the next few years, Upper Styria was to become a key battleground in the struggle between the Socialists and the Communists for the allegiance of Austrian workers. It therefore affords a revealing case study of the volatility of grass-roots Austrian labour politics and the difficulty which the dominant Socialist faction within the ÖGB had encountered in controlling workers as the food situation continued to deteriorate and the initial consensus within the executive began to break down.

Upper Styria was significant to Austria in terms of both politics and economics. Before the Second World War, its mines, foundries and metallurgical plants had been the hub of the Alpine Montangesellschaft steel 'empire', Austria's largest private employer, and the centre of the country's steel industry. The blast-furnaces in its main foundry at Donawitz processed the vast iron-ore reserves from the neighbouring opencast mine at Erzberg, but the area had fallen into decline in the 1920s because it lacked locally produced fuel and since the turn of the century had been forced to rely on imported coal. Despite heavy investment by the Nazi regime in the Hermann Göring Works in Linz, Donawitz and its surrounding area remained the centre of Austria's semi-manufactured steel industry in the immediate post-war period, producing structured steel, rods, bars, track and sheet metal, all of which were essential for Austria's economic regeneration. The future productivity of the region, however, was threatened in May 1945 when Soviet troops occupied Styria and started to strip plants of vital machinery, including a modern continuous rolling mill (*Walzstrasse*) at Donawitz. Despite both this blow and a chronic lack of coal, by March 1946 two blast-furnaces at the Donawitz plant were already in operation using reconditioned old machinery and fuel obtained abroad by barter.[20]

The importance of Donawitz was clearly shown in October 1945, three months after control of Styria had been transferred to the British military authorities and just weeks before the first national elections were due, when, in an effort to cut costs, the local management announced plans to close down two open-hearth furnaces and a triple rolling mill at the plant, laying off 1,000 workers. In response, the Chancellor, Karl Renner, held a meeting with a delegation of Donawitz workers from which he emerged to insist that the firm accept government credits in order to prevent the layoffs. The *Arbeiter-Zeitung* went further and demanded the nationalisation of the company, which duly took place under the 1946 Nationalisation Law.[21]

In addition to its economic significance, Upper Styria had also held a pivotal place in the history of the labour movement. Despite the size of the region's industrial workforce, the fact that it was geographically dispersed had made it difficult for the Socialist Free Trade Unions to curb the indiscipline and militancy of Styrian workers in the early 1920s and, faced with mounting unemployment, they had also failed to sustain membership in the area. In 1928, the Alpine Montangesellschaft management had used intimidation and violence to impose the fascist 'Independent Union' on its employees, breaking the hold of Austria's largest and strongest trade union, the Metalworkers' Union, and undermining the legal position of the entire national union movement. It was in Upper Styria that the *Heimwehr* secured its basic parliamentary mandate in the 1930 general election, and for a time it appeared that the industrial workers of this region had abandoned the SDAP in favour of Austrian fascism.[22] Nevertheless, during a number of illegal strikes in 1933 and the civil war of 1934, Styrian workers had engaged in resolute and protracted resistance to government troops and the *Heimwehr*. The labour leadership had every reason to be aware of their unpredictability.

In 1945 it appeared that, in this respect at least, little had changed. In May 1945, workers at Donawitz and at the neighbouring mines of Seegraben and Fohnsdorf responded to the liberation by holding meetings at which, by show of hands, they elected new works councils for the first time since 1933. This was an attempt to revive the system of grass-roots worker representation which had been set up in the wake of a series of violent strikes and factory seizures towards the end of the First World War, and which had special historical significance for Donawitz. The first unofficial works councils in the Empire had been established in 1917 and 1918, when some of the most obdurate employers, including the Alpine Montangesellschaft, had been forced to negotiate with their employees, having, in extreme cases, temporarily lost control of their enterprises. Later, in April 1919, as the provisional government was drawing up a law to give legal status to the works councils, smelters at the Donawitz foundry had physically ejected the company management from the plant, replaced it with a committee of two manual workers and two engineers, and demanded the immediate socialisation of the entire company.[23] 'Wild socialisation', however, was a sign of 'Bolshevism' to the provisional government, including its Socialist leaders, Karl Renner and Otto Bauer, and threatened to undermine their plans for a peaceful transition to socialism. A compromise was reached when the government agreed to recognise the Donawitz works council retroactively under legislation which had not yet been passed, and the committee dropped its demand for socialisation. When it did reach the statute book on 15 May 1919, the Works Council Law stipulated that all enterprises employing five or more workers should hold elections for shop stewards (*Vertrauensmänner*) and that those with twenty or more workers should set up works councils. Otto Bauer, who was the intellectual leader of the SDAP as well as Chairman of the Socialisation Commission, later described the works councils as the 'germs of a future Socialist constitution of production'; in his concept of the slow transformation of society from capitalism to socialism, the councils would provide workers with the training and experience necessary to enable them to assume control of the means of production.[24] But a rival 'shop-based' network of worker representation was anathema to trade union leaders, who had fought a sustained battle against syndicalism at the end of the nineteenth century and were determined to guard their newly-won status in the new republic. After much trade union intervention, the councils' actual remit under the law became far more limited than had originally been intended, confining them to a largely supervisory role in the workplace. They were to monitor observance of social legislation, provide reports for factory inspectors and ensure that the terms of collective contracts were enforced, although they were debarred from taking part in the negotiations for these contracts, since this powerful function was allocated to the unions alone. In addition, employers were required, if requested, to hold monthly meetings to discuss 'managerial principles' and suggestions for improvements with their works councils, and larger firms employing thirty or more workers were instructed to provide the councils with copies of their annual accounts. Joint-stock companies were also ordered to open up their board meetings to members of the works council.[25] There was little in this law which resembled Bauer's vision of workers acquiring managerial skills in order to advance the social revolution. Nevertheless, until they were undermined at the end of the 1920s, the works councils did provide a democratic local basis for labour politics and were a radical improvement on the situation which had prevailed under the Empire.

The revival of the works councils in Upper Styria in May 1945 was spontaneous, but it had no legal basis, for the 1919 law had been allowed to lapse in 1933. It was, however, not unique. Shop stewards were elected at factory meetings in several plants in Vienna and Lower Austria during the first weeks of May 1945, and the following September the ÖGB organised similar elections in all remaining workplaces, basing these on the provisions of the 1919 law. The results in Upper Styria proved particularly worrying for the Socialists. Although SPÖ shop stewards were to win control of the majority of works councils in the region, in these, the earliest elections, they were beaten into second place by the Communists in Donawitz and Fohnsdorf, while the Seegraben vote was split.[26] In retrospect, the Communist successes are not totally surprising, as the voting took place in the first heady days of the liberation and under Soviet supervision, but the fact that support for the KPÖ continued after the Soviets had handed over control of the region to the British in July 1945 is more puzzling. As well as indulging in looting and rape before they left, Russian troops, as we have seen, had removed vital machinery from the Upper Styrian steel industry and had thus jeopardised the jobs of the very people the KPÖ was mobilising.[27] Nevertheless, these plants, and Donawitz in particular, continued to be regarded as Communist strongholds for some time thereafter. In the November general election, five months after the Soviet withdrawal from the province, the Communist Party polled 14,884 votes in the wider constituency of Upper Styria, 9.24 per cent of its total vote in the constituency and almost twice its national average, resulting in the party's greatest success outside the Russian zone.[28] The election result did not constitute a direct threat to the SPÖ, which still gained 53.3 per cent of the votes in Upper Styria as a whole, but, as relations between the two parties began to deteriorate, the relative success of the Communists here was to grow in importance.

Martin Herz later speculated that the reason for this peculiar development in Donawitz lay in the close relationship which quickly developed between the Communist works council and the management. According to Herz, Josef Oberegger, the plant's managing director, made a pact with Communist shop stewards, agreeing to ad hoc wage increases and allowing the works council to 'determine hirings and firings' in return for assistance in 'conniving' barter deals with Russian-controlled USIA plants.[29] This arrangement was said to have given the Donawitz works council far greater powers than had been granted by the 1919 law. Although Herz's interpretation cannot be verified, two points do give it some credence. The first is that the decision to offer the post of director-general of Donawitz to Oberegger was made by the British authorities in August 1945 and it triggered immediate shop-floor protests: not only was Oberegger a former member of Alpine Montangesellschaft's board of directors, but he had also been a central figure in the Styrian *Heimwehr* in the 1930s, having begun his political career as the *Heimwehr* labour leader in Donawitz, where he had actually led the 1928 campaign to force workers to join the fascist 'Independent Union'.[30] Shop-floor opposition to his appointment was therefore predictable, particularly among older workers who still remembered the industrial terror of the early 1930s. However, when Peter Krauland, the Minister of Property Control and Economic Planning, confirmed Oberegger's appointment as Public Administrator of the newly nationalised plant in 1946, this step was supported by local shop stewards in direct opposition to the national leadership of the ÖGB.[31] The Communist works council had, for some reason, decided to turn a blind eye to Oberegger's past. This was a clear sign of a rift between the national union leaders and the local shop stewards. Second, after crippling fuel shortages in early 1947 had caused the two working blast-furnaces in Donawitz to be damped down, the management secured 50,000 tons of coking coal from Yugoslavia and Czechoslovakia in return for 10,000 tons of railway track.[32] The co-operation of the Yugoslavs in 1947 would, we may assume, have been unlikely without Soviet approval. Neither point is conclusive, but together they do suggest an unusual relationship between former combatants in the industrial warfare of the 1930s.

In 1948, in the run-up to the impending second general election, Herz was still warning about the threat of Communism in Upper Styria and speculating that dwindling support for the Communist Party in the Soviet sector could result in its being the Upper Styrian constituency which provided the Communist Party with the basic mandate required by law for a party to take up seats in parliament.[33] This time he attributed the relative strength of the Upper Styrian KPÖ to its active local leadership, and to its continuing influence over the labour force in the larger units of the Alpine Montangesellschaft such as Donawitz. He painted a starkly contrasting picture of the local leaders of the two left-wing parties: the Styrian Socialist Party was led by elderly party bureaucrats, men such as the sixty-six-year-old Reinhard Machold, and had been weakened by the loss of its most dynamic young leaders in the civil war of 1934. Some of these, for example Koloman Wallisch and Josef Stanek, had died in that struggle.[34] Many others had been active in the Socialist Party's youth group, the *Jungfront*, in the early 1930s, but had emerged as Communist activists in 1945. This group included not only Ernst Fischer and his brother, Otto, who had spent the war years in Moscow, but also Ditto Pölzl, Heribert Hütter and Willi Scholz, who as young Socialists had clashed with local party leaders over their involvement in the illegal strikes of 1933 and who were now all full-time Communist trade union or party workers.[35]

Whatever the reasons for the continuing Communist influence in Upper Styria, its significance became obvious in the spring and summer of 1946 and 1947 as the KPÖ switched tactics nationally to encourage mass protest over the central issue of food. In early 1946 the food situation grew steadily worse and official rations in parts of Austria fell to 700 calories.[36] It was at this point, in February, that the miners in Fohnsdorf walked out, demanding increased rations. The announcement that the first UNRRA shipment was on its way to Austria, weeks before this organisation was to assume responsibility for food distribution in all zones of occupation, was accompanied by a warning that, in the short term at least, this might lead to reduced rations.[37] During March and April, there were further protests in Vienna, the largest on 19 March in the machine shops in the Floridsdorf district in the Soviet sector, but by now simple complaints about the size of the ration were beginning to develop political overtones – the Floridsdorf workers blamed the government for failing to improve the food situation. When workers in a variety of Viennese plants staged a joint protest strike on 9 April, they called on the unions to ensure that immediate improvements were made.[38]

The situation was now critical and the ÖGB made urgent representations to the government, calling for a centrally organised food distribution system, more aggressive policies towards black marketeers and a ban on farmers feeding potatoes and grain to livestock. At the same time it instructed its members not to take direct action.[39] Divisions between the ÖGB and the KPÖ became overt at a meeting of Viennese shop stewards and trade union officials on 16 April 1946 when, in the presence of Chancellor Figl, a Communist attempt to call a general strike was defeated.[40] Later that month, at its first party conference since the end of the war, the KPÖ executive criticised the 'bourgeois parliamentary' form of democracy and called for an increased mobilisation of the masses, while also advocating closer co-operation with Socialist workers. The debate which followed left some delegates with the distinct impression that the party had no clear long-term strategy. This view was later endorsed by a Soviet Communist Party report, which commented that 'the Austrian Communist Party's programmatic theses, adopted at the Party's XIIIth Congress, which define the Party's future policies, set forth in a quite hazy manner the perspectives for a peaceful transition to socialism "without the horrors of a civil war" '.[41] Nevertheless, the XIIIth party conference did mark a change in KPÖ tactics: at the party's next plenary session in June there were harsh criticisms of the weakness of the policy on unions, and as a result new directives were issued instructing party workers to pay greater attention to factory cells as opposed to local community cells.[42] The clearest manifestation of this change was seen later that month, when Communist shop stewards in Styria led out between eight and ten thousand workers in Graz, Liezen, Fohnsdorf and Donawitz in a wave of short protest strikes over the failure of the government to provide adequate rations.[43] Food protests continued elsewhere in Austria throughout the summer of 1946, as printers, tramworkers, metalworkers and miners all held short protest strikes.

The ÖGB leaders, with the exception of the Communists, were, as we have seen, opposed to grass-roots demonstrations. Nevertheless, their political position was strengthened by such outbursts of discontent. In December 1945 the first shop-stewards' conference, held in Vienna, had passed a series of radical proposals, including a call for a centralised ministry of economics headed by a trade unionist. This aspiration was not realised, but, as discontent grew, union leaders mediated between their members, the government and even the Western Allies over the food issue, and as a result their influence increased. On 25 April 1946, at a meeting with trade union leaders, Chancellor Figl announced the creation of a new central food directory comprising government representatives and members of the employers' associations, as well as two trade unionists, who were to monitor decisions.[44] Reporting this development to a shop-stewards' conference four weeks later, Johann Böhm made it clear that the language of class conflict was not yet entirely dead, even within the ÖGB executive. The role of the trade union representatives was, he declared, to prevent employers' bodies from exercising autocratic leadership.[45] Nevertheless, the unions were now involved in policy formulation, although not as yet on an equal footing with the employers. The next stage came at the local level, when, in October 1946, the government set up advisory bodies to assist in the collection and distribution of scarce goods, which this time included representatives of the respective Chambers of Business, Agriculture and Labour. Significantly, the three Chambers were to have equal influence, in other words, 'parity of representation'.[46]

Reports of labour protest declined in the winter of 1946–7 after the basic ration was briefly increased in November to 1,500 calories. A new Law on Collective Contracts, passed in February 1947 and implemented in August, introduced common wage rates across individual industries in all four zones of occupation. It enhanced the power of the ÖGB, conferring on it the sole right to negotiate wages on behalf of all workers, with the exception of those employed in agriculture and forestry.[47] But by this time the economy was again in crisis, due in part to the extreme weather conditions. As temperatures dropped to minus thirty degrees, food supplies fell to critical levels. At the end of January an UNRRA shipment destined for Austria was delayed at sea. One week later officials in Washington informed the Austrian government that it would receive an additional $20,000,000 of food aid as part of UNRRA's new emergency programme to redistribute food to those countries which were in the gravest situation.[48] The grant was welcome and generous, amounting to one half of UNRRA's total emergency budget, but it did little to alleviate the immediate situation. The national government was also encountering mounting difficulty in exerting its authority over local governments, as its attempts to co-ordinate a national food programme were being obstructed by prevarications on the part of the provinces as well as the state of the transport system.

On 11 February, the Food Minister, Otto Sagmeister, informed the Cabinet that the provincial governments had all deliberately failed to deliver the full meat quotas to which they had committed themselves at the last provincial conference. A week later the Chancellor accused the Tyroleans of ignoring the order of the federal minister to supply building materials and, rejecting calls to treat this province as a special case, he exclaimed, 'Either we have a federal state or a sacred and separate Tyrol.'[49] The Styrian government was also withholding its quota of beef carcases, failing to send a single steer and blaming this on lack of transport, but there was a strong suspicion in Cabinet that this was no more than an excuse. The Chancellor recounted the tale of a goods train which had travelled to Fürstenfeld in Styria to pick up meat, only to be forced to return to Vienna empty when railway guards found that local farmers had delivered live rather than slaughtered cattle to the depot. After this, the governor of Styria was summoned to the Chancellery, where Figl threatened to hold back future subsidies to the province until it had fulfilled its promise.[50] He also issued a strongly worded instruction to all the provincial governors, ordering them to attend a special conference on 27 February to discuss the food and energy crisis. But the provincial governments were facing their own difficulties in covering basic rations for their residents.

Food was not the only problem which faced the Austrian people in early 1947. There was also an acute shortage of fuel and electricity, which forced factories to close in the New Year. Drought conditions hit the hydro-electrical industry, which produced 87 per cent of the country's electricity, reducing production in February 1947 to 37 per cent of the level for July 1946.[51] At the same time, the demand for coal had outstripped its supply in much of Europe and the inevitable shortages were then exacerbated by strikes which broke out among miners and metalworkers in the Ruhr in January 1947. This had serious repercussions in Austria, where the mines produced lignite, a low-grade fuel, but where there were no deposits of coal. As a result, the economy depended on imported fuel to run both its railways and its heavy industries. In January 1947, 2,280 factories shut down when coal deliveries from Poland and Czechoslovakia were suspended, and the following month the only blast-furnace in operation in Donawitz was damped down.[52] The government introduced an emergency programme to divert fuel to essential industries, but it was not enough; industrial production fell by a third between July 1946 and February 1947 and, for the first time since 1945, unemployment rose as workers were temporarily laid off. With little or no fuel available to heat homes, half a million people took advantage of the 'warm rooms' set up by the

Viennese authorities, where they were given soup or a warm drink.[53] Inflation was also increasing, fed by wage increases and the rising cost of industrial and agricultural goods, as well as imports.

Despite the short-term crisis unemployment of early 1947, the economy was still suffering from a shortage of labour. Agricultural and unskilled workers were particularly scarce, a consequence of war casualties and imprisonment and the fact that many soldiers had learned a trade in the armed services during the war. There were too many competing demands for labour – on the farms where there were crops to be planted and later harvested, and in the bombed towns and cities where rubble had to be cleared by hand and shovel. The situation was so acute that the provisional government had resorted to limited conscription in June 1945. Initially this was restricted to ex-Nazi Party members and covered the eastern provinces only, but in 1946 the new coalition government reintroduced the Nazi Law on Compulsory Labour as an emergency measure, compelling all men between the ages of eighteen and fifty-five and all single women under forty to work.[54] Nevertheless, in the summer of 1946 the number of job vacancies was double the number of job-seekers.[55] However, the law was applied inconsistently and the figures for those out of work did not include thousands of displaced persons who were living in camps on Austrian soil and receiving rations, and whom the Austrian government were intent on moving on.[56] A British Foreign Office report observed that as a result, 'public opinion has been stirred, partly by propaganda, against foreigners in general and the man-in-the-street is apt to regard them as nothing more than rogues, criminals and black-marketeers'.[57] There were also distinct signs of anti-Semitism: 32,000 of the displaced persons were Jewish survivors who, moreover, were receiving additional rations supplied by the American Joint Distribution Committee, and, unlike other DPs, were specifically exempted from working.[58] Their numbers swelled in the spring of 1947 as Jewish refugees arrived from Rumania, and the following summer a violent and anti-Semitic demonstration broke out when the inhabitants of Bad Ischl in Upper Austria attacked the local DP camp after dried milk was substituted for fresh in rations for local children.[59]

The combination of hunger, lay-offs and an underlying labour shortage was politically volatile in early 1947, at the very time that talks were taking place in London and later Moscow on a possible Austrian State Treaty which would end the occupation. In February, the KPÖ began to call for fresh elections and on 19 March demonstrators took to the streets in Mödling, south of Vienna, and Gmünd, on the Lower Austrian border with Czechoslovakia, demanding food, the resignation of the Figl government and fresh elections.[60] The government responded by sending emergency relief to both areas. In addition, since the beginning of the year thousands of women had been signing petitions and joining demonstrations demanding better rationing and stricter controls on hoarding and black marketeering. The protests were led by Communist women, but found resonance in areas as far-flung as Innsbruck and Klagenfurt, where Communist influence was minimal.[61] On 5 May 1947, following a month in which full food rations could not be issued, deliveries of potatoes failed to materialise. Demonstrators from Simmering, in the Soviet zone of Vienna, marched into the city centre, where they were joined by other workers. According to eye-witnesses, approximately 20,000 people took part in the demonstration, which turned violent when a group of protesters forced their way into the Chancellery, demanding a meeting with the Chancellor. A section of the crowd then marched to the Chamber of Labour and pushed their way into the building. By this time, the Austrian government had become alarmed and Figl made a public request for Allied intervention.[62] The request was denied, but a British military report concluded that the Viennese police had failed to stop the demonstrators from marching into the city because, although a few officers had firearms, there had been a lack of appropriate crowd-control weapons. Describing a meeting between the Interior Minister, Oskar Helmer, and the British Deputy High Commissioner in Austria, General Winterton, it went on:

> General Winterton said that in his opinion the most important question was to equip the Vienna police with some means of competing with a crowd and that for this purpose a truncheon was really more suitable than a lethal weapon. Dr Helmer agreed, but said that the rubber truncheon had a bad reputation in Vienna from Nazi days. . . . General Winterton pointed out that the London police found a wooden truncheon satisfactory and that such a truncheon should be equally suitable for Vienna. . . . Dr Helmer professed to disbelieve this but was nevertheless impressed by the argument and asked General Winterton to obtain sample truncheons from England.[63]

The report added that the British authorities had rejected a call for military intervention in the international First District, because of fears that this would trigger conflict between Allied troops.

In Cabinet next day, ministers blamed the Soviet authorities for preventing deliveries of potatoes from reaching the city and accused them of interfering in police discipline. Figl described the demonstrators as local women and foreigners, Greeks and Albanians, who were intent on wrecking the State Treaty negotiations and undermining the Austrian State itself. The situation, he went on, was dangerous, for the demonstration had had characteristics not previously seen in the Second Republic: he had met a delegation of protesters who had not voiced economic grievances, but had criticised the westernisation of Austrian policy. The demonstration, he maintained, had therefore been politically motivated.[64] Rumours began to circulate that the protest had been a Communist putsch attempt, and these were later repeated by the Vice-Chancellor, Adolf Schärf, who linked the unrest in Vienna to the overthrow of the Hungarian government by Communists that same month.[65] The May demonstration was the first public protest in Austria to be branded a Communist putsch, but it was not the last.

Despite attempts to downplay the economic grievances which had triggered the situation, the government knew it could not ignore the food protests, which had involved working men and women as well as full-time housewives, had crossed zones of occupation, and were often led by elected shop stewards and local politicians. On 29 May 1947, following the protests, government and union leaders held talks with the Allies about raising the daily ration to 1,200 calories immediately and to 1,800 in July.[66] In the meantime, on 7 May in parliament, the Chancellor announced an 'action plan' to produce a 'definitive settlement on the question of wages and prices and on currency reform'.[67] The trade union newspaper, *Solidarität*, reported the speech, adding the phrase 'in co-operation with the ÖGB'.[68] The plan on wages and prices was, however, drawn up in secret by an ad hoc advisory committee, the Economic Commission (*Wirtschaftskommission*), comprising representatives of the ÖGB and the Chambers of Business, Agriculture and Labour, the Economic Partners. The decision on currency reform was postponed until after the Commission had produced its proposals, which it did on 25 July. These were then considered by the Economic Committee of Ministers (*Wirtschaftliches Ministerkomitee*), before being ratified in Cabinet. In order to encourage agricultural production while also exerting control on escalating prices and reducing the influence of the black market, the Economic Commission recommended drastic tariff increases of between 50 and 100 per cent for public utilities such as the railways, postal services, gas and electricity, which had been held artificially low. The price for agricultural goods was to be allowed to rise by an average of 25 per cent, although the increases for bread and sugar were capped at 9 and 13 per cent respectively.[69] The policy was designed to narrow the gap between official and black-market prices and to bring domestic prices, in particular those for agricultural goods, into line with market levels. This was intended not only to encourage agricultural production at a time of food shortages, but also to placate the American government, which had been greatly concerned at the level of food subsidies in Austria. But in order to combat the threat of unregulated and rampant price inflation, the Economic Commission recognised that initial steep increases were necessary. The key was to introduce these in a uniform manner. It was a radical reform which in the existing climate also required protection for consumers. A sliding scale for wages was established which was intended to cover most, though not all, of the anticipated increase in the cost of living, with the provision that the unions would not demand further wage increases for three months unless the cost-of-living index rose by more than 10 per cent during that period.

The 1947 Wages and Prices Agreement was an extraordinary settlement in many respects. It was an exercise in incomes policy formation which sought to contain inflation and stimulate production by introducing what were, by any account, large increases in official prices. The advisory committee that drew it up was appointed by the democratically elected government, but its membership was restricted to the leaders of four peak associations representing the three major economic sectors of business, agriculture and labour. Moreover, these peak associations had by this time been granted statutory rights to act as the sole representatives of their respective economic sectors, the Chambers under the terms of the laws which established them, and the ÖGB under the terms of the Law on Collective Contracts. Their leaders, therefore, had unusual powers; they had been granted exclusive control over the official representation of the interests of the members of their economic sectors, and yet not one of them had, at that point, been elected by those members. Moreover, the creation of the Economic Commission provided these men with a collective role in drawing up recommendations on one of the most important aspects of economic policy. There is little evidence to suggest that the government had considered the long-term consequences of delegating this role to the economic elites, for the decision to set up the Commission had been taken in haste during a period of extreme crisis, and initially it was seen as an informal arrangement. But the strategy of consulting the economic elites was a clear extension of the culture of consensus and parity which the political elites had been fostering since the beginning of the occupation, and over the ensuing four years the Economic Commission was called on to produce four more Wages and Prices Agreements, all of which became law. It continued to operate until 1952, when, as will be shown, the courts ruled that the relationship between the Economic Partners and the government was unconstitutional. And even after this, in 1957, it was resurrected and its powers were augmented.

In 1947, however, the Wages and Prices Agreement was viewed as an emergency measure designed to prevent an imminent economic crisis. Labour leaders, in particular, had taken a considerable risk by endorsing the terms of the agreement. They defended their position by insisting that the nation's productive capacity had been bled dry by the 'Nazi' war and the cost of the occupation. As a consequence, inflation showed signs of spiralling out of control, threatening the value of real wages and thus the living standards of the working class. The Wages and Prices Agreement was the only possible solution to the crisis, for it would stabilise both wages and prices. The ÖGB assured its members that the agreement contained safeguards, citing the clause permitting the unions to submit new wage demands if prices rose.[70] But when the cost-of-living index rose by 14.5 per cent within the next two months, union leaders decided that wage increases could not prevent a further fall in living standards and rejected calls for fresh wage claims.[71] Austrian workers were being asked by their leaders to absorb rising food prices even though the prevailing level of real wages was low. Nevertheless, in the short term, food rather than wages remained the central preoccupation of most of the working population.

The ÖGB described its contribution to drawing up legislation as threefold – influencing policy directly, operating indirectly through the Chamber of Labour, and playing a direct role in policy formation through membership of law-making bodies (*gesetzgebende Körperschaften*) such as the Economic Commission. By 1948 the ÖGB was already calling itself a 'Social Partner', but to many union members it was more a case of poacher turned gamekeeper, a view which was likely to be promoted by the KPÖ.[72]

Two years after the birth of the ÖGB a clear divergence had emerged within the labour leadership. The KPÖ stood alone in refusing to accept the new consensus. Nevertheless, one Communist minister continued to serve in the coalition government until 1947, and Fiala remained Deputy Chairman of the ÖGB. However, despite, or more likely because of, the Soviet presence in Austria, the KPÖ's position was still weak and the Soviets themselves did not recover their faith in the party, even though they did not cease to encourage it to build a base amongst industrial workers by exploiting economic grievances and, in particular, attacking the Marshall Plan.[73] The KPÖ concentrated much of its efforts on the rolling series of works council elections in 1947 and 1948, which became the main arena where the rivalry between the Communists and the Socialists was fought out. Both the strengths and the weaknesses of Austrian Communism proved to be of major significance to the labour movement. While, on the one hand, the KPÖ's policies threatened to undermine political stability, on the other, they actually strengthened the bargaining power of the ÖGB, which was based on the very close relationship between its leaders and the governing elite, as well as on the Federation's ability to contain dissent within the working class. In 1946 and the first half of 1947, unrest over food had not led to serious trouble, despite the periodic inability of the government to secure the ration. Union leaders had successfully argued against large-scale direct action and in favour of negotiations, and had, as a result, increased their influence within government circles. But there was mounting evidence that they had not permanently secured the support of their members. At the 1948 Trade Union Conference, the Minister for Social Administration, Karl Mantler, who was also the leader of the Food-Workers' Union and President of the Viennese Chamber of Labour, argued that wage rises were in fact unnecessary because the prices of many rationed goods were by that time stable and others were actually falling.[74] Sustained long-term economic growth was what was now needed. This required short-term sacrifices by the workers, but would eventually lead to a higher standard of living for all. The implication was that the sacrifice and the resultant benefits would spread across all classes. One woman delegate's response to this argument was that there had been no mention of profits, and that Mantler did not understand the problems workers faced. Women workers in her industry, textiles, took home an average weekly wage of 75 to 80 Schillings. Rations for one person cost between 18 and 22 Schillings a week, so a single working mother with two children had 25 to 30 Schillings left for the rent, electricity and gas. Current wages did not cover the cost of basic essentials, let alone anything bought on the black market, even though prices there were falling.[75]

As time was to show, despite all the urgings of the labour leadership, workers had not yet abandoned the traditional arguments and traditional forms of protest, though the causes of their discontent were changing. When new industrial conflicts arose in 1948, they would return to the strike weapon.

Notes

1   Emmerich Tálos and Bernhard Kittel, 'Roots of Austro-Corporatism: Institutional preconditions and co-operation before and after 1945', in Günter Bischof and Anton Pelinka (eds), *Austro-Corporatism: Past, Present and Future* (New Brunswick, NJ: Transaction, 1996), 43.

2   Lewis, *Fascism and the Working Class in Austria*, 212.
3   Klenner, *Die österreichischen Gewerkschaften*, vol. 2, 1605.
4   TNA/PRO/FO 945/810. J.W. Nicholls to Ernest Bevin, 11 June 1946.
5   Klenner, *Die österreichischen Gewerkschaften*, vol. 2, 1602.
6   Böhm, *Erinnerungen aus meinem Leben*, 197–8. He was elected to parliament and served as Second President of the National Assembly, as well as president of the ÖGB, until his death in 1959.
7   *75 Jahre Kammern für Arbeiter und Angestellte* (Vienna: Verlag des Österreichischen *Gewerkschaftsbundes*, 1995), 34.
8   Klenner, *Die österreichischen Gewerkschaften*, vol. 2, 924.
9   In 1954 the law was changed and the Vienna Chamber of Labour was given superior powers. *75 Jahre Kammern für Arbeiter und Angestellte*, 36–9.
10 *75 Jahre Kammern für Arbeiter und Angestellte*, 37. The law establishing the employers' chamber, the Federal Chamber of Business (*Bundeswirtschafts-kammer, BKW*), was passed on 24 July 1946.
11 TNA/PRO/FO 985/810. J.W. Nicholls to Ernest Bevin, 11 June 1946.
12 TNA/PRO/FO 985/810. J.W. Nicholls to Ernest Bevin, 11 June 1946. In the first election of ÖGB officials in 1948, Böhm was returned as president.
13 TNA/PRO/FO 985/810. W.R.Eley to R. Wilberforce, 1 April 1946.
14 A delegation of British trade unionists visited Vienna in December 1945. TNA/PRO/FO 985/810. J. W. Nicholls to Ernest Bevin, 11 June 1946.
15 *Tätigkeitsbericht 1945–1947 und stenographisches Protokoll des ersten Kongresses des österreichischen Gewerkschaftsbundes* (Vienna, 1948) (hereafter *ÖGB Tätigkeitsbericht 1945–1947*), 3/62, 1/77. The actual figure for December 1946 was 924,274, of whom 75.3 per cent were men and 24.7 per cent women.
16 Weber, *Der Kalte Krieg in der SPÖ. Koalitionswächter, Pragmatiker und Revolutionäre Sozialisten 1945–1950*, 117.
17 *Protokolle des Kabinettsrates*, vol. 3, 199, sitting 24 October 1945.
18 Lewis, *Fascism and the Working Class in Austria*, 74.
19 *ÖGB Tätigkeitsbericht 1945–1947*, 1/17.
20 *Jahrbuch der Arbeiterkammer in Wien*, 1947, 315.
21 *Arbeiter-Zeitung*, (30 October 1945).
22 Lewis, *Fascism and the Working Class in Austria*, 147–201. In order to reduce the influence of splinter parties under its particular system of proportional representation, the Austrian Constitution requires each party participating in an election to win one seat outright before it can receive votes allocated to second- and third-choice parties.
23 Gulick, *Austria from Habsburg to Hitler*, 136–7, ftn. 11.
24 *Ibid.*, 203; Lewis, *Fascism and the Working Class in Austria*, 52–4.
25 Gulick, *Austria from Habsburg to Hitler*, 202.
26 Most candidates stood as representatives of a political party, although many were elected as 'non-affiliated' (*parteilos*). The results were as follows: Donawitz, 10 KPÖ, 9 SPÖ; Fohnsdorf, 10 KPÖ, 5 SPÖ; Seegraben, 7 KPÖ, 7 SPÖ. Herz, *Understanding Austria*, 484.
27 Fritz Weber, 'Go Heavy Metal, Austria!', in Wolfgang Kos and Georg Rigele (eds), *Inventur 1945/55* (Vienna: Sonderzahl, 1996), 302.
28 Rodney Stiefbold *et al.* (eds), *Wahlen und Parteien in Österreich*, vol. 4, *Nationalratswahl* (Vienna: Jugend und Volk, 1966), *passim*.

29 Herz, *Understanding Austria*, 483.
30 Rathkolb, *Gesellschaft in der Politik*, 81, ftn. d; Lewis, *Fascism and the Working Class in Austria*, 157–60; *Wiener Neueste Nachrichten* (18 December 1928). Herz described Oberegger as 'sinister', one of an 'amazing number of Nazis' who were appointed public administrators of nationalised industries. Herz, *Understanding Austria*, 37, 573. An earlier American report stated that the SPÖ had opposed Oberegger's appointment, but that the ÖVP had 'pointed to his years in a Nazi concentration camp'. Rathkolb, *Gesellschaft in der Politik*, 95.
31 Peter Böhmer, *Wer konnte, griff zu. Arisierte Güter und NS-Vermögen im Krauland-Ministerium, 1945–1949* (Vienna: Böhlau, 1999), 59.
32 *Jahrbuch der Arbeiterkammer in Wien, 1948*, 417.
33 Herz, *Understanding Austria*, 484. See also ftn. 22 above.
34 Wallisch and Stanek were hanged by the authorities in February 1934. Ilona Ducynska, *Workers in Arms* (New York: Monthly Review Press, 1978), 38–42.
35 Lewis, *Fascism and the Working Class in Austria*, 181–201. Willi Scholz joined the KPÖ in 1934, and was arrested in December 1934 and released in autumn 1935, after which he spent fourteen months in Moscow. He moved to Maribor (Slovenia) in 1937 and lived from 1938 to 1945 in Britain. Dokumentationsarchiv des österreichischen Widerstands (DÖW), interview 13.100.
36 *ÖGB Tätigkeitsbericht 1945–1947*, 1/17.
37 *Arbeiter-Zeitung* (14 March 1946).
38 *ÖGB Tätigkeitsbericht 1945–1947*, 3/63.
39 *Ibid.*, 1/17.
40 TNA/PRO/FO 945/958. J. W. Nicholls to Ernest Bevin, 30 July 1946: 'On the 16th April a conference of Viennese shop stewards and officials of the Federation passed a motion on food tantamount to a vote of censure on the government. The Federal Chancellor himself was present and got a somewhat stormy reception. I have since been informed that it was only moderating Socialist influence at this meeting which prevented the Communists from proposing a general strike.'
41 Hans Hautmann, Winfried Garscha and Willi Weinert, *Die Kommunistische Partei Österreichs. Beiträge zu ihrer Geschichte und Politik* (Vienna: Globus Verlag, 1987), 350–2. Reports, Informatory Material on the Activities of the Austrian Communist Party. Submitted to A.A. Zhdanov by an official of the Central Committee of the All-Union Communist Party (bolshevik), RGASPI, Fond 575, Op.1, Delo 8, 12 September 1947.
42 Bader contends that the KPÖ changed its statutes to increase the status of the factory cells in May 1946, but this change was actually adopted at the 14th KPÖ congress in 1948. Bader, *Austria between East and West*, 141. Hautmann *et al. Die Kommunistische Partei Österreichs*, 374.
43 TNA/PRO/FO 945/810, J. W. Nicholls to Ernest Bevin, 11 June 1946; *ÖGB Tätigkeitsbericht 1945–1947*, 3/64.
44 *ÖGB Tätigkeitsbericht 1945–1947*, 1/18.
45 *Ibid.*
46 *Ibid.*, 1/20.
47 Prior to this, different systems had applied in different zones. The first wages agreement arrived at in Vienna was published on 12 July 1945, but wage regulation was banned in the US zone until March 1946. *Ibid.*, 3/52.

48 Pomeroy to Figl, Austrian Cabinet Papers, sitting 55, 5 February 1947; telegram from UNRRA Austrian Mission to Figl, 10 February 1947, sitting 57, 18 February 1947. Österreichisches Staatsarchiv, AdR, BKA, Ministerratsproto-kolle (MRP) (hereafter Austrian Cabinet Papers), Figl 1, Box 13.
49 Austrian Cabinet Papers, sitting 57, 18 February 1947. 'Entweder es gibt einen Bundesstaat oder ein heiliges Land Tirol daneben.'
50 Austrian Cabinet Papers, sitting 56, 11 February 1947.
51 Rothschild, *The Austrian Economy since 1945*, 378.
52 *Jahrbuch der Arbeiterkammer in Wien, 1947*, 291. The Czech government offered to send coal in exchange for what it claimed were 'surplus' blast-furnaces in Linz.
53 Wien im Ruckblick (29 March 1947).
54 *ÖGB Tätigkeitsbericht 1945–1947*, 1/74. The law remained in force until 1948, when unemployment began to rise.
55 *Arbeiter-Zeitung* (17 January 1947).
56 During a Cabinet meeting on 18 February 1947, Helmer proposed recruiting workers from among the many 'German' POWs held in camps in Britain who had originally come from the Successor States. Figl pointed out that, as the government had spent months negotiating the removal of the DPs from Austria, they could not now invite 8,000 '*Volksdeutsche*' (ethnic Germans) into the country on the grounds that their labour was required. Austrian Cabinet Papers, sitting 57, 18 February 1947.
57 TNA/PRO/FO 371/70421, Allied Commission for Austria (British Element), 7 January 1948, 'Control of Labour in Austria: April 1945–December 1947', 4.
58 Herz, *Understanding Austria*, 113.
59 Kurt Tweraser, *US Militärregierung Oberösterreich, 1945–1950*, vol. 1, *Sicherheitspolitische Aspekte der Amerikanischen Besatzung in Oberösterreich-Süd, 1945–1950* (Linz: Oberösterreichisches Landesarchiv, 1995), 275–281. The American military authorities prosecuted six Communist Party members for taking part in the riot and sentenced them to long prison terms. The case became politically contentious and the sentences were subsequently reduced. For a review of this demonstration and of anti-Semitic tendencies expressed in Cabinet over the position of Jewish DPs, see Robert Knight (ed.), '*Ich bin dafür, die Sache in die Länge zu ziehen.' Wortprotokolle* (Frankfurt am Main: Athenäum, 1988), 173–90.
60 Rauchenstein, *Der Sonderfall*, 202.
61 Siegfried Mattl, 'Frauen in Österreich nach 1945', in Rudolf G. Ardelt, Wolfgang J. A. Huber and Anton Staudinger (eds), *Unterdrückung und Emanzipation: Festschrift für Erika Weinzierl* (Vienna: Geyer, 1985), 115–17.
62 Austrian Cabinet Papers, sitting 67, 6 May 1947.
63 TNA/PRO/FO/1020/245 ACABRIT to Foreign Office (German Section), 15 May 1947.
64 Austrian Cabinet Papers, sitting 67, 6 May 1947. The reference to Greeks and Albanians hinted at a link with the civil war which was raging in Greece between Communists and Monarchists.
65 Schärf, *Österreichs Erneuerung 1945–1955*, 161–4. Schärf rejected claims by the Foreign Minister, Karl Gruber, that the police had been insufficiently armed, claiming instead that they had had no firearms that functioned. British reports support Gruber's position.

66 AdR, BKA, Auswärtige Angelegenheiten (AA), W.Po. WiEur, Box 87, Marshall Plan, letter from the Minister for Food to the Austrian Ambassador in Washington, 19 September 1947. The funding for this was temporarily blocked by Congress. See Chapter 4, 97-8.

67 *Stenographische Protokolle des Nationalrats*, vol. 3, sitting 7 May 1947, 1408.

68 Hannes Zimmermann, 'Wirtschaftsentwicklung in Österreich 1945–51, am Beispiel der Lohn-Preis-Abkommen und des Marshallplans' (PhD Dissertation, University of Vienna, 1983), 171, 174.

69 Zimmermann, 'Wirtschaftsentwicklung in Österreich', 176–7.

70 *Arbeiter-Zeitung* (1 August 1947).

71 Klenner, *Die österreichischen Gewerkschaften*, 1430–3; Zimmermann, 'Wirtschaftsentwicklung in Österreich', 148–54.

72 *ÖGB Tätigkeitsbericht 1945–1947*, 1/76.

73 RGASPI, Fond 575, Op.1, Delo 8, Reports, Informatory Material on the Activities of the Austrian Communist Party. Submitted to A.A. Zhdanov by an official of the Central Committee of the All-Union Communist Party (bolshevik), 12 September 1947.

74 *ÖGB Tätigkeitsbericht 1945–1947*, 4/113–17. Paradoxically, Mantler resigned from the SPÖ executive later in 1948 in protest at the First Wages and Prices Agreement. Weber, *Der Kalte Krieg in der SPÖ*, 137.

75 *ÖGB Tätigkeitsbericht 1945–1947*, 4/146.

6

Transformation
and confrontation

On 17 September 1948 the *Arbeiter-Zeitung* published an editorial praising the political and moral self-restraint of Austrian workers:

> If, in the year that has passed since the Wages and Prices Agreement was introduced, the Austrian economy has nevertheless made remarkable progress; if today the shops are once again full of goods, if industrial production has risen quite markedly, and if today the appearance of our cities is already entirely different from what it was not so very long ago, then Austria owes this entirely [. . .] to the political and moral self-restraint of our manual and white-collar workers. Whilst terror reigns among our Eastern neighbours, whilst among our Western neighbours strikes, disturbances and ministerial crises follow hot on each other's heels, this small country, Austria, has remained, in spite of poverty and distress, the most tranquil country in Europe.[1]

The editorial had a point, for in comparison with the Communist seizure of power in Czechoslovakia, the blockade of Berlin, the consolidation of Communist rule in Bulgaria, Rumania and Hungary, and even the large-scale strikes in Britain, Italy and France, the situation in Austria was relatively calm. However, there was more than a little wishful thinking in this description of the country's political climate, for the previous twelve months had not passed without strife. There were still sporadic food protests, but these were now less significant than the increasing number of industrial strikes, often triggered by grievances over wages and terms of employment, in particular the implementation of the Law on Collective Contracts. In the autumn of 1947, as we shall see, Socialists and Communists clashed during hotly contested works council elections, workers at the Guggenbach paper factory walked out in protest at the appointment of an ex-Nazi, and agricultural and forestry workers went on strike over their exclusion from the provisions of the Law on Collective Contracts. A strike in the paper industry in November broke out just weeks after a chronic paper shortage had threatened to disrupt the publication of newspapers. Low productivity in the industry was blamed on the under-nourishment of the workers.[2] The following March there was a series of short protest strikes when the government announced that it was unable to raise the basic ration to the promised 1,800 calories, and the Textile and Leather Union called an official national strike of its members in the shoe industry demanding, among other things, a shorter working week. In addition, the spectre of further industrial action loomed as structural unemployment began to rise, threatening to give the lie to the ÖGB's promise to its members of full employment in return for their patience over wage levels.[3]

The real purpose of the *Arbeiter-Zeitung* editorial was clear to see in the newspaper's main article, which appeared alongside it on the front page. This gave the first detailed account of a second Wages and Prices Agreement. The newspaper's praise for the restraint of Austrian workers was actually an appeal to its Socialist readers to support government economic policy and reject increasing Communist militancy. As such, it reflected the mounting alarm that was spreading within the SPÖ hierarchy about the impact which the new Communist strategy of industrial action was having on its own rank-and-file support. The KPÖ, by switching its attention from the street to the shop floor and seeking to mobilise workers on the issue of wages and prices, was challenging the SPÖ's dominance of grass-roots trade unionism, the very core of traditional working-class politics and the one area where the Socialists' position was most vulnerable. In so doing, the Communists were exploiting the SPÖ's major weakness, the contradiction between its traditional role as the sole representative of working-class interests in Austria, and its new role as a partner in and advocate of coalition politics. One of the realities of the new culture of consensus was that it left the field of industrial confrontation wide open to the Communist Party.

Although there were critics of coalition politics within the SPÖ at this time, no group or individual was ready to champion the basic working-class demand for a decent wage while the party's trade union leaders were members of the committee that drew up wages and prices policy and its political leaders were part of the government which put that policy into effect. Moreover, by the end of 1947 debate within the SPÖ had been stifled and it was nigh impossible for ordinary members, or more specifically those who did not share the views of the party's inner circle, to voice any form of dissent, as internal party democracy had been sacrificed on the altar of consensus politics and replaced by a large centralised party machine which was controlled by a small inner clique. The consolidation of power within the SPÖ had followed a similar path to that in the ÖGB, but it had taken a little longer to achieve.

Although the party and the union federation had been created at the same time and, to all intents and purposes, by the same men, the ÖGB's effective monopoly over the establishment of new trade unions gave its leaders greater powers of control. The SPÖ, on the other hand, had to compete with other political parties for both members and votes: it had to woo its supporters and to this end it was necessary to appeal to the traditions and legacy of the SDAP. The problem was that the SPÖ's founding fathers were vehemently opposed to the most fundamental principles of Austro-Marxism and were abandoning the class-based ideology which had been the original party's central tenet. Under the new leadership, class was no longer relevant, for the role of the state in modern society was deemed to be neutral, or, in the words of Adolf Schärf, 'After all, this state is in reality nothing but an administrative machine', serving the interests of all citizens, not just those of the dominant class force.[4] This was an eminently practical position for a political party to adopt in an occupied country, where it was essential to present a united front in order to win independence, and it justified the SPÖ's participation in coalition government. But the renunciation of class analysis also amounted to a complete rejection of the basic principles and policies of the party's predecessor. In 1920 the SDAP had rejected the political compromise which was then on the table and had withdrawn from a coalition government.[5] It had then undertaken a radical experiment in Socialist planning in Vienna, focusing on the interests of its working-class supporters and challenging the conservative policies of the national government. The goal had been to win power through the ballot box by convincing workers that socialism represented a viable political alternative to the bourgeois politics of the national government. The strategy had proved spectacularly successful on several levels: the policies of 'Red Vienna' had won international fame among Socialists and even limited praise from the League of Nations.[6] It had led to a significant rise in the party's share of the vote in the capital itself, which increased from 47 per cent in 1920 to 60 per cent in 1927. Party membership figures had been even more impressive: at its height, over 20 per cent of the city's population were card-carrying members of the SDAP. But the appeal of 'Red Vienna' had failed to win over the provinces, where, in some cases, the Socialist vote had actually fallen. As a result, despite becoming the largest party in parliament in the 1927 general election and retaining this position in the 1930 election, the

SDAP had been unable to secure an overall majority and remained in opposition until the end of the First Republic, even as the country's democratic structures crumbled. According to critics on the right of the party, it had abrogated its responsibility to defend the Republic in order to maintain its ideological integrity.

It was these critics who became the major force behind the formation of the SPÖ. Although the direct political heir to the SDAP, the SPÖ was, as we have already seen, the creation of a handful of people, almost exclusively men, who were co-opted by Karl Renner and Adolf Schärf. Most of them had held office in the SDAP before it had been outlawed in 1934, but they had not belonged to the majority group on the party's national executive, being instead identified with the right wing of the SDAP, which had constantly criticised the radicalism of Otto Bauer and the party chairman, Karl Seitz, in particular. They believed that the party had been wrong to withdraw from the governing coalition in 1920. Even having done so, its leaders should have maintained contact with the Christian Social government and, when the political situation began to deteriorate, should have attempted to find some middle ground on which to negotiate. In true Viennese fashion, Schärf had set up a *Stammtisch* at the Café Herrenhof in the late 1920s, where a group of like-minded Socialist parliamentarians met regularly.[7] This unofficial opposition group had included Schärf, Karl Renner and Oskar Helmer, as well as Felix Stika, Heinrich Schneidlmadl and Franz Popp. In 1933, after parliament had been prorogued, three of these men, Helmer, Schneidlmadl and Popp, had even held discussions with Chancellor Dollfuss, in the hope of limiting his government's move towards authoritarianism. When these talks failed, the group as a whole had held Bauer and Seitz at least partially responsible, while also criticising them for encouraging the escalating violence of the late 1920s and early 1930s.[8] It was these men, who had strongly opposed the basic tenets of Austro-Marxism in the inter-war years, who, accompanied by Theodor Körner, formed the inner core of the SPÖ leadership in 1945 and were determined not to repeat the mistakes of their predecessors.

The political power of the new leadership would, however, still depend on its ability to rebuild the party structure, recruit rank-and-file members and win the votes of Austrian workers and their families, most of whom had previously been loyal to the SDAP. It was for this reason that, despite the eleven-year gap in its tradition of participatory politics, the movement's political heritage remained an essential factor in attracting popular support and so could not be ignored. But, since the legacy of the old party included radical elements that the new leaders found unedifying, the reconstruction of party history which was thus called for had to be handled with care. As a result, Renner and Schärf adopted a policy of partial and selective recollection of the past, tempered with dire warnings about the ever-present dangers which direct action would bring down on the fragile new state and frequent calls for party unity, which had been a major ingredient of Austrian Socialism ever since the birth of the movement in 1889.[9]

These tactics seemed to work. In its first seven months, the SPÖ recruited 360,000 members, or 55 per cent of the SDAP's membership in 1932, the last year such figures were published. But, having failed to win the 1945 general election and having joined Figl's coalition, its leaders intensified the attack on the KPÖ, while rallying working-class support for the Socialist cause. The former glories of the SDAP were recalled along with the achievements of the municipal socialism of 'Red Vienna', all carefully cleansed of the ideology of class conflict which had underpinned both. Party functionaries organised marches and rallies and waved red flags on May Day (International Workers' Day), commemorated the victims of the civil war, and laid wreaths on the Parisian grave of Otto Bauer. But the language of solidarity was changing. The banner headline of the *Arbeiter-Zeitung* on 1 May 1946 read, 'The people with us'.[10] The only mention of workers was found two lines below – 'Long live the unity of the workers in the Socialist Party.' Twelve months later, the newspaper's headline on International Workers' Day made no reference at all to workers and its front page was dominated by a speech by the party chairman, Adolf Schärf, in which he described the celebrations as a 'a true and genuine day of national celebration'.[11]

The concept of party unity was also being subtly altered, along with the nature of the party itself. Although the new party officially adopted the statutes of its predecessor, some of these were reinterpreted in such a way as to limit the role of the rank-and-file and increase the power of the executive, while others were simply ignored. For instance, according to the statutes, all changes to party policy required approval by the party conference. In the past this rule had enabled ordinary delegates to challenge executive proposals from the floor of the meeting, and, in some cases, even to defeat them. As debates at the SDAP party conferences had been relatively open, one result of this method of proceeding was that it had been possible to draft composite resolutions during the course of the debate which reconciled the differing opinions being expressed. This approach had not only acted as a curb on the power of the executive, occasionally forcing it to amend or even withdraw proposals, but it had also helped to preserve party unity, for, once the conference had voted, it became the duty of each and every party member to support the decision arrived at, irrespective of his or her own personal view.[12] The pre-eminence of the conference had reinforced the SDAP's claim to be a broad and democratic party, representing all colours of socialism, and had effectively obviated the danger of schisms and splinter groups such as those which were weakening working-class movements in the rest of Europe. In particular, it had helped to dampen the appeal of the Communist Party during the First Republic, even within the Socialists' radical young left wing.

The original concept of unity, therefore, had meant complete support for party policy, but only after this had been openly debated and confirmed by the party conference. Open debate was, however, unaccept-able to the leaders of the post-war party because it offered a platform to their critics. As a result, the SPÖ executive took new steps to 'manage' conference proceedings. In fact, some of the most important changes made to party policy were never put before conference. The most salient example of this was the question of support for and participation in coalition government, the rejection of which had been, as we have seen, one of the most fundamental principles of the inter-war party. It could be argued that the decision to overturn party policy on this issue was originally a short-term tactical move, adopted by the party executive in the confusion of the first days of the liberation, and that, indeed, it had been extremely successful in ensuring it was a stable government dominated by the SPÖ that wielded power. If this was the case, it did not necessarily represent a fundamental change in party policy. But following the ÖVP victory in the 1945 general election, the executive took the decision to support a permanent coalition without engaging in wider consultation with its members, even though this did undoubtedly constitute such a change and therefore required the approval of conference according to party statutes.[13] Nevertheless, despite heated discussion of the issue within the left wing of the party and among many grass-roots members, the principle of coalition government was never formally put before the conference.

Ignoring the pre-eminence of the conference was only one of several tactics employed by SPÖ leaders to reduce the democratic control of ordinary members over the executive. A second was to present proposals to the conference, but then to refuse to take speeches from the floor, as the statutes demanded, so ensuring that the debate was restricted to speakers who supported the official executive line. In May 1946 an extraordinary conference was convened at short notice to endorse a new party programme of reconstruction (*Aufbauprogramm*) which had been drawn up by three members of the executive, Julius Deutsch, Bruno Pittermann and Erwin Scharf, and was heralded as a 'third way to democratic socialism'.[14] Negotiations over the programme had been fraught, as Deutsch, who had only recently returned from exile in the USA, and Pittermann, who was Junior Minister for Social Affairs, clashed with Scharf over the question of political priorities. Their differences reflected divisions which had existed in the SPÖ since its birth. Deutsch and Pittermann, who at that time represented the majority on the executive, advocated the primacy of foreign policy, a pragmatic approach to policy formation which recognised the limitations imposed on Austrian politicians by the presence of the occupation forces. Foreign affairs, they insisted, had to be the SPÖ's main concern as long as the Allied occupation continued. Domestic policy would therefore take second place until Austrian independence had been achieved. Scharf, who was a member of the party's central secretariat as well as one of the leading figures in the left-wing faction, now called the *Linkssozialisten*, rejected this approach, dubbing it a 'programme of inactivity' and pressing instead for a clear programme of domestic reform designed to improve wages and living standards. But he represented a dwindling section within the SPÖ leadership and his arguments were rejected by the majority on the executive, who endorsed the new programme and recommended it to the conference. However, there was little doubt that, given a free voice, ordinary conference delegates would have reacted angrily to the basic premise of the new programme, namely that the party should concentrate on foreign policy rather than fighting to improve the living standards of its members. The executive was aware that this could lead to a fracas on the floor of the conference room, and the day before the conference was due to take place it pre-circulated a list of fourteen authorised speakers, all of whom duly spoke in favour of the resolution endorsing the programme. But the 1946 conference did not proceed entirely without incident; when the chairman refused to take unauthorised speeches from the floor, once again breaching conference regulations, a number of delegates walked out in protest.[15] It was a futile gesture. The *Aufbauprogramm* was approved by an overwhelming majority and the next day details of it were printed on the front page of the *Arbeiter-Zeitung*. Each of the programme's first three points related to foreign affairs; demands for a planned and democratic economy, a secure supply of food, safeguards against unemployment and increased productivity all took second place. The party called 'upon all people of good will', and referred not to workers or the working class, but to 'working people in town and countryside'. There was no call for the workers of the world to unite. Instead the programme ended with 'Long live the peace-loving community of peoples.'[16]

In order to transform the party from what had originally been a class-based organisation to a 'people's party' (*Volkspartei*), the concept of unity was being reinterpreted to mean unquestioning support for the executive, or, more precisely, for the dominant group within the leadership. This development was summarised quite clearly by Oskar Helmer in 1949 in a letter to Adolf Schärf: 'it has only been possible for the party to be united because what at the start was a very small group of friends stuck unswervingly together; it was this unity which made us strong, and with us also the party which trusted in us'.[17] Having been given this trust, the 'small group of friends' was not about to relinquish control either to the wider party, or to any of the leaders of the SDAP who had survived the war, but who did not share their views. They were particularly anxious about the influence which 'returnees', comrades who came back to Austria having spent the war years in exile or in concentration camps, might have on the party. Some, such as the *Arbeiter-Zeitung* editor, Oskar Pollak, who shared Renner and Schärf's fear of a resumption of the class politics of the 1920s, were welcomed back into the party fold and given positions within the rapidly expanding party machine.[18] Julius Deutsch was also allowed to return and at first joined the party elite. But he was not completely trusted and his requests for a government post or even to be allowed to re-enter parliament were turned down. He was later sidelined by the inner clique following clashes over policy.[19] Others, in particular those who had been specifically associated with Red Vienna, were also viewed with suspicion. In the case of the former SDAP chairman and mayor of Vienna, Karl Seitz, age and incarceration in concentration camps had, however, taken their toll: Seitz was useful as a figurehead representing the glory of Red Vienna and the repression of fascism, while offering no real threat to the policies of the new leadership; he was appointed honorary president of the SPÖ in 1945, but had little actual power.[20] Some returnees were shunned and publicly ostracised for clinging to what Schärf described as dangerous and outdated beliefs, including continued support for *Anschluss* with Germany. Friedrich Adler, the son of the founder of the SDAP, was told that there was no place for him in the new party after he published a series of articles opposing the restoration of an independent Austrian state and criticising the SPÖ's failure to defend working-class interests.[21] But there is also strong evidence that it was the past history of some exiles which made their presence unacceptable to the new party hierarchy in 1945, rather than anything to do with their current political thinking. Hugo Breitner, the former banker responsible for the taxation programme which had financed 'Red Vienna', wrote to Renner in December 1945 asking to be allowed to come home. Although by this time seventy-three years old and in poor health, he still represented the radicalism of the old party and received what he described as a polite refusal on the grounds that his return was not a priority. He died in California in March 1946.[22] Finally, when Bruno Kreisky, who had been a leading member of the Socialist Workers' Youth Association in the early 1930s and a defendant in the trial of Revolutionary Socialists in 1936, travelled to Vienna in 1946 to enquire about the possibility of returning to Vienna on a permanent basis, Renner told him that he would be of greater use to his country if he remained in Sweden.[23]

The potential threat which returnees posed to the reshaping of the party was defused by careful management, but the SPÖ leadership still faced mounting criticism of the ethos of coalition politics from within its own executive. This was in many ways more serious, for it could have provided both grounds upon which to attack the growing centralisation of the party, and a voice for working-class opposition to wage controls. It failed to do either. The most vocal internal opposition came from the *Linkssozialisten* (Left Socialists), the group which emerged from the Revolutionary Socialist wing of the party and included Erwin Scharf, Hilde and Franz Krones and Karl Mark. Initially its members had influence, for Scharf and Hilde Krones had both been co-opted onto the SPÖ executive committee in July 1945 when party activity was still restricted to the Russian zone and the power of the Revolutionary Socialists was still relatively significant.[24] However, when the SPÖ was finally recognised by the Western Allies in the autumn of 1945, its executive was expanded to include Socialist leaders from the provinces, few of whom had anything in common with either the Revolutionary Socialists or the *Linkssozialisten*; indeed, by the time of the 1945 general election, the party's name had, as we have seen, been changed to exclude any reference to the Revolutionary Socialists.

Despite its growing isolation, the Scharf–Krones group became increasingly critical of the party's abandonment of class politics, its dwindling internal democracy and growing bureaucratisation, as well as its ever closer relationship with the ÖVP and the Western Allies. The group saw itself as the true heir to Austro-Marxism and frequently quoted Otto Bauer in its condemnation of the party's move towards the political centre, citing in particular his final book, published in 1936, in which he had advocated an 'integrated socialism' based on closer ties with the Communist Party.[25] The SPÖ's growing hostility to the KPÖ and the Soviet Union became the major bone of contention between the *Linkssozialisten* and the majority on the party executive, whom Erwin Scharf condemned as blatant anti-Communists, out of line with the traditions of Austrian Socialism. The party, he asserted, should return instead to its roots, rebuilding itself from the bottom up and training party workers and its youth wing in order to create an educated tier which would provide democratic scrutiny of the leadership. It should also recreate the vibrant programme of workers' education based on evening classes which had thrived in 'Red Vienna'. But the political circumstances of post-war Austria militated against such romantic idealism. The group was preaching a form of intellectual and cultural socialism which had already been rejected by the new party leadership and for which little support was evident among the rank and file. The membership was more interested in prices, wages and employment than in joining reading groups. When Franz Krones attempted to organise voluntary classes in Marxist theory in Ottakring, one Viennese district where the *Linkssozialisten* had significant influence, few people turned up and the project folded.[26] The group had more success with the SPÖ's youth section, but not enough to challenge the increasing dominance of the right-wing leadership over the party.

The *Linkssozialisten* campaign against the party leadership came to a head during the party conference in October 1947, not long after the announcement of the First Wages and Prices Agreement, when Scharf exploited a last-minute change in the conference agenda to introduce a resolution, signed by forty-four delegates, condemning the government's foreign, economic and incomes policies. Although the resolution identified the ÖVP as the main party responsible for the deteriorating relations with the Russians, as well as the unacceptable living standards, it also accused the SPÖ of complicity. The party leadership was said to have been guilty of forgetting its own election slogan, 'the enemy is on the Right', and of launching a superfluous attack on what was described as the 'laughably small KPÖ'. Success would only be achieved by returning to the great traditions of Austrian Socialism and 'the gloriously militant attitude' of Victor Adler and Otto Bauer.[27]

The 'Resolution of the 44' posed no actual threat to the executive and was defeated by eighty votes in favour to three hundred and ninety-five against. However, it did indicate that discontent within the party was not restricted to a handful of Viennese radicals: of the forty-four who signed the original motion, fewer than half were linked to the *Linkssozialisten* and more than twenty came from the western provinces. The rebellion obviously struck a chord. But it also demonstrated the political vulnerability as well as the incompetence of the left wing and it laid them open to attack as Communist fellow-travellers, or worse: the resolution contained no direct criticism of either the KPÖ or the Soviet authorities, despite the increasing tensions over Russian reparation claims and the establishment of USIA. It is, indeed, noticeable that the signatories did not include one single delegate from Lower Austria or Burgenland, both of which were in the Soviet zone.

However, the 'Resolution of the 44' also epitomised the failure of the left to judge the political climate. The resolution was drawn up within weeks of the announcement of the First Wages and Prices Agreement, at a time when there was not only mounting industrial discontent, but also, as we have seen, the prospect of economic salvation through the Marshall Plan. Despite this, the left did not attempt to mobilise protest and displayed little interest in economic policy per se. Its main target was coalition politics and the impact this was having on SPÖ policy, but it failed to spell out any clear or practical alternatives. The 'Resolution of the 44' did include an indirect attack on the Wages and Prices Agreement, but even this was couched in terms of a general condemnation of economic policies. More importantly, the resolution itself gave the impression of offering tacit support to Soviet claims for reparations.

By the end of 1947 the *Linkssozialisten* had been defeated. Few of the forty-four signatories of the resolution escaped some form of retribution, but the ire of the party leadership was directed at Scharf and Hilde Krones in particular. Within weeks of the conference at which he was re-elected as party chairman, Adolf Schärf announced that the party secretariat was refusing to work with or even talk to Erwin Scharf, and in 1948 Scharf was thrown out of the party. Attempts to remove Hilde Krones from the executive failed, but the party leadership mounted a sustained attack on her political integrity. She committed suicide in December 1948.[28] The danger of a concerted challenge to the leadership from within the party had all but disappeared by the end of 1948, due in part to the machinations and swift actions of Schärf and his colleagues, but also in part to the ineptitude of the Scharf–Krones group. The domination of the party by the Renner–Schärf group was now complete. The inner clique controlled policy-making as well as a rapidly expanding political machine. In addition to the party posts it could provide, the increasing number of government committees and commissions also led to the creation of jobs which were filled by patronage. Left-wing critics within the party were increasingly condemned as crypto-Communists with hidden agendas which threatened the security of the new state. However, it was also the case that the SPÖ had lost its ability to represent working-class dissatisfaction with a system of which it was now part and parcel. In the meantime, the Communist Party, having enjoyed little electoral support in Austria in the late 1940s, was finally recognising the political void which was developing on the shop floor and altering its strategy accordingly. The KPÖ's change of tactics, however, was also a response to growing exasperation in Moscow. In September 1947 the Russian Communist Party issued a withering critique of Communist activity in Austria, in which it urged the KPÖ to take its struggle to the streets: 'experience has shown that the [Austrian] Communists could achieve better results if they were to accompany their parliamentary struggle with the mobilisation of the masses against this or that reactionary measure by the government. Very often, a spontaneous outburst of indignation among the masses takes the party by surprise.'[29] In other words, the Austrian Communists were being accused of failing to take full advantage of the opportunities that were opening up before them.

The first major battle between Socialists and Communists for control of the workplace actually reached its climax in October 1947 when workers throughout the country began to vote in the second series of works council elections. These were the first centrally organised works council elections since the First Republic and also the first to be held under the new Works Council Law, which re-established the basic provisions of the 1919 law, but increased the power of larger councils by introducing a new category of full-time, paid shop stewards in workplaces with over two hundred workers.[30] When the law had been put before parliament in the previous March, the Communist Party had opposed it on the grounds that it was too weak and failed to increase worker participation in either management or decisions on hiring and firing.[31] But the KPÖ's real objective was to launch an attack on its main rival, the SPÖ, accusing it of bowing to pressure from the ÖVP and employers by endorsing a law which promised much but actually delivered little that was different from the existing legislation. At the same time, the Communists invited Socialist candidates to stand for election on joint 'Unity Lists', ostensibly to protect workers from the folly of political factionalism. But the Socialist group within the ÖGB recognised this as a ploy to camouflage party affiliations and thus increase the Communists' chances of success. It firmly rejected the option in July 1947, after which preparations for the election campaign began in earnest.[32]

The works council elections were held in plants and workshops throughout Austria between October and December 1947, but the epicentre of the conflict was once again the industrial region of Upper Styria, where workers cast their votes at the beginning of the election cycle, in late October and early November. The area, still the strongest bastion of Communist support outside the Soviet sector, was the key target in the SPÖ's battle plan. Commenting at the time, Martin Herz wrote that 'the Socialists' fight against the Communists in industrial Upper Styria will go down as an epic in Austrian trade union history'.[33] The SPÖ and its faction in the ÖGB were particularly determined to break Communist control of the works councils in the foundry at Donawitz and the pits at Fohnsdorf and Seegraben. They mounted a fierce campaign, sending ministers and high-ranking union officials into the region, as well as workers from Soviet-controlled plants, who painted graphic pictures of the dangers of Communist domination.[34] Campaigning began at the end of September, just weeks after the announcement of the Wages and Prices Agreement. But any criticism of the Wages and Prices Agreement which the Communists could have used to attack the SPÖ was quickly superseded by the more urgent threat of a cut in the basic ration. In early October the Styrian government announced shortfalls in the delivery of fats, sugar and soap. It accused the national government of issuing seriously over-optimistic targets for the production of fats in the province while ignoring conflicting regulations which prevented these being met, such as the prohibition on the home slaughter of pigs until after the harvest had been brought in. Supplies of lard and butter fell short by over one hundred tons.[35] The ration was cut, and food became the main concern during the run-up to the works council elections. Communist shop stewards seized the moment and called for immediate strike action. On 3 October workers in Donawitz downed their tools, returning to work after a few hours. The Communist Party then organised simultaneous protests in Fohnsdorf, Eisenerz, Donawitz and Zeltweg, its main areas of support. Fohnsdorf workers staged a three-day protest starting on 9 October and they were joined by employees in the other three works the next day.[36] According to a British report, 'these strikes have been well organised, with the object of using the legitimate grounds for complaint (the severe fat ration cut), as a political move to increase Communist popularity in the coming elections'.[37] The same report noted that conservative newspapers were alleging that the strikes were the first steps in a longer Communist campaign of industrial action, but if this was the case, it was nipped in the bud when a Communist proposal to call an official twenty-four-hour protest strike was outvoted at a regional meeting of the Metalworkers' and Miners' Union. But the situation remained precarious and the provincial government met in a nine-hour session to discuss the grievances which had led to the strikes, once more laying blame on the national government.[38]

On 29 October 1947, the 5,500 manual and white-collar workers in Donawitz cast their votes. Eleven Socialist and ten Communist shop-stewards were elected, with the result that the Communist majority which had dominated the council since May 1945 was overturned. The Socialists were jubilant. The victory at Donawitz was feted on the front page of the *Arbeiter-Zeitung* and by the party's national executive, which sent a telegram congratulating the workforce.[39] The SPÖ went on to secure 68 per cent of the votes cast in Styria as a whole and to win control of the works councils in Fohnsdorf and Seegraben, the final bastions of Communist strength. This was the culmination of the 'epic' to which Herz referred.

The victory was, however, less clear-cut than it seemed. During the election campaign in Upper Styria, each side accused the other of physical intimidation, but there is stronger evidence that the results which were published by the ÖGB and repeated in the Socialist press were manipulated, for they differed significantly from those issued by the Styrian Chamber of Labour. The discrepancy arose from the ostensible political affiliation of candidates. Despite their failure to get this approach adopted in the major plants, Communists in a number of smaller workplaces did fight the elections as 'Unity List' candidates. The Chamber duly divided the votes cast into five categories, SPÖ, ÖVP, KPÖ, Unity List and non-affiliated. The ÖGB chose to acknowledge only four categories, assigning 'Unity List' candidates almost arbitrarily to one of the other categories. As 'Unity List' candidates were, without exception, sponsored by the KPÖ, this substantially reduced the number of votes the Communists were reported as having gained. For instance, in Graz the combined vote for KPÖ and 'Unity List' candidates was 18.9 per cent, but, according to ÖGB figures, only 3.8 per cent of works council places were won by Communists. Conversely, the actual percentage of votes cast for non-party candidates was only 7.8 per cent, but this group was deemed to have secured 34.4 per cent of the places.[40] The ÖGB's figure for the final result in Styria was that the Communists obtained 13.8 per cent, but this omitted the 6.3 per cent of the vote which went to Unity List candidates. This obfuscation had no practical significance, because the works councils were independent bodies and their members did not require ÖGB endorsement. It did, however, allow the Socialists to record a greater victory over the Communists than they had actually achieved and meant that the Communists' attempt to increase their influence by arguing that these elections should be above party politics had seriously backfired.[41] All in all, the SPÖ success in the Upper Styrian works council elections was momentous and it was followed by similar results throughout Austria.[42]

In the autumn of 1947, the SPÖ leadership had much to celebrate. Despite food shortages and strikes, the Communist attempt to challenge the Socialist position as that truly representative of the Austrian worker by exploiting local economic grievances had resulted in the loss of the KPÖ's major industrial base in Austria. In addition, the last Communist Minister, Karl Altmann, resigned from the government on 17 November.[43] The SPÖ's own left wing was becoming increasingly isolated and, at the same time, there were clear signs that its dire warnings that the policy of consensus would alienate the party's working-class base were unfounded. Austrian workers, it seemed, were reassured by the argument that the SPÖ and the ÖGB would protect their interests. There was no adverse reaction to the implementation of the First Wages and Prices Agreement, and the Socialists' success in the works council elections came after it had become clear that the Agreement was proving far more successful in holding down wages than prices. On 2 October the ÖGB executive announced that the cost of living had risen by 14.5 per cent over the previous two months, far in excess of the 10 per cent level at which the trade unions were permitted to put forward fresh claims for wage increases, the so-called 'safeguard clause'. Nevertheless, union leaders voted to waive this right on behalf of their members, repeating the mantra that higher wages alone would not protect living standards, and demanded in its place government measures to stabilise the currency, direct supplies of raw materials to the production of essential goods and to introduce of stricter price controls.[44]

But, if the Socialists had won this battle for control of the workers, the war was not yet over. The Communists took solace from two aspects of the works council elections: their vote was higher than they had achieved in the 1945 general elections, and they had performed significantly better in the larger factories in Styria, Lower Austria and Vienna. Their conclusion was that the policy of concentrating on industrial issues was successful and should be extended.[45] In early 1948 the KPÖ set up 'action committees' to co-ordinate industrial protest over the continuing food crisis and encouraged strikes at the beginning of March when the government admitted that it was yet again unable to meet its promise to raise the basic ration to 1,800 calories.[46] The revitalisation of Communist attempts to foster discontent was, however, not the only problem which labour leaders and the government were to encounter in 1948.

In the autumn of 1947 and the spring and summer of 1948, the ÖGB's ability to defend workers' rights was severely tested when it encountered its first experience of widespread industrial action. The main grievances were over wages, terms of employment, and the reluctance of employers to implement the new Law on Collective Contracts. This came into force in September 1947 and gave legal status to such contracts, introducing common wage rates across industries and in all four zones of occupation. It enhanced the power of the ÖGB, conferring on it the sole right to negotiate on behalf of all workers, with the exception of those employed in agriculture and forestry.[47] Agricultural and forestry workers were the first to strike, over their exclusion from the legislation, but the main problem for the trade unions was the difficulty of persuading employers to enter into and conclude negotiations. In November, 6,000 paper workers walked out over delays in settling their collective contract.

But the most important protests of 1948 broke out at the beginning of March and they involved issues of food, wages and conditions. The first wave came after an official announcement issued on 3 March that, despite government assurances that it was to be increased, the food ration would actually contain no meat in the following week. This sparked factory-gate meetings in Vienna and Lower Austria, while Communist activists set up the first 'action committees' to organise short protest strikes. Fighting broke out in Wiener Neustadt during one such protest and, coming just days after reports that the Communists had seized control of the Czech cabinet, this led to rumours that the KPÖ was planning to orchestrate a campaign of civil strife in Austria.[48] On the same day as the announcement of the ration cut, shoeworkers began an official strike involving the industry's total workforce of 5,800 employees, 55 per cent of whom were women or youths. They were demanding a shorter working week, one free working day a month with pay for women workers who also ran households (the Domestic Day – *Wirtschaftstag*), and the right of shop stewards to be consulted on issues of hiring and firing. Despite the fact that it had been officially recognised by the ÖGB, the strike was run by a committee of shop stewards in the shoe industry. The strikers' demands involved improvements in working conditions, particularly for women workers, but none was unique to the shoe industry, and the first two, the forty-four-hour working week and the Domestic Day, had already been included in collective contracts which had been agreed in other sections of the textile industry. The shoeworkers suspected that the employers had a hidden agenda. Their union, the shoeworkers' section of the Textile and Leather Union, had for the previous six months been trying and failing to negotiate a collective contract with their employers on the basis of the new law. The union accused the employers of bad faith, and argued that, on the advice of the Chamber of Business, the dispute was being used to test the commitment of the ÖGB to collective contracts. If the unions were to give way in this case, more employers would refuse to conclude collective agreements. In a secret ballot held on 2 March, 2,829 members of the Shoe-Workers' Union voted in favour of strike action, with twenty against and twelve blank papers.[49]

The strike lasted for eight weeks and ended in a partial victory for the workers – the forty-four-hour working week was conceded, but the employers rejected the other two demands and the Textile Union leaders concurred in this. This decision led to a furious row within the ÖGB. The fact that the Federation had recognised the strike as official, despite its general condemnation of industrial action, indicates the importance it attached to on the issue – collective contracts were a central feature of its approach to industrial relations and were crucial to its monopoly of trade union activity. They had to be defended. But there was also a political division within the Textile and Leather Union – the leaders of the main union were predominantly SPÖ, while the shoeworkers' section contained a strong Communist element and was led by Gottlieb Fiala, the increasingly isolated Communist Deputy Chairman of the ÖGB.[50] Throughout the strike, Fiala and his supporters fulminated against government policy on wages and prices, and attacked Socialist ministers and union leaders for capitulating to the employers by accepting 'coalition politics'.[51] They accused Böhm and the ÖGB of giving only half-hearted support to the strike. The ÖGB executive condemned the committee of shop stewards which ran the strike, and the *Arbeiter-Zeitung* carried articles describing solidarity actions as unnecessary and unhelpful.[52] The paper also focused exclusively on the demand for a forty-four-hour working week, following a majority decision within the ÖGB not to support either the Domestic Day or the extension of shop-stewards' powers.[53] For their part, the strikers condemned Böhm for issuing a press statement at a crucial stage in the negotiations in which he suggested that the strike could have been avoided, and opposed calls to extend the demand for shorter working hours to other industries.[54] The Minister for Food, a member of the SPÖ, suspended the strikers' supplementary rations on 9 April.[55] The strike finally came to an end when Chancellor Figl intervened. On 28 April, 1,829 strikers, half the original number, voted in a second ballot, with 912 in favour of the offered settlement, and 716 against.[56] Some weeks later, Böhm responded to his critics by arguing that the strike had been a success, because it had achieved the forty-four-hour working week. There was no mention of the other two demands, just as there had been no reference to them for many weeks in the Socialist newspaper.

The shoeworkers' strike represented the first large-scale direct confrontation between labour and capital in the Second Republic. The employers had been testing the ÖGB's determination to defend collective contracts, and the Federation had fought back. But Böhm's claims of victory were exaggerated – 80 per cent of workers in the textile industry had already been working a forty-four-hour week before the strike began. Moreover, the strikers had only gained one of their demands. Neither of their other two demands, the improvement in working conditions for female workers and the enhancement of shop-stewards' powers, was particularly radical, and throughout the strike employees in other industries staged short solidarity protests and organised shopfloor collections, indicating that the shoeworkers had clear support amongst other rank-and-file workers. Nevertheless, non-Communist union leaders gave the strike little more than tepid support and refused to back more than the one key demand. They were torn by conflicting interests. On the one hand, as trade unionists, it was imperative that they defended their right to collective contracts. But, at the same time, they did not want to undermine the economic policies which they had helped to draw up, nor to encourage social instability.

Although the strikes of March 1948 had been triggered by domestic economic issues, they were taking place at a point when political tensions in the region as a whole were reaching dangerous levels. Communists now controlled the government in Hungary and the situation over Berlin was deteriorating.[57] But it was the proximity of the strikes to events in Czechoslovakia in February which triggered panic among political and labour leaders in Austria. On the first day of the shoeworkers' strike, the front page of the *Arbeiter-Zeitung* was devoted to the latest ration crisis, but readers were also urged to pay heed to the fate of their northern neighbour and to boycott Communist action committees.[58] On 9 March, as Böhm attended the opening of the Marshall Plan talks in London, ÖGB leaders mounted a verbal attack on the committees, saying they were modelled on the Czech factory committees which had been used to undermine democracy by unleashing terror in the factories. Members were warned that they should shun all unauthorised meetings and ignore anonymous phone calls from bogus trade unionists pretending to represent the movement: the Austrian labour movement was Socialist.[59] Those who chose to ignore these warnings and take part in the action committees were threatened with expulsion from the ÖGB. At the same time, the Ministry of the Interior issued a statement declaring that the activities of the action committees were illegal and 'may lead to violations of the penal code'. Ferdinand Graf, Junior Minister for the Interior, approached the American and British authorities asking for assurances that they would intervene to quash any attempt by the Communists to stage a putsch in Austria.[60] He presented them with figures indicating that the KPÖ had a long-term strategy to unleash mayhem in Austria and had expanded its USIA 'shock troops', the armed and trained *Werkschutz*, from under one thousand to between eight and ten thousand, including members of the action committees. This move, he believed, had arisen from the failure of the Russians to sustain their early dominance of the Viennese police.[61] The Soviets, he claimed, were training armed units in USIA plants in order to challenge the authority of the Austrian police: 'it would appear that they [the Soviets] may have decided to discredit and intimidate the Police and Gendarmerie in the Soviet Zone so that at a convenient moment there may be an adequate excuse for ordering the assumption of their duties by Communist armed men'.[62] The action committees were therefore being implicated in a much more serious plan than merely organising food protests. The intention of all such protests, according to Graf, was to destabilise internal security. This was a conclusion with which the ÖGB agreed. At the end of the shoeworkers' strike, the Socialist leaders of the parent Textile Union dismissed opposition to the result as Communist-inspired. The problem was that, as the liberal *Wiener Zeitung* pointed out, many of the most outspoken critics of the outcome of the strike were in fact Socialists.[63]

The ÖGB, having been compelled to support the strikers, had yet acted as a moderating influence upon them. Subsequently, the Federation's opposition to all forms of industrial action increased, in tandem with its growing involvement in economic policy-making. Strikes and demonstrations were routinely dismissed as the work of Communist saboteurs whose only aim was to bring down the democratic system and replace it with a 'people's democracy'. But the grievances which triggered labour protest were not going to go away. Moreover, the KPÖ leadership now believed that it had finally identified an important chink in the SPÖ's armour which it could exploit to breach the traditional Socialist hegemony over Austrian working-class politics. The Socialists appeared to be attempting to achieve the impossible, namely, to reconcile the long-term interests of the state with the short-term interests of manual and white-collar workers. So far they had been successful, but the reactions of workers to the food protests and the shoeworkers' strike suggested that support was wavering. This was a weakness which the KPÖ tried to capitalise on, distancing itself from the SPÖ's left wing by abandoning attempts to establish a Popular Front, and openly advocating a People's Democracy as the only alternative to western domination and the exploitation of the workers.[64] In order to achieve this, the Communists sought to place themselves at a head of the campaign for a much more substantial increase in wages than the government was prepared to concede, so as to gain increased support for their political line under the guise of spearheading a basic working-class economic demand. The KPÖ's attacks on the SPÖ intensified, focusing on the Marshall Plan and the government's economic policy, for which it also blamed both the SPÖ and the ÖGB, and stepping up its campaign against the Wages and Prices Agreement. In April 1948 it finally responded to the ÖGB's failure to implement the safeguard clause in the Wages and Prices Agreement by mounting a concerted campaign for a general wage increase of 25 per cent in large companies to be announced by 15 September, while during the summer of 1948 Communist shop stewards organised strikes in Vienna, Styria and Lower and Upper Austria in support of this claim.[65]

The timing was inauspicious for the government. Industrial productivity was declining, thus threatening to jeopardise exports and hence negate the economic forecasts on which the submission for Marshall Aid funding had been based. In addition, agricultural prices rose steeply in May and June, at the very time that the government was coming under increasing pressure from the ERP to reduce food subsidies.[66] There was little alternative but to resort once again to economic controls. On 24 August the Chancellor revealed that representatives of the three Chambers and the ÖGB were meeting in the Economic Commission to negotiate the Second Wages and Prices Agreement.[67] This time, however, the government and the ÖGB went on to the offensive, arguing that the earlier Agreement had protected Austria from the ravages of inflation and social and political chaos. Ten days later it was announced that the basic ration would be increased to 2,100 calories from 13 September.[68] Newspapers published details of the progress of the negotiations and the *Arbeiter-Zeitung* ran a series of articles on the positive impact which the new rationing system would have on women, war-invalids and ex-POWs. The link between rations and the need to control wages and prices was not made explicit, but the paper claimed that without a new Agreement it would be impossible to improve the supply of food.[69] The Second Wages and Prices Agreement was unveiled on 16 September. Under this Agreement wages were increased by 6 per cent, subsidies on milk and milk products, meat and meat products and fats were reduced, and households with dependent children were given a tax concession of 23 Schillings per month. The result was an increasingly bland diet based on carbohydrates, and a rise of 18.5 per cent in the cost of living between September and October.[70]

The announcement of the Second Wages and Prices Agreement coincided with the deadline set by the KPÖ for acceptance of its 25 per cent wage claim; it had threatened to call a series of protest strikes if the claim was not met. On 9 September Karl Maisel, the Minister of Social Affairs, President of the Metalworkers' and Miners' Union and Vice-President of the ÖGB, addressed a meeting of Socialist shop stewards in Leoben to press the case for the Agreement. In this speech he used the word 'putsch' to describe the planned Communist strikes. The local Styrian SPÖ newspaper, *Neue Zeit*, went further.[71] Three days after the Leoben meeting, it published details of what it alleged was a Cominform directive calling for rebellion in the Upper Styrian town of Kapfenberg. It reported that local women had been instructed to stage a violent demonstration which Communist activists would use to trigger strikes and revolt throughout the region and then the entire country. The day before the *Neue Zeit* revelations appeared, 158 workers who had supported the Communist wage claim had been sacked 'for economic reasons' at the Boehler works in Kapfenberg. Protest meetings were held throughout Upper Styria and Graz, as well as in Vienna and Upper Austria. Shop stewards in Donawitz were prevented from holding a meeting and the managements there and in Kapfenberg called out the police to protect their plants from what they now declared to be an attempted putsch. According to the Communist *Volksstimme*, British troops in Styria were also put on alert.[72] Johann Böhm joined the attack on 14 September, accusing 'Communist provocateurs' of orchestrating strikes and demonstrations in order to sabotage the final stages of the negotiations on the Second Wages and Prices Agreement. Two days later, in the build-up to the announcement of the Agreement, the *Arbeiter-Zeitung* informed its readers that the Communist strikes had failed even in Upper Styria, where, it alleged, at a mass meeting in Donawitz, Communist shop stewards had been forced to call off the strike, blaming this on the 'cowardice' of the workers.[73] By the time the actual content of the Second Wages and Prices Agreement was made known on 17 September, there was little prospect of further industrial protest.

Nevertheless, the years 1947 and 1948, far from ushering in a greater degree of calm and stability, were fraught with incident, and indeed represent a turning point in post-war Austrian history. This was a period of constant industrial protest, when the differences between the ruling parties and the KPÖ widened into a gulf. The authorities' growing anti-Communism, the chief domestic cause of which was the KPÖ's attempt to place itself at the head of worker discontent, took on added intensity from the fact that 1948 saw the Cold War come to its first peak.

Notes

1 '*Wenn die österreichische Wirtschaft in dem Jahr das seit dem Lohn-Preis-Abkommen vergangen ist, immerhin bemerkenswerte Fortschritte erzielt hat, wenn heute die Geschäfte wieder voll Waren sind, wenn die industrielle Produktion so deutlich gestiegen ist und wenn heute das Bild unserer Städte doch schon ganz anders aussieht als vor noch gar nicht so langer Zeit, so verdankt das ganz Österreich der österreichischen Arbeiter und Angestellten, der politischen und moralischen Besonnenheit unserer Arbeiter und Angestellten. Während bei unseren östlichen Nachbarn Terror herrscht, während bei unseren westlichen Nachbarn Streiks und Unruhen und Ministerkrisen einander jagen, ist dieses kleine Österreich, trotz Armut und Bedrängnis, das ruhigste Land Europas geblieben.*' *Arbeiter-Zeitung*, 17 September 1948.
2 *Arbeiter-Zeitung*, 4 September 1947, 6 September 1947; *ÖGB Tätigkeitsbericht 1945–1947*, 3/71–2. For details of the Law on Collective Contracts see p. 117.
3 *ÖGB Tätigkeitsbericht 1950*, 380. The number of people seeking work rose from 39,759 in September 1947 to 51,851 in September 1948 and then shot up to 93,650 by the end of December 1948.
4 '*Dieser Staat ist doch in Wirklichkeit nichts anders als ein Verwaltungsapparat*', *Parteitagsprotokolle der SPÖ*, 1945, 86.
5 Bauer believed that the state was neutral in crisis periods when the 'Balance of Class Forces' weakened the strength of the dominant class. At this point it was possible for the workers to win control of the state through the ballot box. See Lewis, *Fascism and the Working Class in Austria*, chapter 4.
6 W. T. Layton and Charles Rist, *The Economic Situation of Austria. Report to the League of Nations* (Geneva: League of Nations, 1925), 41–2, 110–11, 158–62.
7 Maria Mesner, ' "Weil ein anfänglich sehr kleiner Kreis von Freunden unbeirrt zusammen gehalten hat". . . . Die Umorientierung der SPÖ unter Renner und Schärf', in Erich Fröschl, Maria Mesner and Helge Zoitl (eds), *Die Bewegung. Hundert Jahre Sozialdemokratie in Österreich* (Vienna: Passagen Verlag, 1990), 477–8.
8 Karl Stadler, *Adolf Schärf: Mensch, Politiker, Staatsmann* (Vienna: Europa Verlag, 1982), 98.
9 The SDAP was established at the Hainfeld Congress (30 December 1888–1 January 1889). For two decades before this the movement had been fraught by schisms between Moderates advocating a democratic path to socialism, and Radicals who believed that violence was essential. Victor Adler succeeded in uniting the Moderates and Radicals by formulating a compromise party programme which ruled out neither strategy, but which emphasized the primacy of class and party unity.
10 'Mit uns das Volk', *Arbeiter-Zeitung*, 1 May 1946.
11 '*Es lebe die Einheit der Arbeiter in der Sozialistischen Partei*', *Arbeiter-Zeitung*, 1 May 1946; '*Ein echter und treuer Staatsfeiertag*', 1 May 1947. Bauer died in Paris in 1938. On 12 February 1948, the fourteenth anniversary of the civil war, the SPÖ organised a major rally and laid his ashes to rest in Vienna's Central Cemetery alongside the graves of the founders of the SDAP, Victor Adler and Engelbert Pernerstorfer. *Arbeiter-Zeitung*, 12 February 1948.

12 In 1932 a group of young Socialists, including Ernst and Otto Fischer, formed
    a separate organisation, the *Jungfront*, following disagreements about their role
    in the campaign for local elections. They later accepted general supervision by
    the SDAP, but were granted limited autonomy. At the 1933 party conference
    Jungfront delegates challenged the leadership's failure to call a general strike
    in response to the suspension of parliament, forcing Otto Bauer to identify
    four specific government actions which would trigger an armed response by
    the party. Anson Rabinbach, *The Crisis of Austrian Socialism: from Red Vienna
    to Civil War 1927–1934* (Chicago, IL: University of Chicago Press, 1983),
    112–20.
13 Mesner, ' "Weil ein anfänglich sehr kleiner Kreis von Freunden" ', 482.
14 Weber, *Der Kalte Krieg in der SPÖ. Koalitionswächter, Pragmatiker und
    Revolutionäre Sozialisten 1945–1950*, 82. This book provides a detailed account
    of the process by which democratic control of the SPÖ was weakened.
15 Weber, *Der Kalte Krieg der SPÖ*, 82–3.
16 'alle auf, die guten Willens sind'; 'die werktätigen Menschen in Stadt und
    Land'; 'Es lebe die Friedensgemeinschaft der Völker', *Arbeiter-Zeitung*, 8 May
    1946.
17 'die Einheit der Partei nur möglich gewesen ist, weil ein anfänglich sehr kleiner
    Kreis von Freunden unbeirrt zusammen gehalten; diese Einheit hat uns stark
    gemacht und damit auch die Partei, die uns ihr Vertrauen schenkte' Mesner,
    ' "Weil ein anfänglich sehr kleiner Kreis von Freunden" ', 476. A similar pattern
    of rebuilding the Socialist Party from the top down appears to have emerged
    in at least some of the provinces. For a discussion of Upper Austria and Linz
    see Brigitte Kepplinger and Josef Weidenholzer, 'Die Rekonstruktion der
    Sozialdemokratie in Linz 1945–1950', in *Historisches Jahrbuch der Stadt Linz,
    1995*, 13–68.
18 Pollak had been the editor of the *Arbeiter-Zeitung* throughout most of the life-
    time of the First Republic and had been on the right of the SDAP. In the
    summer of 1934 he had approached Schuschnigg, offering to work with the
    government in return for the restoration of limited democratic rights. He
    did so without the knowledge of the SDAP. Berg *et al*, *The Struggle for a
    Democratic Austria*, 129. He spent the war years in London and established
    close connections with the Labour Party. He was reappointed as editor of the
    Arbeiter-Zeitung on his return in the summer of 1945.
19 Deutsch, *Ein weiter Weg*, 378–85, 391–3. Deutsch was critical of the party's
    increasingly close relations with the western Allies, which, in his opinion,
    threatened the possibility of Austrian neutrality.
20 Nevertheless, Seitz was not beyond criticising the concentration of power in
    the new Republic. In 1945, shortly after his return, he was said to have
    commented in a meeting of the party executive: 'In den kaiserlichen Zeiten
    wurden Gesetze mit der Klausel verlautbart: 'Mit Zustimmung beider Häuser
    des Reichsrates finde ich anzuordnen wie folgt . . .', aber jetzt: die Vollmachten
    des Kaisers hat der Renner, die Vollmachten des Abgeordnetenhauses hat der
    Renner, und die Vollmachten des Herrenhauses hat wieder die Regierung
    Renner.' ('In the days of the Empire, laws were published bearing the phrase:
    "With the approval of both houses of the Reichsrat, I decree as follows . . ."
    But now it is Renner who possesses the plenipotentiary powers of the Emperor,

Renner who possesses the plenipotentiary powers of the House of Deputies, and once again the Renner government which possesses the plenipotentiary powers of the Upper House.' Stadler, *Adolf Schärf*, 198.

21 Schärf, *Österreichs Erneuerung 1945–1955*, 186–92.

22 Mesner, ' "Weil ein anfänglich sehr kleiner Kreis von Freunden" ', 480.

23 Berg *et al*, *The Struggle for a Democratic Austria*, 228. Kreisky (who was Chancellor of Austria from 1970 to 1983, recalled being asked by one Socialist official if he would like to manage an abattoir. It was a joke, 'but in fact it hit the nail on the head, for everything was there for the asking, any post at all, even that of the abattoir'. He was actually offered the undefined position of Special Attaché in Stockholm and did not return to Austria until 1951. Mesner suggests that anti-Semitism may have played a role in the refusal to allow some Jewish Socialists to return. Mesner, ' "Weil ein anfänglich sehr kleiner Kreis von Freunden" ', 480.

24 Weber, *Der Kalte Krieg der SPÖ*, 25.

25 Otto Bauer, *Zwischen zwei Weltkriegen? Die Krise der Weltwirtschaft, der Demokratie und des Sozialismus* (Bratislava: E. Prager, 1936). Weber, *Der Kalte Krieg der SPÖ*, 40–6.

26 Weber, *Der Kalte Krieg der SPÖ*, 57.

27 'der glanzvollen kämpferischen Haltung', Weber, *Der Kalte Krieg der SPÖ*, 158.

28 Weber, *Der Kalte Krieg der SPÖ*, 211–4.

29 RGASPI, Fond 575, Op.1, Delo 8, 12 September 1947.

30 Klenner, *Die Österreichischen Gewerkschaften*, vol. 2, 1568.

31 The *Volksstimme* published a series of articles on this in the second half of March 1947. *Volksstimme*, 12, 14–16, 26–30 March 1947.

32 TNA/PRO/FO 1020/113, Short Brief on Industrial Unrest in Styria, 16 October 1947; *Tätigkeitsbericht des ÖGB 1945–1947*, 3/68.

33 Herz, *Understanding Austria*, 483.

34 *Ibid.*, 484.

35 TNA/PRO/FO 1020/113. Short Brief on Industrial Unrest in Styria, 16 October 1947.

36 *Ibid*. The strikes in Donawitz and Zeltweg lasted for twenty-four hours, but the Eisenerz miners stayed out for only one hour.

37 *Ibid*.

38 *Ibid*. The motion was defeated by 95 votes against to 71 for, with 60 members abstaining.

39 *Arbeiter-Zeitung*, 31 October 1947.

40 Bader, *Austria between East and West*, 147–8.

41 British reports on the 1952 works council elections suggest that little had changed by then. In March the fourth political party, the Verein der Unabhängigen (VdU), withdrew its list of candidates for the Donawitz election. The Communists won the vote, and the Socialists demanded fresh elections, alleging fraudulence and intimidation. In the second election in July, the VdU withheld its list until the last moment, then handed it to a Communist official who took the list into an adjoining room and promptly jumped out of the window with it. The VdU names did not appear on the ballot sheet – but the

Socialists still won the election by 2011 votes to the Communists' 1983. TNA/PRO/FO LAB 13/582.

42 The only national figures, published by the ÖGB, are SPÖ 62 per cent; KPÖ 6.8 per cent; ÖVP 3.6 per cent; non-affiliated 27.6 per cent, but, for the reasons outlined above, these are unreliable. *ÖGB Tätigkeitsbericht 1945/47*, 1/15.

43 Altmann cited his opposition to the currency reforms as the grounds for his resignation, although there was speculation that the real cause had been the KPÖ's renewed opposition to the Marshall Plan. Herz, *Understanding Austria*, 298.

44 *ÖGB Tätigkeitsbericht 1945–47*, 1/24–5. *Arbeiter-Zeitung*, 3 October 1947.

45 'Bilanz der Betriebsratwahlen', *Weg und Ziel* (January 1948).

46 TNA/PRO/FO LAB 13/581, Labour Attaché's monthly report, December 1948.

47 Different systems had applied in different zones. The first wages agreement concluded in Vienna was published on 12 July 1945, but wage regulation was banned in the US zone until March 1946. *Ibid.*, 3/52.

48 Herz, *Understanding Austria*, 365.

49 *Der Abend*, 2 April 1948.

50 Kodicek, the General Secretary of the Union, was also a Communist. Support for the Communists was strongest amongst miners and leather workers. RGASPI, Fond 575, Op.1, Delo 8, 12 September 1947.

51 *Protokoll des Achten Arbeiterkammertages abgehalten am 18. und 19 März 1948*, Vienna, 1948, 32–5.

52 *Arbeiter-Zeitung* (13 April 1948).

53 *Der Abend*, 14 May 1948. The latter had been a major Communist demand during the parliamentary debate on the Law on Collective Contracts.

54 The accusation was levelled by Kodicek in an article published in *Die Arbeit*, 6 June 1948. Böhm had responded to criticisms of the ÖGB's position in the strike during the first ÖGB congress, which was held in Vienna on 18–23 May 1948. He asserted that the Federation's executive had been taken by surprise when the strike broke out and that it could not afford the three million Schillings which the action had cost. Such 'fun' (*Spaß*) could take place once, but no more. *Tätigkeitsbericht des ÖGB 1945–1947*, 4/263.

55 *Österreichische Zeitung*, 9 April 1948.

56 *Wiener Zeitung*, 29 April 1948.

57 The Communists seized power in Hungary in May 1947 and in Czechoslovakia in February 1948. The Berlin blockade began on 24 June 1948, but on 2 April the *Arbeiter-Zeitung* published a report stating that the Soviet authorities were preventing the Western Powers from entering the city.

58 *Arbeiter-Zeitung*, 3 March 1948.

59 *Arbeiter-Zeitung*, 6–10 March 1948.

60 Herz, *Understanding Austria*, 350.

61 Helmer, the Minister of the Interior, had fought a long and relatively successful campaign to remove Communists from the Viennese police force, but the Austrian government was putting pressure on the Allied Control Council to agree to arm the police. At the beginning of March, Graf asked the Americans to issue weapons unilaterally. Herz, *Understanding Austria*, 249.

62 TNA/PRO/FO, 1020/453. Communist Armed Bodies in Austria. Letter from Lieutenant-General A. Galloway (Allied Commission for Austria, British

Element) to Ernest Bevin, 25 March 1948. Graf's estimates of the number of trained and armed *Werkschutz* members were rejected by the Americans and the British, although the British Foreign Office encouraged journalists to publicise the Austrian claims.

63 *Wiener Zeitung*, 29 April 1948.

64 Hautmann, Garscha and Weinert, *Die Kommunistische Partei Österreichs: Beiträge zu ihrer Geschichte und Politik*, 359.

65 Ronald Gruber, 'Der Massenstreik gegen das 4. Lohn-Preisabkommen im September/Oktober 1950' (PhD Dissertation, University of Vienna, 1975), 97–8. Zimmermann, 'Wirtschaftsentwicklung in Österreich, 270.

66 Rothschild, *The Austrian Economy since 1945*, 53–6; Zimmermann, 'Wirtschaftsentwicklung in Österreich', 264, 272–4. Agricultural prices rose by 66–68 per cent in May and June.

67 The talks had already been underway for some time, as Gottlieb Fiala disclosed during a meeting of the ÖGB executive on 19 August. Gruber, 'Der Massenstreik', 98.

68 Despite this announcement, the Cabinet when it met on 28 September was still divided over its ability to provide the extra calories. The main obstacle was the attitude of the Americans and the British. Karl Gruber, the Foreign Minister, pointed out that the proposed ration was higher than the current ration in Britain. He also endorsed the Italian practice of basing rations on prices rather than calories. Austrian Cabinet Papers, sitting 28 September 1948, 26–7.

69 *Arbeiter-Zeitung*, 14 September 1948.

70 Gruber, 'Der Massenstreik', tab. 2/6.

71 *Neue Zeit* (Graz), 12 September 1948, reprinted in Gruber, 'Der Massenstreik', 99.

72 Gruber, 'Der Massenstreik', 100. The surviving British documents throw no light on this subject, although there is one report of '158 alleged Communist representatives' arriving in Graz on 13 September to meet the leader of the Styrian ÖGB. TNA/PRO/FO 1020/486, 13 September 1948.

73 *Arbeiter-Zeitung*, 14 and 16 September 1948. Herz reported on the Communist strike attempt in saying that it was intended to start in Upper Styria and spread, but that only workers in the Steyr works in Linz actually went out on strike and then for one day only. The KPÖ, he reported, was particularly disappointed by USIA managers who refused to sanction strikes in their plants. Herz, *Understanding Austria*, 543.

7

Rising tensions

In 1949 the Iron Curtain finally clanged down across Central Europe. The North Atlantic Treaty Organisation was inaugurated in April and in May the West German parliamentary council passed the Basic Law establishing a separate West German state. One week later, Stalin announced the birth of the German Democratic Republic, thus marking the official division of Germany.[1] Austria was now unique – the only country which was still jointly administered by all four former Allies and, consequently, the one state in which east and west would continue to confront each other face-to-face during the early years of the Cold War. But in 1949, as the actual process of division took its course, it was still not clear where or on which side of Austria the Iron Curtain would fall. Alongside the consternation which this uncertainty created, there were also fleeting glimmers of hope: negotiations on the State Treaty resumed in March and by July there were signs that a successful conclusion ending four years of occupation could be reached. Throughout that year Austrian newspapers carried reports of barbed-wire entanglements being constructed along the borders with Czechoslovakia and Yugoslavia and of mines being laid along the Hungarian border. But although such stories did indicate that the Soviet leadership had, for the moment, accepted that the Communist sphere of influence would not include Austria, they offered no certainty that the Soviet Union would be prepared to loosen its grip on Austria in either the short or the long term, nor did they increase Austrian internal security or reassure public opinion. There was still too much cause for alarm. Since 1947 the Russians had been kidnapping opponents of the new Communist regimes in Eastern Europe who had sought a safe haven in Austria, and then whisking them across the border. In 1948 this tactic took an extraordinary turn, when three Austrian government officials, including the head of counter-intelligence in the Ministry of the Interior, Anton Marek, and the head of planning in Peter Krauland's Ministry for Property Control and Economic Planning, Margarethe Ottillinger, were abducted, the latter while on official business and accompanied by her boss.[2] The next year there were several more reports of Austrians disappearing without trace, presumably having been kidnapped.

On the domestic front, 1949 was an important election year. The Republic's second general election was held on 9 October and the second round of works council elections began in the same month. The SPÖ had much to gain and it started campaigning early, on New Year's Day. Describing itself as the party which stood for freedom and justice for working people, it quickly set up an election fund and invited supporters to contribute. It even revived some of its former radicalism, at least on the surface, reminding workers that it was not only the party of Victor Adler, but also of Koloman Wallisch. Indeed, the Socialists' 1949 commemoration of the 1934 civil war was dominated by the memory of Wallisch, the radical leader of the 1927 Bruck an der Mur 'soviet' and civil war hero, culminating in a ceremony held on 22 February in Bruck an der Mur which was attended by many party dignitaries, including Schärf, the party Chairman and Vice-Chancellor, and the government ministers Maisel, Migsch and Sagmeister.[3] Karl Renner sent a wreath. There was more than a hint of irony in this, for, when alive, Wallisch had represented the type of grass-roots radicalism which the new party leadership abhorred.[4] However, this was an election year and the SPÖ had high hopes of gaining an outright victory. Its leaders realised that, in order to win, the party had to distance itself from its coalition partner and only real rival, the ÖVP. In these circumstances, verbal support for working-class heroes (who by this time were long dead) was acceptable if it appealed to the party's core constituency.

The SPÖ's decision to support demands for the legitimisation of a fourth political party, the *Verein der Unabhängigen* (Association of Independents/VdU), was a similar exercise in political expediency and one which, at first glance, appears oddly perverse. The VdU was founded on 26 March 1949 without the approval of the Allied Control Council.[5] Its leaders, Herbert Kraus and Gustav Canaval, were both conservative journalists who were well known for their campaigns against the de-Nazification laws and who appeared to have little in common with the SPÖ.[6] The setting up of this new party was, in fact, a direct consequence of the relaxation of these laws, which had, as we have already seen, divided offenders into two categories, those who were 'seriously implicated' by reason of having held party office or the like, and those who had merely been ordinary party members and hence were deemed to be 'less implicated'. Each group had been barred both from voting and from working in the civil service and liberal professions.[7] By June 1948, the coalition government estimated that approximately one third of the entire Austrian population was affected in one way or another by these legal restrictions, either directly or indirectly, as in the case of relatives of former Nazis, and they were aware of the disruption such a large cohort of disenfranchised citizens might well cause. Consequently, ministers decided to restore civic rights to the 'less implicated'. The immediate result was the addition of over half a million names to the electoral register, who joined approximately the same number of first-time voters and returning prisoners-of-war who had also been unable to vote in 1945.[8]

The sudden surge in the number of voters had obvious implications for the 1949 general election. The most pressing question was whether the prevailing restrictions on the number of political parties should also be lifted in order to cater for this enlarged electorate. Although there were clear democratic reasons for arguing that restricting political organisations was an infringement of civil liberties, the loudest call for the right to form a new party came from Kraus and Canaval, whose party was created specifically to represent the interests of the former Nazis. Both the ÖVP and the SPÖ had supported the change in the de-Nazification Law and the re-enfranchisement of the 'lesser' Nazis, but, for purely pragmatic reasons, they differed in their responses to its implications. The ÖVP leadership calculated that the majority of former Nazi members would be unlikely to vote for the SPÖ and therefore represented a substantial pool of potential votes which it could mobilise to increase its share of parliamentary seats. However, a new party which was specifically designed to represent this group posed a distinct threat, for it might also lure away some of the ÖVP's own less committed supporters. In January 1949, at a meeting of ÖVP provincial and national leaders, Julius Raab pointed out that, although their party had won a narrow majority of seats in 1945, the ÖVP vote had actually been lower than the combined SPÖ/KPÖ vote. There was a danger, he went on, that the SPÖ would make considerable gains in the forthcoming election if, as expected, the KPÖ vote collapsed.[9] The solution was to unite bourgeois voters in a single stand against the threat of a people's democracy and to convince them that the ÖVP was the only party which could undertake this task. The rallying call would be anti-Marxism, branding the SPÖ as fellow-travellers with Communism. On the other hand, the advent of a new, far-right party might split the centre-right vote and lead to the defeat of the ÖVP. By way of bolstering this argument, ÖVP leaders claimed that an increase in the number of political parties in Austria would destabilise the political situation in general, but their more immediate purpose was to persuade the Allied Control Council to withhold recognition of the VdU.

The SPÖ, by contrast, was fully in favour of the fourth party, for exactly the same reason. Adolf Schärf, in particular, was convinced that the new right-wing party would increase the SPÖ's chances of winning the general election by luring voters away from the ÖVP, and he went to some lengths to achieve this goal. In January, he approached Ernest Bevin, the British Foreign Secretary, asking that the Western Allies should withdraw their objections to the formation of new parties. Three months later, having received no reply, he wrote again requesting Bevin to 'give the matter your urgent consideration'. He played down the possibility that such a decision would undermine the 'grand coalition', the form of government which the Allies preferred: 'Even if ten new parties should take part in the next elections there would be no danger to the formation of a state coalition government of the two main parties which everybody consideres [*sic*] necessary for the present.' The presence of new parties would not change the outcome, Schärf contended, for the political history of Austria indicated that two parties would always dominate. However, the internal stability of the country was 'due first and foremost to the fact that the Austrian workers maintained their traditional allegiances to the cause of democratic socialism. ... Thus we were successful in defeating all attempts by the Communists to split the Austrian working class.' The ÖVP's 1945 electoral victory had been ensured by the Allies' decision to permit only three parties, two of which were on the left, which had been to the ÖVP's advantage in 1945, 'giving the People's Party a monopoly of all anti-Socialist votes'. He warned Bevin that:

> if the Western Allies should insist on preventing the formation of other parties, this will be interpreted by the Socialist workers as the desire of the Western Powers under all circumstances and against the fundamental ideas of democracy to maintain and strengthen the power of conservative and reactionary forces in Austria, and vice versa the People's Party will claim that they alone enjoy the support of the Western Allies even of the British Government.

This, he added, would in turn bolster Communist claims that the only alternative to reactionary politics was a people's democracy. Moreover, the dangers would spread further than Austria: 'The attitude of the Western powers in this matter will be judged by those workers in the "peoples' democracies" in the light of communist propaganda [no full stop] I feel it is not to [*sic*] much to say that the reputation of democratic socialism as the only alternative to Communism as represented by the Labour Party may be seriously impaired.'[10] This letter was addressed by one Socialist to another. It was clearly an informal approach, for, contrary to diplomatic custom, the letter is written in English, opening with the words 'my dear comrade Bevin'. It also contains several errors of punctuation and grammar. There is little doubt that Schärf was engaging in a piece of private initiative on a matter which involved national politics and should properly have been handled through official channels. Moreover, despite the letter's expressions of support for the coalition government, it is highly unlikely that Leopold Figl, the Chancellor, would have known, let alone approved, of actions on the part of his Vice-Chancellor which were intended to reduce the ÖVP vote. Still, on 26 August the Allied Control Council agreed to transfer responsibility for recognising new political parties to the Austrian government, although the French and Soviet Elements both expressed reservations and threatened to bar any parties which put forward 'Nazi' candidates from campaigning in their respective zones.[11]

Despite the arrival of the VdU, the two major issues which dominated the election campaigns of 1949 were the State Treaty negotiations and the economy. Negotiations on Austria in the Council of Foreign Ministers had broken down in May 1948 when, in the wake of the Czech 'coup', the Americans had recoiled at the prospect of withdrawing before Austria had been allowed to rearm.[12] Preliminary talks reopened in London the following February and were then adjourned to the meeting of Foreign Ministers in Paris in May. The early signs from Paris were good. The Russian Foreign Minister, Vyshinsky, initially agreed to abandon support for Yugoslav claims to Austrian territory, and to restore 'German assets' to Austrian control in return for payment to the Soviets of $150 million.[13] The sting was in the tail. He then insisted that the process should be staggered over a six-year period. Nevertheless, the Western Allies agreed and, on 21 June, just days before the date of the election was announced, the *Arbeiter-Zeitung* published a front-page story giving details of what its editors believed would be the final settlement. But the report was premature. Alan Bullock's account of the last day of the conference paints a vivid picture of what then happened:

> On the final evening, after the communiqué had been signed, champagne had been drunk and the participants had dispersed, Vyshinsky sent out a message calling for the Council to reconvene. He had, it was learned privately, received instructions in the roughest terms from Moscow to get a change made in the Austrian agreement. So back they had to come. Arriving after a very good dinner at the same time as Acheson, Bevin

seized the American's arm as they stepped out of the creaking lift and (according to one of Acheson's favourite stories) asked him:

'Do you know The Red Flag? The tune's the same as "Maryland, my Maryland". Let's sing 'em together as a sign of solidarity, as we Labour blokes say.

And so we did, robustly, arm-in-arm, walking through the sedate Second Empire anterooms, with the final bars at the very entrance of the meeting-room.'

When Vyshinsky made his request, Bevin congratulated him on a new record. Soviet agreements were fragile things, but today's was the frailest yet. It had not even survived the day.[14]

Any possibility of a settlement had now passed. When the deputy Foreign Ministers met in New York in the autumn, the Russians raised the question of payment for the food aid which they had distributed in 1945 (known as 'the dried peas payment') as a pretext for rejecting the terms of the Treaty, much to the relief of the Pentagon and the French authorities.[15]

Throughout the whole of 1949 and even at the most promising stage of the State Treaty talks, the Austrian government remained deeply sceptical about Soviet intentions. At the beginning of the year Oskar Helmer, the Minister of the Interior, warned that the withdrawal of western troops from Austria in the wake of an agreement on the Treaty could trigger a Communist putsch there. When details of the proposed compromise were published in June, Figl complained that the $150 million which Austria would be obliged to hand over to the Soviet Union was yet another unwarranted burden.[16] During that summer, with the Treaty negotiations still in limbo, there were frequent reports of Soviet troops once again stripping factories and plants, removing as much machinery as they could before the occupation ended.[17] But the Soviets were not the only problem. In addition, throughout 1949, the government was faced by a mounting balance of payments problem which led to friction with the ECA mission in Vienna, but for which, in public, it sought to hold the Soviet authorities largely responsible. In 1948, as has been shown in Chapter 4, the head of the ECA Mission in Vienna, Westmore Willcox, had rejected Austrian budget proposals on the grounds that the figures on which they were based were seriously flawed and did not comply with the criteria laid down in the Marshall Plan. The Figl government responded by maintaining that the occupation created unique circumstances which rendered Austria a special case. The most important factors it raised were the costs to the Austrian budget both of the occupation and of providing food and shelter for over half-a-million refugees or displaced persons whom the country had been forced to accommodate, as well as the loss of tax revenue and profits from those sectors of the economy which were controlled by the Russians: the Soviet authorities had not only appropriated German assets, but were also refusing to pay Austrian taxes.[18] In fact, the most critical burden for the economy was the cost of the occupation, which, initially, was borne exclusively by the Austrian Treasury. This had amounted to 2.8 billion Schillings in 1946, over half of which had been paid to the Soviet Union.[19] The negative impact of the USIA concerns on the Austrian economy combined with the Soviet share of the occupation costs gave the Austrian government solid grounds on which to attack the USSR for undermining the reconstruction of the Austrian economy. Moreover, in June 1947 the American government made the welcome announcement that it would not only cover its own occupation costs in future, but would also return $300 million it had received from the Austrian government since 1945. But this decision represented only a partial solution to Austria's economic problems, for the other three Allies continued to insist on payment.[20] Matters finally came to a head in February 1949, when the Figl government introduced a new tax levied on incomes over 2,000 Schillings per annum, to cover the occupation costs, putting the blame for this firmly on the Soviets.[21] The KPÖ's reaction was to accuse Figl of deliberately whipping up anti-Soviet sentiment.

Without doubt, the occupation costs were a huge burden for Austria to bear. Nevertheless, there were other structural problems in the economy which had become increasingly obvious during the first year of Marshall Aid. Unemployment was beginning to rise. The figures had begun to climb in the autumn of 1948 and in February 1949 they reached 7.02 per cent of the workforce. The number of people who were registered as seeking work was now almost three times higher than it had been in February 1948. Moreover, although seasonal factors brought the figure down in the spring and summer, and there was an actual increase in employment, the number of those out of work was increasing at an even faster rate. It was clear that the days of full employment were over. By February 1950 almost 10 per cent of Austrian workers were registered as unemployed.[22] In addition, productivity remained a serious concern and was affecting the balance of payments. By the end of 1948, domestic agriculture was still producing only 55 per cent of domestic demand, so that almost half of the country's food supplies had to be imported and paid for in foreign currency. Exports were also disappointing, for, although industrial productivity was improving overall, productivity per worker remained at just 75 per cent of the 1937 level.[23] The consequence was that Austria was still importing far more than it was exporting: despite the fact that the trade gap, the difference between the value of exports and the cost of imports, had decreased considerably since 1947, it remained critically high at $267.2 million.[24] In its first budget proposals for 1949, the proposals which Willcox had rejected, the Figl government had assumed that the shortfall in the balance of payments would be covered by Counterpart funds. But at the beginning of 1949, Willcox's successor, Clyde King, confirmed US objections to the fiscal plan and withheld the 1949 release of Counterpart funds, leaving the government with an even more chronic balance of payments problem and a dollar shortage.[25] An ERP report on the revised Austrian proposals which the Americans demanded was presented in May 1949. It maintained that, despite the relatively low level of living standards in that country, 'a comprehensive investment programme compels Austria, however, for the time being to rest content with the achievement of this minimum and to devote the future increase in national income which will be achieved with the assistance of the ERP almost exclusively to increasing investment'. There would be no funds to boost employment.[26] Specific requests for the release of Counterpart funds to finance house building, thus stimulating employment and addressing an urgent social need, were turned down. By this time the budget deficit was 2.5 thousand million Schillings. The ECA accused the Austrian government of camouflaging normal expenditure by transferring costs to the extraordinary budget, in the mistaken hope that, in the end, these would be covered by Counterpart funding. It repeated calls for an increase in the level of purchase taxes and for cuts in public expenditure to be achieved through the reorganisation of the railways, reducing the size of the civil service and abolishing all remaining subsidies. The Figl government was faced with a dilemma. Its economic programme depended on Marshall Aid, but the apparent consequences of this were rising prices and increasing unemployment which threatened to provoke widespread public protest and hence serious political instability. It responded on 8 May by announcing a Third Wages and Prices Agreement which, like its predecessors, was negotiated by the three Chambers and the ÖGB, with meetings, once again, taking place in secret. The new Agreement increased rates for public utilities and rail travel, introduced new taxes on incomes and capital, and raised purchase tax. Food credits and some of the remaining subsidies on coal and grain were abolished and in compensation wages were raised by a flat rate of 0.30 Schillings per hour or 60 Schillings per month, combined with an overall 4.5 per cent wage increase. Civil servants, along with employees in the hotel and restaurant industry, were temporarily excluded from the pay rises. In order to sugar the pill, social insurance was increased, with a rise in child allowance from 23 to 37 Schillings and, for the first time in Austrian history, the introduction of old age pensions for manual workers.[27]

The ÖGB and the SPÖ were also placed in a difficult position. Despite all their protestations about the success of the previous Agreements, it was clear that these had not produced a stable economy: indeed, there were now persuasive grounds for believing that they had restrained wages while having relatively little effect on prices. There were also strong rumours that the announcement of the Third Wages and Prices Agreement was yet another tactical manoeuvre by the ÖVP to destabilise electoral support for the SPÖ: while their own supporters in industry, trade and agriculture welcomed the reform and would pass price increases on to the consumer, the ÖVP calculated that the Agreement would unleash a storm of indignation amongst Socialist voters, forcing the SPÖ onto the defensive before the election, and ultimately losing it votes to the KPÖ. Schärf, an avid collector and disseminator of political rumours, claimed that he had been reliably informed that ÖVP leaders were secretly astounded at the ease with which they had been able to convince their coalition partners to support the new Agreement.[28]

It was a foregone conclusion for the Socialists, who could not criticise either government economic policy or ECA pressure in public without implying misgivings about the Marshall Plan, thus playing directly into the hand of the Communists. They were now, however, faced with task of convincing their voters that there was no alternative. Johann Böhm immediately gave public support to the Third Wages and Prices Agreement. On the day details of the Agreement were announced, the *Arbeiter-Zeitung* quoted him at length. There was, he maintained, no choice if the government was to reduce the deficit and boost economic recovery. The abolition of subsidies on sugar and grain would hurt in the short term, but the alternative was inflation. In an attempt at jocularity, he agreed that the price of pork would also rise, but how many manual or white-collar workers, he asked, ever saw pork?[29] He went on to assert that workers would be protected from rising prices by wage increases, just as he had after the announcement of each of the two earlier Agreements, but added that this time they would also benefit from the introduction of the pension reforms: the implication was that the pensions were dependent on the implementation of the Agreement. Finally, he linked increasing taxes and prices, which were an integral part of the Agreement, to the occupation costs, which were not, pointing out that the Occupation Costs Tax would also come into force during the following weeks.[30] When workers felt the pinch over the coming year, they should blame the Soviet Union and not the ERP.

But if Böhm appeared confident in public, he was less buoyant in private. In August he wrote to Figl pointing out the important role which the ÖGB had played in wooing support for the Marshall Plan, but also emphasising that this was at the cost of alienating sections of its own membership. Some trade unionists were beginning to hold the Federation responsible for the least positive repercussions of Marshall Aid. At this point it becomes clear that Böhm was also well aware of the leverage which the situation afforded the labour movement. The wider membership, he went on, was unhappy with the limited influence which workers had over the use of ERP funds, and they were demanding greater representation on the bodies responsible for economic decision-making. This was a salient example of tactical manoeuvring on the part of the ÖGB president, for although there is no evidence of rank-and-file pressure to extend the political influence of the labour leadership, it was a very obvious goal of Böhm and his colleagues. And the ploy was successful. Soon after, a representative of the Chamber of Labour joined the Ministry of Economic Planning. It was another step in the journey towards the Social Partnership.[31]

The introduction of the Third Wages and Prices Agreement and the disputes with the ECA mission in Vienna created a potentially dangerous climate in which to fight the general election. The attitude of the Americans finally became too much for the conservative Chancellor, for, together with the failure of the Treaty negotiations, the intransigence of ECA officials clearly demonstrated the narrow limits of Austrian autonomy: in July Figl dispatched a formal complaint to the State Department concerning what he described as King's 'offensive' behaviour.[32] But the situation was even more delicate for the Socialists. Once again, the Socialist Party's role as a coalition partner precluded it from exploiting grass-roots dissatisfaction with both escalating unemployment and rapid price rises. This was left to the opposition, which now included not only the KPÖ, but also the VdU, the most significant of the new parties to have been authorised in 1949.

The Third Wages and Prices Agreement soon proved to be no more successful in solving the country's economic problems than its two predecessors had been. Prices continued to rise, and in the week in which the election date was actually announced, meat deliveries to Vienna dried up completely. As the election campaign got underway, the SPÖ tried to distance itself from the mounting crisis by condemning the ÖVP for supporting 'cartels', which it blamed for increases in the price of flour, and by attacking ÖVP ministers for refusing to release dollars to pay for more imported food.[33] It also reverted to accusations of ÖVP collusion with former Nazis and chose this moment to bring a legal action against the former *Heimwehr* leader, Ernst-Rüdiger von Starhemberg, accusing him of treason.[34] But its campaign lacked vigour, as did those of the other two original parties. The ÖVP stuck to its theme that a vote for the SPÖ was tantamount to a vote for Communism. The Communists, on the other hand, formed an electoral alliance, the *Linksblock*, with the small Socialist Workers' Party which Erwin Scharf had set up, and concentrated on opposition to the Marshall Plan and to the Third Wages and Prices Agreement. But it was the appearance on the scene of the fourth party, the VdU, which had the greatest impact on the election. Claiming that it would protect the 'ordinary people' (*kleine Leute*) from the corruption of the two big parties, it denied any direct links with the Nazi Party, but, unsurprisingly, did target the newly enfranchised former Nazis and their families. It also opposed the nationalisation of private firms, ignoring the situation in which this had been carried out, and attacked government economic policy for creating the budget deficit which had led to the Third Wages and Prices Agreement. Finally, it promised to end the housing shortage.[35] The VdU's campaign was a notable success. On 9 October, election day, the party polled just under half-a-million votes, 11.6 per cent of the national total. But its performance in three western provinces was even more spectacular: it won over 20 per cent of the votes in Carinthia, Voralberg and Upper Austria. Its greatest victory was in Linz where over a quarter of the electorate supported the new party. The result was devastating for the three original parties. The *Linksblock* fared even worse than had the KPÖ in 1945, winning only 5.06 per cent of the votes and ending up in fourth place, behind the VdU. The ÖVP captured the support of 44.03 per cent of the electors, 5.76 per cent fewer than it had achieved in the first election, and lost its overall majority in parliament. It was, however, the SPÖ, which had had such great expectations of reaping the reward from a split right wing, that became the prime victim of the emergence of the new party. Its suffered a loss of 5.78 per cent of the total vote, marginally greater than that of the ÖVP.[36] The result was a continuation of the two-party coalition government, as Schärf had predicted in his letter to Bevin, but not one which the SPÖ controlled. It was a jolt which reinforced the Socialists' political battle against the Communists, but which also forced both the party and the ÖGB to reassess their attitude to wage restraint in an attempt to resume the mantle of champion of the working class.

Notes

1 On 1 June 1948, the Western Allies had made public their intention to set up a separate West German state, thus triggering the Berlin blockade. Tony Judt, *Postwar: A history of Europe since 1945* (London: Penguin, 2005), 145–7.

2 Herz, *Understanding Austria*, 421–6, 502–3, 549, 607–8. Ottillinger had played an important role in the Austrian application for Marshall Aid. Both she and Marek were held in Russia on spying charges and only released in 1955.

3 Koloman Wallisch was born in Hungary in 1889, took part in the 1918 revolution and moved to Bruck an der Mur in 1921, where he became secretary of the SDAP. During the Schattendorf protests of 1927, he threatened that 'the instant workers' blood flows in Bruck, so too will bourgeois blood', which led to the myth that a soviet had been set up in the town. He was executed in February 1934. Lewis, *Fascism and the Working Class in Austria*, 132–8. See also the biography written by his wife; Paula Wallisch, *Ein Held stirbt* (Graz: Verlag der Sozialistischen Partei Landesleitung Steiermark, 1946).

4 *Arbeiter-Zeitung*, 1 January and 6, 13, 20, 22 February 1949.

5 Wilhelm Svoboda, *Die Partei, die Republik und der Mann mit den vielen Gesichtern: Oskar Helmer und Österreich II. Eine Korrektur* (Vienna: Böhlau, 1993), 100.

6 Canaval, who had been imprisoned in Dachau during the war, was editor-in-chief of the *Salzburger Nachrichten*. Kraus was head of the Salzburg Institute of Economics and Politics and had worked as a foreign correspondent of the Nazi *Südost-Echo*, which Herz described as a 'cover for the SS-SD'. Herz, *Understanding Austria*, 176–7, 181–2.

7 Under the National Socialism Prohibition (Interdiction) Law of May 1945, Austrian former Nazis were required to register: 428,249 had done so by February 1946. Anton Pelinka, *Out of the Shadow of the Past*, 30.

8 4,193,733, votes were cast in 1949, 976, 379 more than in 1945. The question of Austrian denazification is explored in Dieter Stiefel, *Entnazifizierung in Österreich* (Vienna: Europa Verlag, 1981). Austrian POWs were released earlier than German POWs by the British. (I am indebted to Gillian Clarke for this information.) By 1948 all 335,270 Austrian POWs had been released from French, British and US camps, most returning in 1945 and 1946. The Soviets, however, delayed their release and by 1949 only 136,270 Austrian POWs had returned from Soviet captivity. Ela Hornung, 'The Myth of Penelope and Odysseus: An Austrian Married Couple Narrate their Wartime and Post-war Experiences', in Duchen and Bandhauer-Schöffmann, *After the War*, 56.

9 'Stenographisches Protokoll der Tagung der Landesparteisekretäre und Sekretäre der Bünde [der ÖVP] in Schloss Wartholz am 6. Jänner 1949'. Schärf Papers, Box 43, 4/281.

10 Schärf to Bevin, 19 (no month is given, but internal evidence indicates that it was April) 1949. Schärf Papers, Box 31, 4/222. Schärf first met Bevin in London in April 1946, when he lobbied the British Foreign Secretary on the Austrian situation before Bevin left to attend a meeting of the Council of Foreign Ministers (CFM) in Paris. Bevin, who was already sympathetic to the Austrian cause, tabled a motion at the Paris conference seeking to establish a definition of 'German assets'. The motion was vetoed by the Russians. He continued to

champion Austrian independence in subsequent CFM meetings, but was finally forced to concede in December 1949. Bullock, *The Life and Times of Ernest Bevin*, vol. 3, 264–5, 385, 697.

11 *Arbeiter-Zeitung*, 27 August 1949. The British Element on the Allied Control Council proposed the change, which General Keyes, the American High Commissioner, initially opposed. Keyes was then 'directed' by the State Department to support the proposal, even, if necessary, reintroducing it himself. 'Memorandum for transmission to General Keyes on the Department of State's position respecting Political Parties in Austria', 12 August 1949, NA, US State Department, Civ. RG 59, Subject Files Austria Desk (Arthur Compton Files), Box 8, File A 800. State Department officials were also concerned lest any confusion about the legal status of new parties should present the Soviets with a pretext for subsequently challenging the results of the general election. The Schärf Papers contain a typed note, dated 13 August 1949, by the French Minister of the Interior, Jules Moch, concerning an approach that he, Moch, had made to the French Military Commander in Austria, General Béthouart, asking him to persuade the French Foreign Minister to overturn a decision to ban the VdU from campaigning in the French sector. The note is headed 'Innenminister J. Moch gab mir am 13.8.1949 folgende Information für Dr. Schärf u. Dr. Helmer', Schärf Papers, Box 31, 4/222. Svoboda gives a detailed account of the SPÖ's endeavours to secure recognition of the VdU; Svoboda, *Die Partei, die Republik und der Mann mit den vielen Gesichtern*, 98–107. Six other new parties were also authorised at this time.

12 Bullock, *The Life and Times of Ernest Bevin*, vol. 3, 628–30; Bischof, *Austria in the First Cold War*, 116–7. In 1948 the Americans began to set up secret arms caches and to train Austrian police.

13 Rolf Steininger, *Der Staatsvertrag: Österreich im Schatten von deutscher Frage und Kaltem Krieg 1938–1955* (Innsbruck: Studien Verlag, 2005), 107–8.

14 Bullock, *The Life and Times of Ernest Bevin*, vol. 3, 697. Dean Acheson had been appointed American Secretary of State in 1948.

15 Bischof, *Austria in the First Cold War*, 110–11.

16 *Arbeiter-Zeitung*, 30 January 1949. Helmer's speech provoked a robust response from Julius Deutsch. *Arbeiter-Zeitung*, 9 February 1949, 23 June 1949.

17 For reports on the State Treaty negotiations, see *Arbeiter-Zeitung*, 21 June, and for the dismantling of plant by the Soviet authorities, see *Arbeiter-Zeitung*, 13–25 August, 2 September, 13 September 1949.

18 Bischof, *Austria in the First Cold War*, 92.

19 *Ibid.*, 84; 191, ftns 55 and 56. In September 1946 the Allied Control Council decided that the occupation costs should be less than 25 per cent of the total Austrian budget. This was reduced to 15 per cent in December 1946. By 1949 the occupation costs accounted for 3 per cent of the national budget. Klaus Eisterer, 'Austria under Allied Occupation', in Steininger, Bischof and Gehler, *Austria in the Twentieth Century*, 202.

20 The French, British and Soviet governments did not relinquish their right to payment until 1953.

21 *Arbeiter-Zeitung*, 23 February 1949. Günter Bischof has suggested that the value of foreign aid which Austria received amounted to just less than the combined value of the occupation costs and all transfers to the USSR. Quoted

in Seidel, 'Austria's Economic Policy and the Marshall Plan', in Bischof, Pelinka and Stiefel (eds), *The Marshall Plan in Austria*, 252.

22 *Jahrbuch der Arbeiterkammer in Wien 1948*, 369–74. The Arbeiterkammer calculated its own unemployment figures until 1950, when it began to publish figures issued by the Ministry of Social Affairs. Comparisons of the figures for 1947 to 1949 suggest that the Ministry's figures were consistently lower than those of the Arbeiterkammer. *Jahrbuch der Arbeiterkammer in Wien 1950*, 380. The official figure for February 1950 was 8.3 per cent, while the Arbeiterkammer figure was 9.7 per cent.

23 Allgemeines Memorandum zum revidierten Jahresprogramm 1949/1950 (ERP report on the revised Austrian proposals, 1949/1950) May 1949, AdR, BMfsV, SA II, Box 215, 12932/49.

24 In 1947 the value of imported goods was 303.17 per cent of the value of exports; it was 216.9 per cent in 1948 and 189.7 per cent in 1949. Seidel, 'Austria's Economic Policy and the Marshall Plan', 255. For details of the 1949 trade deficit with specific countries, see *Jahrbuch der Arbeiterkammer in Wien 1949*, 324–31.

25 Chapter 4, p. 99. Counterpart funds were accrued from the sale of US goods in the recipient countries for local currency and were deposited in accounts which, in theory, were administered by individual governments. In practice, the release of counterpart funds required the agreement of the ECA mission which imposed stringent criteria.

26 Allgemeines Memorandum zum revidierten Jahresprogramm 1949/1950, 2. Between April 1948 and December 1949 Austria received $387.54 million in Marshall Aid funding, $199.5 million as foodstuffs, $26.6 million as fuel, $63.5 million as raw materials and semi-manufactured goods and $33 million as machinery. *Jahrbuch der Arbeiterkammer in Wien 1950* (Vienna, 1950), 194.

27 Rothschild, *The Austrian Economy since 1945*, 57–8.

28 This is apparent from a private undated and untitled memo on the VdU found in the Schärf papers. It was apparently written between May and October 1949. Schärf papers, Box 43 4/283. According to Schärf, the rumours were relayed to him by members of the Viennese ÖVP.

29 The comment was odd. In April workers in Upper Styria had staged a strike in protest at the provincial government's decision to raise the price of pork. The national government intervened and insisted that the price rise was rescinded. *Arbeiter-Zeitung*, 16 April 1949.

30 *Arbeiter-Zeitung*, 8 May 1949.

31 Mähr, *Der Marshallplan in Österreich*, 158.

32 Karl Ausch, *Erlebte Wirtschaftsgeschichte: Österreichische Wirtschaft seit 1945* (Vienna: Europa Verlag, 1963), 186–7; Mähr, *Der Marshallplan in Österreich*, 188–9. The written complaint was delivered by the Austrian ambassador in Washington and a verbal account was conveyed to the American authorities in Austria by telephone by Josef Schöner, who was by then a senior official in the Austrian Foreign Ministry.

33 *Arbeiter-Zeitung*, 1 July 1949.

34 *Arbeiter-Zeitung*, 1 July, 3 July, 17 August 1949.

35 Brigitte Kepplinger and Josef Weidenholzer, 'Die Rekonstruktion der Sozial-demokratie in Linz 1945–1950', *Historisches Jahrbuch der Stadt Linz*, 1995, 37–8.

36 Stiefbold *et al.* (eds), *Wahlen und Parteien in Österreich: Österreichisches Wahlhandbuch*, vol. 4.

8

The putsch
that never was

If the appearance on the scene of the fourth party had unforeseen consequences for the SPÖ's performance in the general election, it also had repercussions for the Socialists in the works council elections. The Socialist faction in the ÖGB had overlooked the influence of one specific group of VdU supporters, part of the half-a-million Displaced Persons (DPs) then living in Austria. These were the *Volksdeutsche*, German-speaking refugees, who constituted by far the largest group of DPs.[1] They included a strong contingent of Sudeten Germans, many of them staunch Catholics and German nationalists, who had been expelled from Czechoslovakia after the war. The majority of the *Volksdeutsche* were living in the American sector of Upper Austria, in and around Linz and Steyr, where they were employed as industrial workers, having been recruited in the immediate post-war years to fill a major gap in the labour market. More specifically, they replaced the thousands of foreign slave and forced labourers who had been transported to Austria during the war by the Nazi regime in order to provide labour power in the steel industry and who had then been repatriated after the war ended.[2] The DPs were initially housed in camps run by the Western Allied authorities in their respective zones, but in 1948 the Americans handed all responsibility, including the provision of accommodation, food and clothing, for refugees in their zone to the Austrian government, and the British and French quickly followed suit. As the cost of running DP camps would inevitably add to the demands on an already over-burdened Austrian economy, the government quickly introduced incentives to encourage refugees in general, and the *Volksdeutsche* in particular, to leave the camps, get jobs and rent rooms with Austrian families.[3] As a result, DPs had a significant impact on the character of the workforce in some of Austria's largest and most important industrial plants. By 1949, 20 per cent of the workforce at the VÖESt plant (*Vereinigte Österreichische Eisen- und Stahlwerke*, formerly the Hermann Göring works) in Linz, were foreigners, mostly *Volksdeutsche*, as were many of the workers in the neighbouring nitrate (*Stickstoff*) and electricity plants.[4]

Many *Volksdeutsche* held right-wing nationalist sympathies which made them an obvious target for the VdU. The fact that they were not Austrian citizens and so did not have the right to vote in either local or national elections, did, however, limit their political significance. On the other hand, they could take part in works council elections, which were open to all employees, irrespective of nationality. So, too, could one other significant group of newly recruited workers who shared the political tendencies of the *Volksdeutsche*, but who did enjoy full civil rights after 1948 – the 'lesser' former Nazis. Their appearance on factory floors in Austria had been yet another consequence of the 1946 de-Nazification Law which had not only deprived them of the franchise, but had also excluded them from employment in the civil service and the liberal professions. But it had not prevented them from taking up any of the manual jobs which were readily available in the early years of the Second Republic.[5] As a result, in areas where there was a particularly acute labour shortage, the workforce was likely to include relatively large numbers of highly educated former members of the NSDAP. This was the case in Linz, where the combination of ex-Nazis and *Volksdeutsche* was the major reason for the resounding success of the VdU there in the 1949 general election. However, the most pertinent example was Kaprun in the province of Salzburg. It was here that in 1938 the Nazis had begun construction of a vast dam and hydro-electric plant, which was still unfinished at the end of the war. After building work resumed in 1947, Kaprun became the symbol of Austrian post-war industrial reconstruction and 'the most important single Counterpart funded project of the Marshall Plan' in that country.[6] But the project required thousands of building workers, and a combination of low rations, the site's dangerous working conditions and the poor reputation of its management, who were unable to procure adequate supplies of food, clothing and footwear, discouraged potential applicants. Initially, managers supplemented the small regular workforce by bringing in prison labour, as well as using volunteers from youth groups. But in 1948 the Americans closed an internment camp in nearby Glasenbach and freed hundreds of ex-Nazis, many of whom found work at Kaprun. Later that year the police reported that 80 per cent of workers employed on the project were ex-Nazis.[7] The symbol of modern Austria was also a stronghold of VdU support.

The formation of the VdU and the fact that many of its potential supporters were employed in key industrial plants posed a particular problem for the SPÖ. In the works council elections, Socialist trade unionists now found themselves fighting on two fronts, against both the Communists and the VdU. Moreover, the Communists were continuing to increase their efforts to mobilise support among shop stewards. In March they antagonised the ÖGB by calling a shop stewards' conference to protest against the occupation tax, which they alleged was an 'army tax' designed to bleed workers at a time 'when the profits of entrepreneurs are growing at an unprecedented rate'.[8] Böhm attempted, unsuccessfully, to prevent this conference from taking place by arguing that only the ÖGB had the authority to call such a meeting. But in making this move he had ignored the terms of the Works Council Law which specifically protected the independence of the councils from the Federation; the ÖGB possessed extensive powers, but it had no legal control over the activities of shop stewards, a weakness which the KPÖ would exploit again in 1950, as we shall see later in this chapter.[9] The Communists' main campaign in 1949 for both the general election and the election of works councils began in May, following the announcement of the Third Wages and Prices Agreement, when they trebled the print-run of the *Volksstimme* and targeted workers' housing estates in Vienna with leaflets carrying the slogan 'let the rich pay' and calling for more widespread strikes and demonstrations in support of sweeping wage increases. According to a Cominform report, on 17 May one hundred thousand workers demonstrated against the Third Agreement in Vienna, seven thousand in Linz and five thousand in Wiener Neustadt.[10] In Donawitz, where there had been complaints that Socialist shop stewards were failing to represent workers' interests, the Communists linked protests over the new Wages and Prices Agreement to calls for early works council elections in the plant. The situation at the plant escalated and, after violence had broken out during a factory meeting on 16 July, Socialist members of the provincial assembly refused to work with the Communists. Eight Communists were expelled from the Metalworkers' and Miners' Union, and the Communists' provincial leaders were reported to have reprimanded several of their own shop-stewards, while also urging members not to disrupt either ÖVP or VdU meetings.[11]

The 1949 round of works council elections began in October, shortly after the general election. According to the *Arbeiter-Zeitung*, the results were a resounding success for the Socialists, but its editors created this impression by ignoring almost all plants where the party's vote fell. The newspaper did report the first and most startling outcome in Austria, which was that at Kaprun, where the VdU won nine of the seventeen mandates.[12] But it did not mention Linz, where workers at the VÖESt plant overturned a Socialist majority, electing fourteen VdU candidates as opposed to twelve Socialists and two Communists (the latter standing as members of the *Linksblock*), and where the Socialists lost their majorities in both the nitrate and electrical plants. Nor did the newspaper record that the Socialists were only able to retain control of the VÖESt works council by forging an unprecedented alliance with the KPÖ, combining the votes for their respective candidates to produce an overall majority which resulted in a Socialist shop steward being appointed chairman.[13] On the other hand, the SPÖ response to Communist proposals to form a similar anti-fascist front at Kaprun, which it threw out on the grounds that one type of anti-democratic dictatorial party was as bad as another, was emblazoned across the paper's front page.[14] This partial (in both senses of the word) reporting of the works council elections and the inconsistent response of local shop stewards to VdU victories both indicate a growing rift between SPÖ leaders and at least some sections of the party's rank-and-file. The *Arbeiter-Zeitung* attributed the Socialists' defeat at Kaprun to bullying on site, as well as to the number of ex-Nazis and *Volksdeutsche* who were employed there, comparing the situation at the hydro-electric project to what it described as the Communist culture of intimidation in Upper Styria before 1947, which, it claimed, the SPÖ had since managed to transform. This turned out to be an ill-starred comparison to make, for just weeks later the Communists regained control of the Donawitz works council, increasing their vote from 2,121 in 1947 to 2,898, while also making gains in Eisenerz, where the VdU helped to overturn a solid SPÖ majority. True to form, the *Arbeiter-Zeitung* ignored both these latter outcomes, although it did print the results for Seegraben and Kindberg, where support for the SPÖ rose.[15]

Despite the protestations of the *Arbeiter-Zeitung*, the SPÖ's influence on the shopfloor had been declining nationally since 1947, when, according to the ÖGB's own figures, Socialists had won 62 per cent of seats on the works councils. This fell to 55.1 per cent in the 1949 round. The Socialist faction lost votes to the VdU, as did the ÖVP, but despite Soviet manoeuverings over the State Treaty, the KPÖ vote remained stable and even increased marginally, from 6.8 to 6.9 per cent.[16] The VdU's overall performance was unspectacular, at less than 1 per cent, but, as we have seen, it scored important victories in several key plants. The overall outcome was a disturbing one for the SPÖ, particularly when combined with the party's disappointing performance in the general election, and it brought about a serious reassessment of ÖGB policy. The Federation could no longer ignore the signs of increasing impatience among its members over rising prices. In October, in the wake of the British devaluation of sterling and in the face of well-founded rumours that the Schilling would soon follow suit, prices did begin to rise dramatically once more: figures issued by the Institute for Economic Research in December indicated that they had increased by 10.7 per cent over the previous three months.[17] Although bread and flour rationing ended in that month, potatoes were disappearing from many markets; in some regions, the police were called out to enforce official prices and thwart illegal profiteering. On 11 November, as protest strikes were breaking out all over the country, some led by Socialist shop stewards, Böhm warned the three-day-old government that the Federation could no longer support its economic policy and called yet again for stringent measures against cartels and profiteers.[18]

Just six months after he had given a public assurance that the Third Wages and Prices Agreement would not affect workers adversely, Böhm was forced to concede that he had been wrong. Police reports emanating from both Vienna and the provinces in January 1950 stated that popular discontent over the government's handling of the wages and prices question was reaching dangerous levels.[19] But neither Böhm nor the ÖGB executive would go so far as to call for a general wage increase to rectify the disparity between wages and prices, though the Communists immediately adopted this demand. Instead, at a meeting with government officials in January, Böhm pressed for the introduction of a new law against cartels, a piece of legislation which was also advocated by the ECA. In return, he said, the ÖGB would resist calls for a national wage claim. According to an American report, 'the Federation, together with Socialist party leaders, initiated immediately a public relations program designed to impress the workers with the wisdom of the anti-wage demand policy'.[20] The trade union and Socialist press carried articles re-emphasising the folly of wage increases and the need for price controls, and their leaders also exerted pressure on party newspapers to stifle debate on the wages question.[21] But the wording of the ÖGB's commitment to wage restraint was highly significant. It referred to national claims only. There was no mention of local claims, which provided a loophole for trade union leaders. Citing a clause in the Agreement which sanctioned the 'realignment' of wages for workers in specific industries or areas where wages were conspicuously low, the Federation went on to give tacit support to that anathema to centralised trade unionism, local wage negotiations: employers and local works councils began to negotiate individual pay 'supplements' (*Nachzieh-verfahren*), thus avoiding a formal breach of the Wages and Prices Agreement. This compromise, which was publicly endorsed as a means of alleviating the plight of the poorest workers, was a curious step for the ÖGB to take and it is doubtful whether its leaders had fully realised what a Pandora's box they were now opening. The Federation had been built on the premise that the strength of the movement depended on the centralisation of power and control over its membership and it had fought hard to establish its monopoly over collective bargaining. Now, as its grip on the local labour movement appeared to be slipping, it agreed to delegate responsibility for negotiating 'top-up' pay deals to local shop stewards over whom it had no official control in a bid to pacify rank-and-file discontent, while still claiming that the overall strategy of wage control must be maintained. In theory, at least, the ÖGB remained a loyal member of the Economic Commission, the body responsible for drawing up the Wages and Prices Agreements. But the tactic backfired and actually precipitated labour activity. Shop stewards in individual plants began to campaign for local wage rises, drawing up petitions in support of their specific claims and in many plants, including VÖESt, Steyr and Donawitz, leading their colleagues out on strike. In December 1949, building workers staged demonstrations demanding interim payments. In Graz twenty-one demonstrators were charged with damage to persons and property and were later sentenced to what American observers described as 'draconian' prison terms.[22] A stream of local demands and petitions followed throughout the spring and early summer of 1950, many of them backed by further strike threats. Styrian farm workers and builders walked out when talks in their province failed to produce rises equalling those which had been won in the eastern provinces, as did metalworkers and miners in Vorarlberg. White-collar workers in private firms demanded parity with colleagues in the public sector. The decision to negotiate local wage deals on the basis of 'special cases' unleashed an avalanche of claims. In July, American sources reported that 'about half the total wage earners will benefit from these wage adjustments. An average total wage increase of about 6 per cent is estimated, the effect of which would be to add about 600 million Schillings a year to the total wage costs.'[23] Employers were complaining about the wage explosion and threatening to resist further claims.

This was not a good moment to contemplate further increases in the cost of living, but by the summer of 1950 the government was under overwhelming pressure to raise grain prices. The problem was twofold. The official prices of rye and wheat, the staple grains, had been kept level for two years for obvious political reasons, and were only 250 per cent higher than they had been in 1937. In contrast, other agricultural prices had risen to between 500 and 1,600 per cent of their 1937 levels and, most seriously, producers could earn more for a kilo of animal fodder than for a kilo of wheat for bread-making: farmers were complaining that they were selling grain at 40 per cent of their production costs and that it was more profitable for them to distil the grain into schnapps or feed it to farm animals than to deliver it to the flour mills.[24] It was also necessary for the government to subsidise imported grain in order to maintain the official price, which it did by means of the variable exchange rate which had been introduced in 1949. While the commercial exchange rate was 21.30 Schillings to the dollar, the rate used to calculate the cost of grain was 8.80 Schillings. This subsidy was financed by the release of Counterpart funds. As a result, grain was sold in Austria at prices which were far below those prevailing on the world market. This was a situation which, for different reasons, neither Austrian farmers nor the ECA were willing to see continue. The Americans were already deeply suspicious of the entire system of economic policy formation in Austria, and in particular of the role of the Economic Partners in the Economic Commission, which, they maintained, restricted free competition. Austria's new political oligarchic culture of elite consensus ran counter to the American concept of free-market economics: 'The resulting politico-economic system may be described quite accurately as a corporate state. The various Chambers should be deprived of their direct political and administrative influence and restricted to *de facto* rendering of technical services.'[25] More specifically, the ECA was demanding the complete abolition of grain subsidies and the introduction of a uniform rate of exchange and had set a deadline for 1 July, ruling out the future use of Counterpart funds to secure cheap food. It also supported proposals, submitted in April 1950 by the Lower Austrian Chamber of Agriculture, to raise the price of a kilo of rye from 0.75 to 1.3 Schillings and of a kilo of wheat from 0.90 Schillings to 1.5 Schillings. The issue remained under discussion for weeks in the Ministerial Economic Committee and was raised again on 20 June at a meeting which was chaired by the Chancellor and attended by representatives of the three Chambers, but not of the ÖGB.[26] The main point of contention was not whether the prices of grains should be raised, for it was generally agreed that this could not be avoided, but how the price rises should be financed and whether they should be accompanied by a commensurate wage rise. When the discussion became deadlocked, the Chancellor and the Finance Minister were reported to have turned to Strommer, the Chairman of the Conference of Chambers of Agriculture, demanding to know if he actually wanted an overall wage increase. Upon being told, 'yes', they answered flatly that they did not.[27] The matter was referred back to the Economic Commission which was instructed to present a unanimously agreed solution within one week. The Chancellor reminded those present that 'points 1 to 3 should, however, not be made the subject of public discussion'.[28] The whole process of negotiation was to take place in secret.

The ÖGB had warned of the dangers of introducing a fresh Wages and Prices Agreement at this time. Indeed, at the meeting of the Ministerial Economic Committee, the chairman of the Chamber of Labour lamented the absence of a Federation representative, commenting that the current level of 'calm' in the factories was entirely due to the restraining influence of union leaders. The government was also worried about the likely public reaction to the announcement of yet more price and wage controls, but it had no other viable option. The acting head of the ECA in Vienna, John Giblin, was unwilling or unable to sanction any delay in or modification of the abolition of subsidies, either of which would have lessened the blow, although his negotiations with government ministers went on until the very last moment. But, unable to find any other solution to the economic crisis, and despite Böhm's opposition, on Friday 22 September the Economic Commission agreed the terms of the Fourth Wages and Prices Agreement. The wholesale price of wheat was raised by 58 per cent, that of rye by 46 per cent and that of sugar beet by 35 per cent. The cost of a kilo of bread in the shops rose by 26 per cent, of flour by 64 per cent, of white rolls (*Semmel*) by 59 per cent and of sugar by 34 per cent. Coal, electricity and tram ticket prices were also increased by 25 per cent. Wages were scheduled to go up by 10 per cent, though pensioners and those who earned less than 1000 Schillings per annum were to receive increased supplements. Child benefit and social welfare payments were also raised.[29]

Plans to make a formal announcement the following Tuesday, after Cabinet ratification of the Agreement, which would have given union and SPÖ officials the weekend in which to sell it to their members, were scuttled on Saturday 23 September, when the Communist *Volksstimme* published the story. At this point the paper did not call for strike action, and the following Monday, 25 September, when work continued as normal, politicians may have been reassured that their fears of a violent reaction had been exaggerated. Metalworkers in the VÖESt steelworks in Linz did stage a one-hour protest that day, as did some railway workers, but the reaction appeared to be generally low-key. The custom of not bringing out newspapers on Mondays may have contributed to this apparent calm, for the situation changed on Tuesday. As the news spread, workers at plant and factory gates throughout Austria voted by show of hands to walk out. That day, between 20,000 and 30,000 people demonstrated in the centre of Linz.[30] A crowd of 15,000 turned out in Steyr. Both towns were in the American zone. In Lower Austria, in the Soviet zone, the police reported on 26 September that workers in the USIA plants were on strike and persuading or intimidating other workers into joining them. There were demonstrations in Wiener Neustadt, Mödling, St. Pölten, Neunkirchen and Zistersdorf.[31] The same day, workers in Vienna's Soviet zone held factory-gate meetings and downed tools. Post office and telephone workers also walked out, although, according to a report which reached the Soviet Foreign Ministry in January 1951, the city's railway and tram workers ignored the strike call.[32] The police reported that by 11 a.m. 16,000 workers were converging on the Ringstrasse, accompanied by lorries carrying Communist shop stewards who were denouncing the Wages and Prices Agreement through loudhailers.[33] Their goal was to demonstrate on the Ballhausplatz, outside the Chancellor's office, as the Cabinet met to ratify the Agreement. But the Cabinet meeting had been brought for-ward by two hours in order to avoid the demonstrations, and by the time the protesters arrived they were told that the only minister who was still in the building was Chancellor Figl.[34] Fighting broke out as demonstrators tried to burst through police cordons. Reluctantly, Figl agreed to meet a strike delegation. The crowd dispersed at about 1 p.m. after Communist speakers announced that there would be a meeting of the city's shop stewards that evening and urged the protesters to go home, but to make sure that they turned up for work the next morning. The following day, 27 September, Communist newspapers reported that the strike had been suspended pending a national meeting of shop stewards which would be held in the working-class district of Floridsdorf, in the Soviet zone of Vienna, on Saturday 30 September. But the call to hold off went unheeded in Linz, where workers resumed the strike, smashing windows in the town hall and attacking the city's Chamber of Labour, while shouting for the resignations of the provincial leaders of both the Chamber and the ÖGB.

The KPÖ's decision to call a halt to the first wave is one of the most curious aspects of the 1950 strikes. In the first place, the protests constituted the strongest upwelling of anti-government feeling since the end of the war. Second, the issue at stake, namely opposition to the Wages and Prices Agreement, lay at the heart of the KPÖ's political platform, and had the added attraction of encouraging public hostility to the Marshall Plan. Third, little tactical advantage was to be gained from calling off a widespread strike movement which appeared to be gathering national momentum. And, finally, the party's executive committee could not have been certain that the strikers would pay any heed to its directive, as indeed many did not, for, despite repeated government allegations, Communists had not taken the lead in the earliest protests. In fact, the first demonstrations took place in Linz and Steyr, in the American zone, where, as has been shown, there was very little support for Communism.[35] The main force behind the protests of these Upper Austrian workers was the VdU, whose shop stewards led the procession on 27 September which culminated in some of the worst violence of the entire episode. Their actions had not, it is true, been endorsed by the national leadership. Rumour has it that, on hearing of the attack on the Linz Chamber of Labour, Kraus, the leader of the VdU, at once travelled to the city and ordered his members to call off the strike. Nevertheless, the strike continued both here and in Steyr, although neither VdU nor SPÖ shop stewards played any further role in it.[36] This did not prevent the local SPÖ newspaper, *Tagblatt*, from printing in its 29 September issue a speech by Karl Maisel, the Minister for Social Administration and Chairman of the Metalworkers' and Miners' Union, berating his union's members for not realising 'that you are being used, not in order to achieve a wage-rise, but to ensure success for outright putsch attempts by the Communists and their allies in the VdU'.[37] This is the first mention of the mythical Communist 'putsch' of 1950.

Events in Upper Styria, where the Communists did enjoy significant support, confirm the impression that the strikes erupted spontaneously, leaving the KPÖ executive in a state of disarray. On Saturday 23 September, the day the party press published details of the Agreement, Gottlieb Fiala, the Communist Deputy Chairman of the ÖGB, hurried to Styria to urge local party leaders to call an immediate strike, at the very latest for the following Monday. He was told that they needed a few more days to prepare, but he returned to Vienna unconvinced of their capacity for decisive action and informed the KPÖ's executive committee that in his opinion the Styrian comrades would not manage to pull it off (*nicht durchkämen*).[38] His report confirmed already existing fears that, should the strike continue, it would be limited to the Soviet sector, and he persuaded the executive that time was needed to mobilise support elsewhere. His error became clear the very next day, when news came in that the strike had broken out again in Upper Austria and that workers in Donawitz and Fohnsdorf had also walked out. In fact, the workers in Linz and Steyr did not return to work until 3 October. Within twenty-four hours, most of the major plants in Upper Styria and Graz had also joined the protest and chosen delegates to attend the shop-stewards' meeting in Vienna on the coming Saturday.

The first strike wave was largely over by the evening of Thursday 28 September. During the preceding four days, localised strikes had broken out in every Austrian province except Carinthia, and had involved between 120,000 and 200,000 people, or between 6 and 10 per cent of the country's entire working population.[39] Some protests lasted for less than an hour and others for several days. Many Socialist shop-stewards who opposed the protest in principle resorted to the lesser evil of proposing short stoppages in order to defeat calls for all-out strikes. But there were very few parts of the country where some form of strike action did not take place, with the mines, machinery and steel plants in Upper Austria and Upper Styria and the factories in Vienna itself seeing the most large-scale protests. They took place in different areas at different times, and even, as we have seen, on different days. They were all unofficial, for the ÖGB withheld recognition, condemning them in public for being purely politically motivated. Böhm, however, presented a different case in a letter he wrote to Figl on 30 September, the day of the shop-stewards' conference. The 'deep dissatisfaction' of the workers, he claimed, could be attributed only in part to the Communists.

> It was to a large extent caused by the fear that fresh price increases would follow in the wake of the new Agreement. This fear became reality sooner than might have been expected. Even though the new Agreement has not yet come into force, we are already getting numerous reports of price increases and the hoarding of goods. These reports are, understandably, causing panic buying, and this chaotic state of affairs is making the workers and employees yet more agitated and bitter. If we fail to call a last-minute halt to these developments, disaster will inevitably ensue.[40]

He called on the Chancellor to take drastic steps to prohibit all unjustified price rises, failing which the ÖGB would have no choice but to issue a new wage demand.

Böhm's intervention was not disclosed to the public and the Federation became the prime target of the protesters in some areas, condemned by many of its members for having been a major collaborator in the formation of the government's economic policy. Although strike demands differed to some extent across the country, they invariably included the abandonment of wage controls and immediate wage increases across the board, as well as denunciations of ÖGB leaders. This was the most significant explosion of popular discontent in Austria since the civil war of 1934, and remains the most serious strike wave in the history of the Second Republic. But, at least in the view (or hopes) of the KPÖ, the protests had not ended; they had merely been postponed.

The controversial conference of shop stewards was held in the vast assembly hall of the Floridsdorf railway engine factory on Saturday 30

September. According to police estimates, 3,700 people turned up, roughly 10 per cent of the total number of elected shop stewards in Austria, but critics complained that not all of those present were actually legitimate members of works councils. This was undoubtedly true, for the SPÖ and ÖGB instructed their people to stay away from the meeting, denouncing it as a Communist-fascist trick which lacked any credibility.[41] Workers in many plants where official shop stewards opposed the strike had, during the previous week, reacted to this by electing delegates at impromptu factory meetings.

Police reports of the conference are not detailed. Their attempts to infiltrate it were thwarted by the police officers' union, whose members acted as stewards at the entrance to the building. US secret service records are more informative. Their people did get in, and reported a split within the Communist leadership. Two leaders, Franz Honner and Ernst Fischer, argued against further strikes, and this line was reported to have been backed by Johann Koplenig, the Communist Party Chairman, while Fritz Neubauer, a member of the executive committee, and the Secretary-General, Friedl Fürnberg, both of whom were more rigid party stalwarts, argued successfully in favour. Resolutions were passed calling for the abandonment of the Wages and Prices Agreement, a 20 per cent tax-free pay increase, a price freeze, and strike pay to come out of the coffers of the Trade Union Federation. The meeting also issued an ultimatum threatening a general strike if the government did not agree to its demands by midnight on 3 October.[42] The government responded by saying that it would not negotiate with the meeting's delegates, as the ÖGB was the only legitimate representative of labour. It refused to budge from this position.

In the days leading up to 4 October, a propaganda war broke out in the newspapers and on the radio, with the Communists using the Soviet-controlled RAVAG transmitter, and their opponents using the Rot-Weiss-Rot station. On 3 October, the government issued a statement calling on workers to oppose the strike in the name of 'Freedom and Democracy' and warning of sabotage and bloodshed. The survival of the Wages and Prices Agreement was not at stake, it declared, but that of Austria was. The shop-stewards' conference had been unrepresentative, merely acting as a front for the Communist Party executive committee. The statement did not use the word 'putsch', but the Communists were accused of attempting to overthrow democracy and abolish the democratic republic. It was also made clear that strikers would lose pay for time lost.[43] Trade union leaders were not as reticent. On the same day that the government statement was released, Böhm addressed a meeting attended by more than three thousand Socialist shop stewards and told them that:

> the plan was to depose the leadership of the Trade Union Federation and also the governing bodies of the individual trade unions by means of a putsch, and then to attempt to do the same with the Federal Government. Indeed, there were even people on the Central Committee of the Communist Party who were entertaining the idea of setting up a provisional government to take over control of the State.[44]

This conference passed a resolution which explicitly stated that the Communist plan was to seize control of the trade union movement, to overthrow the government and set up a People's Democracy.[45] From this point forward, there were few occasions when political and union leaders did not describe the strike wave as a putsch attempt.

The beginning of the second strike wave on 4 October was violent. In the middle of the night, strikers in Wiener Neustadt, in the Soviet zone, seized the post office and were ousted by Austrian police reinforcements who had been brought in from Vienna. This led to a direct confrontation between the Austrian authorities and the Soviet commandant, who ordered the police to withdraw and hand the post office back to the strikers. In Donawitz, twelve shop stewards were arrested and charged with sabotage for attempting to extinguish the blast-furnaces. The police occupied all major works in Donawitz, Graz and Steyr.[46] By midday, however, conservative and Socialist newspapers throughout the country were insisting that the strike had been a total failure, confined to the USIA plants, or at least to the Soviet zone. Even here, it was claimed, support had been involuntary. Workers were said to have been intimidated by barricades set up in six Viennese districts (II, IV, XX, XXI, XXII, XXV) with the connivance of the Soviet authorities. Soviet jeeps were said to have been sighted leading the 'thugs'. Soviet troops were reported to be massing on the Czech border. In response, the leader of the Building Workers' Union, Franz Olah, organised a band of his members to confront the strikers, issuing them with wooden clubs and knuckle-dusters. He also made a deal with the industrial and employers' federation to ensure that wages would be paid, offering union funds as guarantee.[47]

The strike disintegrated on 5 October amid claims that, by refusing to bow to terror, the country had averted a planned putsch. Olah was singled out as the hero of the hour, feted for thwarting attempts to drag Austria into the Soviet sphere.[48] But did the events of September and October 1950 indeed amount to a putsch attempt? On 12 October, in conversation with the British Under Secretary of State at the Foreign

Office, Lord Henderson, Chancellor Figl gave a detailed account of the Communist 'plan':

> It was first to seize and block all communications, telegraph, road and rail, between Vienna and the British Zone at Wiener Neustadt and between the capital and the United States and the French Zones at St Pölten. Once Vienna was cut off an attempt would have been made to seize the government or at least the Chancellor in the Ballhausplatz and through Russian control of RAVAG broadcasting network force the Chancellor at pistol point to announce the resignation of the Austrian Government, after which a self-appointed Government would have installed itself, claiming of course to be based on the democratic will of the people. The object of the outbreak at Linz in the American Zone was to try to get the United States forces involved, and thus give the Russian forces a precedent and an excuse for open intervention in their zone.[49]

But, without concrete proof of a plan to seize power, the case remained circumstantial. In a nine-hour debate in the Austrian parliament, also on 12 October, government politicians repeated the putsch claim time and again.[50] To some speakers, the evidence rested on the nature of Communism itself, in the shape of its revolutionary theory which preached the violent overthrow of the bourgeois state. The very fact that the Communists wanted a revolution at some stage, combined with the Communist seizures of power in Hungary, Poland and Czechoslovakia, proved, they asserted, that these events constituted an Austrian putsch attempt. Government spokesmen concentrated on the reports of violence and sabotage, of 'flying pickets', or '*Rollkommandos*', who moved from area to area on lorries with Soviet number plates, and of the intimidation of non-strikers, particularly women workers, who had been unable, it was said, to withstand the aggression. The strike, they claimed, had begun in the Soviet USIA plants and had only spread as a consequence of the terror tactics employed by the Communists. Oskar Helmer, the Minister of the Interior, described those who attacked the Linz Chamber of Labour as 'putschists', the implication being that these people had stormed the building in order to overthrow the state, threatening the primacy of elected power by demanding the resignations of Johann Böhm, and the President of the Chamber of Labour, Karl Mantler. The assumption that a challenge to organised labour was also a challenge to democratic power was often repeated over the following months and years, not least by trade union leaders.[51] The fact that the Linz demonstration had been led by local members of the VdU rather than by the KPÖ was neatly circumvented by references to collusion between Communists and fascists. The final evidence of a Communist conspiracy was said to be the role of the Soviet Forces, namely their refusal on 26 September to allow the redeployment of one-thousand Austrian police officers from their zone into the centre of Vienna to control the demonstration taking place there, the actions of the Soviet commander in Wiener Neustadt on 4 October, and the use of Soviet vehicles to transport strikers.

According to official statements, the strikes had been pre-planned and orchestrated by the Communist Party with the support of the Soviet Union and had been defeated by the tenacity of the Austrian people. A closer examination of events throws doubt on this interpretation. Although the Communist Party had mounted a campaign against the prices and wages strategy throughout 1949 and 1950, it had not created the genuine hostility towards wage restraint in general which prevailed among workers, nor their outrage at learning that the Fourth Wages and Prices Agreement had, once again, been negotiated in secret. The government was fully aware of the workers' attitude, which was precisely why secrecy had been necessary in the first place. Moreover, despite the official line, neither the scale nor the pattern of the protests support allegations of conspiracy. During the two waves of strikes, just under 10 per cent of the Austrian workforce as a whole took part in some form of protest, far more than the Communists could muster even in the general election. VdU and SPÖ members played important roles, the latter in direct contravention of their party's instructions. The strikes were uncoordinated. The Communist Party leadership was not even able to present a united front at the Floridsdorf shop-stewards' meeting, where one section argued unsuccessfully for the abandonment of strike action. If there had been a plan for a putsch, it was badly bungled. The supporting role of the Soviet forces is also open to question. The refusal of the Soviet military to redeploy Austrian police from their zone and the events in Wiener Neustadt, both of which were condemned as 'Soviet intervention', should also be seen in the context of the Soviet-Austrian dispute over jurisdiction: the Soviet Element had come into conflict with the Austrian government over the question of the extent of police powers on several occasions before the 1950 strikes. Indeed, the surprising point about the role of the Soviet authorities during the strike is their inactivity. This also applies to the Soviet plants. In his memoirs of the period, Ernst Fischer recalled that during the first strikes many USIA plants closed for only twenty-four hours because managers refused to sanction lost production resulting from strike action.[53] Waldbrunner, the Minister of Transport and Nationalised Industries, remarked sardonically that this was 'the "ultimate" in labor tactics when workers, coming off an eight hour shift, are transported to other factories and paraded as strikers'.[53]

The most telling evidence is to be found in the twenty-four-page report of January 1951 written to the Soviet Foreign Ministry, referred to above.[54] While praising the actions of the 'Austrian working masses' in their opposition to 'the American imperialists and their Austrian lackeys', the account of the outbreak of the strikes, their size and the subsequent chronology of events differs little from local police reports. There is, of course, greater emphasis on the Austrian government's use of force to break the strike, no reference to the role of VdU shop stewards in leading the first strikes, although they are condemned for breaking them later, and repeated claims that this was an economic rather than a political protest. But throughout the report there are criticisms of the role of the Communist Party executive, and the conclusion contains a detailed list of errors committed by the party. The executive is accused of misreading the situation from the start. It had originally planned to call a strike for 2 October, more than ten days after its own press had broken the story of the announcement of the Fourth Wages and Prices Agreement. Having then been 'compelled by the course of events to issue a strike call for September 26', it was unable to rally sufficient support.[55] The writers of the report even consider that the 'timing for holding the meeting [on the Ballhausplatz on the morning of 27 September] proved to have been badly chosen. It would have been more efficacious to devote the day to meetings in the districts, encouraging the factories to strike, widening the movement, and to move to the centre after work was over. Had that been the case, thousands of workers could have joined the demonstration without being on strike.'[56] The implication is that the goal was to rally support for the protest, rather than to confront the Cabinet. As it was, the 'meeting was comparatively poorly attended, although the mood of those who took part was bellicose and upbeat'. The executive is accused of having left the demonstration too early.

The decision to call off the first wave of strikes is described as 'an error of tactics', which gave the 'reactionary forces' time to regroup. The KPÖ, says the report, was poorly organised and failed to liaise with the regions. Indeed, it lacked essential information on which plants were on strike and at what time and was not even capable of mobilising full support within the Soviet sector, where, 'workers in the Soviet factories may be sure that they will not suffer repression by the directors for having participated in strikes'.[57] But the report also refutes claims that the protests even amounted to a general strike, on the grounds that they were sporadic, partial and lacking in cohesion. The strikers had, the report concludes, failed to achieve the specific goal of destroying the Wages and Prices Agreement, but, having begun as an economic movement, their actions had intensified the class struggle, shown their

opposition to the Marshall Plan, and 'acquired great political significance'. The KPÖ is given moderate praise for placing itself at the head
of the most active members of the working class, but is reminded that
it will not succeed in winning over the majority of Austrians until it can
rally support among poor farmers and women.[58] There is no indication
in this report that the Soviet authorities had any expectations of a
successful Communist putsch.

Nor were the Western Allies convinced that such a thing had been
on the cards. At the end of October, the British High Commissioner,
Sir Harold Caccia, informed the Foreign Secretary that 'we have no
evidence to show that the communist [*sic*] Party had decided on this
occasion to make a determined attempt to carry out such a plan'.[59] The
American Chargé d'Affaires, Walter C. Dowling, concurred, reporting
that:

> There was a strong impression that the Communists were surprised by
> their momentary success on September 26 and 27 and unprepared to
> exploit it. This would indicate that the demonstration was organised in
> accordance with a general policy of provoking labor unrest but that the
> Cominform's master planners had not intended this to be the day for
> their capture of Austria. The impression that these demonstrations were
> a local effort and not a Moscow managed puppet show was strengthened
> when the Communist leadership split at the meeting.[60]

Nevertheless, Günter Bischof argues that, whether or not there was an
orchestrated Communist plan to seize power in 1950, the 'putsch' threat
caused genuine alarm in Austria at the time.[61] Without doubt, many
Austrians were convinced that, in its second stage, the strike had been
transformed into an attack on the state. Support for the strike on 4
October was weaker, although no concessions on the wages and prices
issue had been gained. Engineering workers at the Floridsdorf plant,
where the resolution to call the second strike had been passed, decided
to work and there were even rumours that the announcement that time
lost during the second wave would not be counted as sick-leave put off
some who had joined the earlier strike.[62] But government statements
denouncing the protests as a 'putsch' do appear to have been accepted
by the working population in the long term.

Did the government itself believe in this interpretation? The Cabinet
papers suggest that it did not. The Cabinet met three times during the
course of the strikes, on 26 September to approve the Agreement, on
3 October and in a special session on 5 October. At none of these
meetings was the possibility of a putsch discussed. The word was not

even mentioned. At the first meeting, the one which had been brought forward by two hours, the Cabinet was told that a demonstration in Vienna had been planned, streets were blocked, and Soviet military posts were only letting USIA lorries into the city. The Soviets' refusal to allow the redeployment of Austrian police was also noted. Oskar Helmer, the Minister of the Interior, reported that Communists and the Soviet authorities appeared to be working together and there was a danger that they would 'succeed'. Chancellor Figl commented that he thought calm would return to the city in a few days. At this stage, the government seemed to believe that the strike was a threat to civil order, but no more. Police were issued with neither riot gear nor helmets, there were no proposals for the evacuation of the government and the Cabinet went on to discuss details of the economic agreement, even after Helmer had reported that five thousand demonstrators were marching on the Chancellery.[63]

American sources report that Figl was less calm by lunchtime, when he requested US intervention.[64] The Americans prevaricated; although American and British troops remained on the alert throughout the period, they were never used. Helmer and the Vice-Chancellor, Adolf Schärf, remained adamant that Western Allied assistance would not only exacerbate the situation, but would also undermine years of work to re-establish Austrian independence; the Austrian authorities had to be seen to be putting their own house in order.

The atmosphere in the second Cabinet meeting one week later was more tense. Helmer reported that the Viennese police and reservists had been armed and ordered to meet violence with violence and that the strike was receding. But two remarks by the Foreign Minister, Karl Gruber, indicate the general attitude of the Cabinet. Responding to Helmer's report, he told the meeting that it was imperative to inform the Allied Control Council of any Soviet interference with government orders: 'I believe that the more we show that they are involved, the more the Russians will distance themselves.' He went on to comment on the situation in Korea, where undeclared war had broken out in June: 'Without doubt, the Russians are planning a rapprochement with the Western powers, although it is uncertain if this will happen now.' Such a rapprochement would be important for Austria, which would become a test of Russian goodwill. He went on to discuss long-term tactics for increasing US military aid to Austria.[65] These comments were made the day before the October strike was due to start. They are not the words of a man who feared that the Soviet authorities were involved in an imminent coup attempt. But they were uttered in the privacy of the Cabinet. After this meeting the government issued a call to the people in which the strike movement was, finally, denounced as a 'putsch'.

Two days later, in the third meeting, Helmer reported on the Soviet intervention in Wiener Neustadt, saying, 'The fact is that the Russians have intervened. It appears that they have no serious aims, for if they had, they would have seized the train stations and government offices as well as the post office.'[66] Gruber supported this assessment, arguing that if the Russians had wanted to use force, the Austrians would have been completely unable to stop them. The Soviet intervention was, he said, more probably an act of intimidation, designed to cover a retreat, but the pressure on the Russians had to be kept up, using the Allied Council as well as the press and radio. All communiqués should emphasize the right of the Austrian authorities to enforce law and order in all zones, including the Soviet, and should stress that the Soviets had intervened in Austrian domestic affairs, contravening the Allied Control Agreement. The Chancellor's comments are also revealing: 'Either they [the Soviets] should be forced to show their hand, or they should be brought down a peg or two.'[67] The following week Figl's spirits were even higher, as he spoke of using the parliamentary debate to expose the Communist Party and attacked provincial politicians for under-estimating his government.[68]

The Cabinet papers show that the Austrian government did not fear a Soviet-backed coup and that it knew that without Soviet backing such a coup could not succeed. They also show that members of the Cabinet, particularly Helmer and Gruber, realised that these events could be put to good use. The putsch label was adopted for political purposes. Initially the hyperbole was designed to deflect criticism of the new Wages and Prices Agreement, about which there was obvious anxiety. There were many references in Cabinet to the strength of popular opposition to the wage controls, which, according to Helmer, even went deep into the bourgeoisie. The speed at which the first strikes were called off seemed to have come as an unexpected, but welcome, relief. Labelling the next wave as a 'putsch' effectively trumped public hostility to wage restraint by raising the spectre of a greater threat, thus relieving the government of the necessity to defend its economic policy. In the longer term, the putsch label gave grounds for a purge of Communist sympathisers within the trade union movement and the police force, as will be shown in the next chapter. Communists were accused of having conspired against the state, a far more serious accusation than that of having led an illegal strike. The Soviet position was also attacked. The battle over jurisdiction in the Soviet zone was resumed with vigour and with the backing of the Allied Council. Relations with the Western Allies were also strengthened. On the one hand, the Austrian government had demonstrated that it was capable of quelling unrest without outside assistance. On the other, the threat of a putsch emphasised Austria's precarious political position. This would be used in negotiations with the Americans over increased military and economic aid.[69]

At the beginning of October, the British ambassador criticised the Austrian government for having been 'caught napping' during the first wave of strikes.[70] It is clear that from the start of that month, at least, this was not the case and that the government was able to exploit the situation with great skill and speed. The real, and very pressing, fear was that the Republic could be destabilised by the unrest, especially as it was known that prices could not be held and that unemployment would rise in the winter months. But there is no indication that the Austrian government ever believed that the strikes were part of a putsch plot. On the contrary, the Cabinet was aware that the Soviet authorities did not support an escalation of protest. Yet the putsch label was successful in deflating support for the economic strike and in turning the tables against the Soviets in the Allied Council. These were the main reasons for its adoption in 1950. It was also extremely popular, reflecting an image of Austria as the David who had withstood the Soviet Goliath. That is one reason for the longevity of the legend.

Notes

1 Gabriela Stieber, 'Die Lösung des Flüchtlingsproblems 1945–60', in Thomas Albrich, Klaus Eisterer, Michael Gehler and Rolf Steininger, *Österreich in den Fünfzigern* (Innsbruck: Österreichischer Studienverlag, 1995), 87. There were 520,591 refugees in Austria in July 1948, 327,506 of whom were *Volksdeutsche* and 19,283 of whom were Jews. The other categories were South Tyroleans and non-German-speaking refugees.
2 Oliver Rathkolb, 'Private Commissions', in Bischof, Pelinka and Lassner (eds), *The Dollfuss/Schuschnigg Era in Austria*, 249–57.
3 Gabriela Stieber, 'Die Lösung des Flüchtlingsproblems 1945–60', in Albrich *et al.*, *Österreich in den Fünfzigern*, 73–6.
4 Kepplinger and Weidenholzer, 'Die Rekonstruktion der Sozialdemokratie in Linz 1945–1950', 27.
5 *Arbeiter-Zeitung*, 16 October 1949.
6 Georg Rigele, 'The Marshall Plan and Austria's Hydroelectric Industry: Kaprun', in Bischof *et al.* (eds), *The Marshall Plan in Austria*, 335.
7 Georg Rigele, 'Kaprun. Das Kraftwerk des österreichischen Wiederaufbaus', in Kos and Rigele (eds), *Inventur 45/55*, 319.
8 RGASPI 575/1/78. 'Reports, informational memoranda on the workers' and Communist movement, the economic situation of Austria, England, drawn up

in the Central Committee of the All-Union Communist Party (bolshevik), in consultation with the Information Bureau, on November 16–17, 1949. The unity of the working class and the tasks of the KPÖ', 7–9. The accusation was that the revenue would be used to rebuild the armed forces.

9   *Arbeiter-Zeitung*, 27 March 1949.
10 RGASPI 575/1/78, 'Reports, informational memoranda on the workers' and Communist movement', 10.
11 TNA/PRO/FO 1007/333, Allied Commission for Austria (British Element), Monthly Political Reports Styria 1949.
12 *Arbeiter-Zeitung*, 16 October 1949.
13 Kepplinger and Weidenholzer, 'Die Rekonstruktion der Sozialdemokratie in Linz 1945–1950', 38–9.
14 *Arbeiter-Zeitung*, 19 October 1949.
15 Soviet and British reports contained the same results, although the Eisenerz result is only found in the former. RGASPI fond 066, op. 31, papka 152, delo 58, 'Bericht über die Arbeit der Abteilung für Soziale Verwaltung des Sowjetischen Elements der All'. Kommission für Österreich für das 4. Quartal 1949; TNA/PRO/FO 1007/333, Allied Commission for Austria (British Element), Monthly Political Reports Styria 1949.
16 See Chapter 6, ftn. 42; after 1950 the US authorities became very interested in the works council elections and compiled a detailed report comparing results in 1947 and 1951. 'Austria. Works Council Election Results. Confidential, 18 December 1951', US National Archives (NA), Record Group 59, Records of Western European Affairs, Subject Files Austria (hereafter NA, RG 59). 863.06/12–1851.
17 The Schilling was devalued on 21 November 1949 and a system of multiple exchange rates was introduced. *Arbeiter-Zeitung*, 4 December 1949.
18 *Arbeiter-Zeitung*, 11 November 1949.
19 Lageberichte der Sicherheitsdirektionen, 31.1.1950. A copy of this is held in the Schärf-Helmer Correspondence, Schärf Papers, Box 44, 4/287.
20 NA RG59, 863.06/2–2350 Austrian Labor Report, 23.2.1950.
21 On 24 August 1950 Otto Probst wrote a letter to the editor of the Tyrolean newspaper, *Volkszeitung*, conveying Johann Böhm's displeasure at the publication of an article on wages: 'He [Böhm] thinks that it would be dangerous for our Party press to start making trouble over the wages question.' 'Er [Böhm] meint, daß es gefährlich sei, wenn unsere Parteipresse in der Lohnfrage zu zündeln beginnt.' The editor replied that 'what is said in this article expresses in a subdued way what shop-stewards have been saying at all the conferences.' 'die Feststellungen dieses Aufsatzes sprechen in einer gedämpften Form aus, was die Vertrauensmänner in allen Konferenzen … ausgesprochen haben.' Probst Correspondence, SPÖ Documents, Verein für Geschichte der Arbeiterbewegung, Vienna.
22 NA, RG 59, 863.06/8–1750, Austrian Labor Review for July 1950. 17.08.1950.
23 *Ibid.*
24 Ronald Gruber, 'Der Massenstreik gegen das 4. Lohn- Preisabkommen im September/Oktober 1950', 125.
25 NA, RG 59, 863.054/3–850, Austrian Labor Report, March 1950.

26 Socialist members of the Economics Committee had fiercely opposed a Fourth Wages and Prices Agreement, arguing that the trade unions already had difficulties maintaining industrial peace. Negotiations were then passed to the three Chambers. Protokolle des Wirtschaftlichen Ministerkomitees, 20 June 1950. AdR, (BKA), (AA), Box 6, sitting 76.

27 AdR, BKA, Wirtschaftliches Ministerkomitee, Box 6, sitting 76, 20 June 1950.

28 *Ibid*. 'Hinsichtlich der Punkte 1 bis 3 ist aber kein Gebrauch nach aussen zu machen.'

29 Gruber, 'Der Massenstreik gegen das 4. Lohn- Preisabkommen', 124.

30 An internal KPÖ report on activities in the VÖESt plant estimated that twenty thousand took part in the demonstration in Linz on 26 September. 'Vereinigte Österreichische Eisen- und Stahlwerke, Linz, Gedächtnisprotokoll der Betriebsorganisation der KPÖ über den Streik', signed Schneiderbauer, Institut für Zeitgeschichte, Vienna, Material Knoblehar. No date. According to Ernst Epler, there were approximately thirty thousand present. Ernst Epler, *Der Grosse Streik* (Vienna: Stern-Verlag, 1965), 39.

31 Epler, *Der Grosse Streik*, 60.

32 'The strike movement in Austria, 26 September–5 October 1950', Foreign Policy Archive of the Russian Federation (AVP RF), Fond 066, Opis' 32a, delo 6 (Austrian Section), list 1, 23 January 1951. An excerpt from this document appears in Wolfgang Mueller, Arnold Suppan, Norman Naimark and Gennadi Bordjugov (eds), *Sowjetische Politik in Österreich 1945–1055. Dokumente aus russischen Archiven* (Vienna: Verlag der Österreichischen Akademiie der Wissenschaft, 2005), No. 71, 685–711, where it is dated 16 December 1950.

33 'Streiks und Kundgebungen in Wien am 26., 27. und 28.IX.', Polizeidirektion Wien, AdR, BMfI, 132.011–2/50.

34 The official government figure was 2,140. Information, 1 October 1950, Bundespolizei Wien, AdR, BMfI, 132.015–2/50.

35 Figl maintained that the KPÖ had deliberately started the strike in the American zone in order to precipitate US intervention and establish a precedent for Russian intervention in the Soviet zone. TNA/PRO/FO 371/84924, Ref 9032. C 6869/12/3, 30 October 1950, Sir H. Caccia to Ernest Bevin. In parliament Figl claimed that the factories which had come out on strike were Communist dominated.

36 Gruber, 'Der Massenstreik', 239–42.

37 'Dass man Euch benützt, nicht um eine Lohnforderung zu erreichen, sondern um regelrechte Putschversuche der Kommunisten und ihrer Verbündeten vom VdU durchzusetzen', *Tagblatt*, 29 September 1950, quoted in Gruber, 'Der Massenstreik', 239.

38 *Ibid*., 147, 188–9, 192. Fiala's role was confirmed by Gruber in interviews with Otto Fischer, Franz Marek and Friedl Fürnberg.

39 To put the size of the September strike into some sort of context, a comparison may be made with the June Uprising in East Germany in 1953, which was triggered by government announcements of changes to productivity targets; there 300,000 to 372,000 workers went on strike, representing between 5.5 and 6.8 per cent of the total workforce. Mary Fulbrook, *The Fontana History of Germany 1918–1990. The Divided Nation* (London: Fontana, 1991), 191.

40 'Zum grossen Teil ist sie ausgelöst worden von der Befürchtung, daß im Gefolge der neuen Vereinbarung nun neuerliche Preissteigerungen einsetzen würden. Diese Befürchtung hat sich rascher erfüllt, als man annehmen durfte. Noch bevor das neue Abkommen in Wirksamkeit getreten ist erhalten wir eine Fülle von Nachrichten über Preisssteigerungen und Warenhortungen. Diese Nachrichten lösen begreiflicherweise Angstkäufe aus und durch diesen tollen Wirbel wird die Erregung und Erbitterung der Arbeiter und Angestellten noch weiter gesteigert. Wenn nicht in letzter Minute dieser Entwicklung Einhalt geboten werden kann, so sind verheerende Folgen unvermeidlich!' Böhm to Figl, 30 September 1951, VGA, Helmer papers, Heft 4, Mappe 1/III.

41 AdR, BKA, MRP, sitting 219, 26 September 1950. It is worth noting that, in contrast with Böhm's condemnation of the shop-stewards' meeting in March, this time the ÖGB did not claim it had the sole prerogative to convene such a conference.

42 'The Communist Attempt to Promote a General Strike in Austria from September 26 to October 7 1950', 30 March 1951. Office of Intelligence Research (OIR) Report No. 5461, NA, RG 59.

43 Government proclamation, 'Österreichischer, Mitbürger! In den letzten Tagen versuchen die Kommunisten unsere demokratische Republik zu gefährden.' ('Austrians, fellow-citizens! In the last few days the Communists have been attempting to endanger our Republic.') BMfI, 134.938–2/50. 3 October 1950.

44 'Es war geplant, durch einen Putsch die Leitung des Gewerkschaftsbundes und auch die Vorstände der einzelnen Gewerkschaften abzusetzen und dann das gleiche auch mit der Bundesregierung zu versuchen. Ja, es haben sich im ZK der KP schon Menschen mit den Gedanken getragen, eine provisorische Regierung einzusetzen, die die Führung des Staates zu übernehmen hätte.' Resolution der sozialistischen Betriebsratskonferenz vom 3.10.1950. BMfI, 132.015–2/50.

45 *Arbeiter-Zeitung*, 4 October 1950.

46 Epler, *Der Grosse Streik*, 126–34.

47 Helmut Konrad and Manfred Lechner, *'Millionenverwechslung'. Franz Olah. Die Kronenzeitung. Geheimdienste* (Vienna: Böhlau, 1992), 58–62; Wilhelm Svoboda, *Franz Olah. Eine Spurensicherung* (Vienna: Promedia, 1990), 77.

48 *Arbeiter-Zeitung*, 6, 7, 8 October 1950. The 'putsch' myth has survived. Olah was awarded Austria's highest honour, the Grosse Goldene Ehrenzeichen mit Sterne, in March 2005, as celebrations began for the 50th anniversary of the State Treaty and the 60th anniversary of the Second Republic. It was also Olah's 95th birthday. The Federal Chancellor, Wolfgang Schüssel, described Olah thus: 'He was and is an exemplary patriot.' He went on to praise Olah's 'determined efforts in defence of democracy', as a result of which it had been possible to frustrate Communist revolutionary plans in Austria in the 1950s. Schussel: 'It was his personal courageous intervention which saved Austria.' ('Sein persönliches mutiges Eingreifen hat Österreich gerettet.'), *Salzburger Nachrichten*, 29 March 2005. For details of Olah's controversial political career in the 1960s, see Helmut Konrad and Manfred Lechner, *'Millionenverwechslung'. Franz Olah. Die Kronenzeitung. Geheimdienste*.

49 Sir H. Caccia to Ernest Bevin, 30 October 1950. TNA/PRO/FO 371/84924 Ref 9032. C 6869/12/3.

50 *Stenographisches Protokoll des Nationalrates der Republik Österreich*, sitting 31,12 October 1950, 1091–169.

51 Klenner, *Die österreichischen Gewerkschaften*, 1469.

52 Fischer, *Das Ende einer Illusion. Erinnerungen 1945–1955*, 310.

53 'The Communist Attempt', (OIR) Report No. 5461, NA, RG 59, 4.

54 'The strike movement in Austria, 26 September–5 October 1950', AVP RF, Fond 066, Opis' 32a, delo 6 (Austrian Section), list 1, 23 January 1951.

55 *Ibid.*, 2.

56 *Ibid.*, 4.

57 *Ibid.*, 3. The inclusion of this phrase suggests that not all USIA employees believed this to be the case.

58 *Ibid.*, 23–4.

59 Sir H. Caccia to Ernest Bevin, 30 October 1950, TNA/PRO/FO 371/84924 Ref 9032. C 6869/12/3.

60 Dowling to the State Department, 'Wage-Price demonstrations of September 26–October 5, 1950', 17 October 1950. NA, RG 59 763.00/10-1750. He was referring to the Floridsdorf shop stewards' meeting on 30 September.

61 Günter Bischof, 'Austria looks to the West: Kommunistische Putschgefahr, geheime Wiederbewaffnung und Westorientierung am Anfang der fünfziger Jahre', in Albrich *et al.*, *Österreich in den Fünfzigern*, 186.

62 It was pointed out in Cabinet that the Chancellor's insistence that workers should not have to provide a sick note for the first three days of illness made it difficult to discipline those who had taken part in the protests. Figl replied indignantly that he had meant this provision to cover illness, not going on strike. AdR, BKA, MRP, sitting 221, 11 October 1950.

63 AdR, BKA, MRP, sitting 219, 26 September 1950.

64 'The Communist Attempt', (OIR) Report No. 5461, NA, RG 59, 2.

65 'Ein Probefall zum Beweis guten Willens', AdR, BKA, MRP, sitting 220, 3 October 1950.

66 AdR, BKA, MRP, sitting 220a, 5 October 1950.

67 'Entweder sie decken die Karten auf oder sie sollen eine Dämpfung erfahren', *Ibid.*

68 AdR, BKA, MRP, sitting 221, 11 October 1950.

69 Anton Staudinger, 'Zur Geschichte der B-Gendarmerie', in *Österreichische Militärische Zeitschrift*, vol. 5, 1972, 343–8. After the 1950 strikes, Marshall Aid Counterpart funds were released for job creation schemes. Frequent references were made to the danger of political instability in Austria, if unemployment were to rise too high, e.g. 'dependence on US aid is inevitable. The effects of curtailment of aid are predictable from recent experience. Costs and prices rise. With decreasing real wages the workers become restive: the tempo of Communist and extremist efforts is increased. The volume of investment and building activity falls, and unemployment rises. Since these are politically intolerable conditions, inflationary financing is the Government's only recourse.' The Employment Problem in Austria, October 1950. NA, RG 59, 863.06/10–2550.

70 Sir H. Caccia to Attlee, 9 October 1950. TNA/PRO/FO, 771/84923.

9

The aftermath

The main public debate on the strikes took place, as we have seen, in parliament on 12 October. By this time government ministers had consolidated their account of events. Chancellor Figl opened the proceedings with a lengthy and passionate speech which concentrated on the second phase of the protests, the October strikes, alleging widespread use of terror by the Communists and extensive Soviet interference. Citing the incident at Donawitz, he spoke of 'brutal, naked terror'. Communist accounts of events were summarily dismissed: 'a more infamous distortion of the facts has not been perpetrated in Austria except by the Nazi regime'.[1] Helmer spoke next, adding even more lurid accounts of the incidents during which the 'putschists', he maintained, had employed intimidation and violence and had engaged in acts of sabotage in order to undermine the economy and bring down the state. Repeating claims that Communist shop stewards had attempted to close down the blast-furnace at Donawitz and had been prevented by the combined actions of the security forces and workers, he announced that the perpetrators had been arrested. He went on to list numerous examples of Soviet interference in policing in Vienna and Lower Austria, after which he unveiled a collection of weapons which he said had been used during the disturbances, and concluded by reporting that 115 policemen and 21 gendarmes had been 'more or less seriously injured'.[2] Böhm and Pittermann, the General Secretary of the ÖGB, also spoke; both defended the Wages and Prices Agreement while condemning the 'wild terror' of the Communists.

Communist deputies, including Honner and Fischer, attempted to refute the claims made by the governing parties, but the story was now set in aspic. The official version of the strikes of 1950 was that they had constituted an orchestrated attempt to overthrow the state – which according to the law amounted to treason. It is therefore surprising that there were no successful prosecutions of any perpetrators. Many arrests were made under the 1870 Combinations Law and the 1936 Security of the State Law, the twelve Communist shop stewards from Donawitz being among those detained, but, despite the best efforts of the authorities, no one was actually brought to trial.[3] Nor was anyone held legally accountable for the attack on the Chamber of Labour in Linz. This is, perhaps, the most telling evidence that the 'putsch' of 1950 was, indeed, a myth.

The absence of proof did not deter the government, and later the wider public, from reiterating claims that Austria had repulsed the Communist threat and defeated a Soviet-backed coup. The strikes themselves became known as the 'October strikes', with the result that the main emphasis fell on early October, which witnessed the action called by the KPÖ, while the first wave of protests was virtually airbrushed out of public memory. The 'putsch' was far too valuable to be dispensed with, for it served as an awful warning of the fate to which this small state might succumb should the Soviet Union's influence in Europe expand. Here was a grim scenario which Austrian politicians were able to exploit during subsequent negotiations with the American government and the ECA, as well as in appeals to its own people. The repercussions of the 1950 strikes were to prove deep and widespread.

Relations between the Austrian authorities and the American government were considerably strengthened by the latter's response to the strikes, although, privately, the State Department did not accept the official Austrian verdict on the disturbances. The Office of Intelligence Research produced a report in March 1951 which concluded that:

the seizure of political power by force, the aim impugned [*sic*: imputed] to the Communists by the government, was definitely beyond the designed scope of the strike action and by far exceeded the strength of the Communist agitators. Helmer's statement that seizure of the labour unions would have enabled the Communists to carry out a putsch was essentially designed for consumption by the conservative People's Party. Not only were the Communists very far from taking control of the labor unions, but the security organs of the state remained firmly in the hands of the cabinet, so that even a temporary success of the labor agitation would not have resulted in a seizure of power.

Decisive interference by the Soviet authorities in their zone could have resulted in a Communist seizure of power. It is well known that this course is open to them, but, so far, they have shown no evidence of embarking upon it, or upon its corollary, the partitioning of Austria on the German pattern. The very fact that the Soviets extended only limited aid to the agitators, knowing full well that the Communists alone could not seize power, leads to the conclusion that the latter pursued only a limited goal.[4]

On the other hand, the Americans recognised that the stance adopted by the Austrian government afforded an excellent example of resistance to the very real Soviet threat.[5] When Figl lodged a complaint with the Allied Control Council over unwarranted Soviet interference in Austrian domestic affairs, he was supported by the Western Elements led by the American members, who then issued their own formal protest.[6] In December the American High Commissioner, Walter Donnelly, held a meeting with Figl, Helmer, Gruber and Schärf to review 'Operation Squirrel Cage', that is to say, the policy adopted in 1948 which ensured that food reserves were secretly held in storage with a view to distributing them in the event of a Soviet blockade of Vienna.[7] The thorny issue of arming the Austrian gendarmerie was also raised; when Helmer complained that, unlike their British counterparts, the American authorities in Salzburg had prevaricated over issuing arms and equipment to Austrian officials, Donnelly promised immediate action. According to Franz Olah, the 1950 strikes also triggered the formation of a clandestine 'secret army' whose task would be to defend Austria in the event of a Communist attack; this force was financed from the USA.[8]

The failure of the 1950 strikes also altered the relationship between the Austrian government and the Soviet authorities. Helmer reacted to the Soviet response to the strikes and demonstrations, and in particular to the confrontation between the Soviet commander and Austrian police in Wiener Neustadt on 4 October, by sacking Communist police officers, including five district commanders in the Soviet sector of Vienna who had refused to obey the orders of the Austrian government during the strikes. The Soviets protested on the grounds that, under the terms of the 1946 Allied Control Agreement, they were responsible for policing in their own zone, and demanded the reinstatement of the officers.[9] The dispute dragged on for some time, but the Austrian government did not cave in. As a result, the police force was purged of Communist members and Soviet authority in the Russian zone had been successfully challenged.

The failure of the strikes also provided the ÖGB with an opportunity to rid the trade unions of many of their Communist functionaries. Gottlieb Fiala not only lost his position as Deputy Chairman of the Federation, but, in addition, he was expelled from the Textile Workers' Union, along with that union's General Secretary, Egon Kodicek. The General Secretary and two other members of the White-collar Workers' Union executive committee, four members of the executive committee of the Public Employees' Union, including its vice-president, the deputy chairman of the Building Workers' Union, and three secretaries of the Metalworkers' Union were also dismissed. According to Fritz Klenner, a total of eighty-five trade unionists were expelled from their unions, resulting in the exclusion of the Communist Party from all leading positions within the labour movement.[10] The Building Workers' Union went further and banned any member of the KPÖ from holding office in its organisation, while the Union of Journalists expelled the editors of all nine Communist newspapers, including Ernst Fischer, and dismissed its own Communist functionaries. But retribution was not restricted to prominent Communists. Twenty-two Communist shop stewards were sacked by their employers, including all twelve Communist members of the Donawitz works council. The most widespread punishment was inflicted on workers in Linz and Steyr, where 350 participants in the strike lost their jobs, and in the aluminium works in Ranshofen, where 90 workers were sacked. The VÖESt management avoided criticism for having failed to produce a legal case against the strikers by announcing that immediate and large-scale redundancies were required on economic grounds.[11]

One of the most important consequences of the 1950 strikes was that the US State Department reassessed its attitude toward the ÖGB. Its earlier complaints that the Economic Partners, including the trade unions, had too much influence over policy formation were now replaced by open admiration for the Austrian labour movement. The 1950 Annual Labor Report for Austria praised the Federation for having:

made a valuable contribution to the reconstruction of Austria. This contribution is not only measured in terms of the defense of, and the improvement of, the workers' standard of living, but also in terms of the Federation's contribution to general economic recovery through its understanding of basic economic facts and its adoption of a statesman-like economic program designed to aid all segments of the population through real economic recovery in Austria.

Referring to the strikes, it went on, 'it was to a large extent the workers of Austria themselves who stepped into this violent situation when the Communist objectives became clear, and who destroyed this threat when the Soviet Occupation Forces handicapped the Austrian police'.[12]

Böhm was characteristically quick to grasp the opportunities which the ÖGB's new status offered him. On 6 October he and Proksch attended a meeting in the ECA Mission with King and Giblin during which he gave his assessment of the events of the previous week. The ÖGB had been strengthened by the unquestionable loyalty which non-Communist workers had shown to their leaders during the strikes, he maintained, but this could not be relied upon in the future; there continued to be fears and doubts about the problems of inflation and unemployment which might well dishearten his members and allow the Communists to regain the 'prestige and following which they had lost during the past ten days'.[13] He then called on the ECA to support an employment programme, to be financed from Counterpart funds, which should include the injection of 100 to 150 million Schillings into the Production Unemployment Relief Programme, raising the funding for house building from 45 to 100 million Schillings in 1950 and to 200 million Schillings in 1951, and increasing investment in apprenticeship schemes in order to ease youth unemployment. He justified these proposals on the grounds that the tapering off of food subsidies had reduced the ECA's level of social expenditure, and argued that greater emphasis should now be placed on relieving unemployment. The fact that Böhm made this appeal so soon after the strikes had been broken is yet another example of his skill as a negotiator, this time with the Americans. He was fully aware that the ECA's remit was to reduce social investment and increase capital investment. Earlier requests by both the ÖGB and the government to increase Counterpart funding for house-building projects and job-creation schemes had been rejected by the ECA, whose officials had insisted that any additional expenditure in these areas should come out of the ordinary budget. But in the meanwhile the situation had changed, and on 6 December, following Soviet protests in the Allied Control Council at the Austrian government's failure to stem unemployment, the State Department sent a telegram to the American Legation in Vienna: 'DEPT giving urgent consideration to unemployment relief measures including works program . . . and agrees situation warrants assistance with counterpart.'[14] At the beginning of 1951 the ECA did agree to release 150 million Schillings of Counterpart funds for 'an extensive construction program of apartment buildings'. The State Department insisted that 'this emergency program' should only consider labour-intensive projects and called on the ECA to release the funds as soon as possible, as well as to ensure that sufficient foreign currency was made available to defray the cost of the necessary raw materials.[15] The intervention by the State Department followed a letter sent by Böhm to Donnelly on 20 January 1951 asking that the normal procedure by which Counterpart finds were released in stages should be waived in this case. The 'release letter' was duly issued on 23 February.[16] The State Department had finally come to realise how dangerous an impact high unemployment in Austria would have on the political stability of both that country and the entire region.[17]

At the same time as he was consolidating the relationship between the ÖGB and the Americans, Böhm was also seeking to augment the role of labour in economic policy-making by expanding the powers of the Economic Commission. In February 1951, delegates to a conference of Socialist shop stewards passed a resolution calling for the creation of a new top-level economic body which would have responsibility for the distribution of raw materials, for currency reforms, and for the allocation of Marshall Aid, adding the stipulation that the primary purpose of such aid should be to stimulate employment. In reiteration of the central principle of parity which had been established in 1946, the requirement was included that workers should be represented on this body on an equal footing with the employers.[18] The resolution was based on an ÖGB proposal which had been submitted to the Cabinet some weeks previously. In April, following heated debate in parliament, a package of new laws was passed. The first of these set up an Economic Directorate comprising all Cabinet Ministers with the exception of the Ministers for Justice and Education. The Economic Partners, the three Chambers and the ÖGB, and the Austrian National Bank, would form a committee to advise the Directorate. The remaining new legislation contained regulations on foreign trade, transport, the distribution of raw materials, food rationing in the event of an emergency, and prices, which comprised the basic remit of the new body.[19] The Economic Directorate represented a significant step along the path towards the future Social Partnership model, for, unlike its predecessor, the ad hoc Economic Commission, it was designed to function as a permanent statutory body. Although it was required to report to parliament each quarter, the Directorate was granted direct responsibility for almost all aspects of economic policy formation. As a result, the influence of the Economic Partners, including the ÖGB and the Chamber of Labour, now extended far beyond the issue of wages and prices control and, moreover, it now had a basis in law. Böhm's dream of an unassailable role for labour in economic policy formation appeared to have become reality.

The position of the trade union leadership had been appreciably strengthened by the failure of the 1950 strikes, but, like its predecessors, the Fourth Wages and Prices Agreement did not succeed in stemming price rises. Not only were prices on the world market rising substantially in response to the Korean War, but German, Czech and Polish producers also put up the price of coal, adding significantly to the cost of Austrian imports. Moreover, as Marshall Aid was due to end in 1952, the government was once more faced with heavy pressure from the ECA to phase out the last remaining subsidies. In February 1951 the trade unions embarked on another series of individual wage negotiations which raised the wage level by between 10 and 12 per cent.[20] But, despite the proven inefficacy of earlier Wages and Prices Agreements, by that spring Federation leaders had become convinced that there was no alternative but to start negotiations for a fifth Agreement. According to an American Labor Report, informal talks actually began in April 1951, but they were delayed when the presidential election which was held on 6 May failed to produce an outright winner.[21] A second round of elections was set for 27 May. On 21 May, just one week before the run-off election, *Solidarität*, the official ÖGB newspaper, disclosed that the Economic Partners were about to begin a new round of discussions. The Partners met on 20 June, but when they failed to agree, negotiations were transferred to the new Economic Directorate. After a number of 'long and stormy sessions', a compromise was reached and details were released at a series of regional conferences of trade unions and shop stewards on 12 and 13 July.[22] On 14 July, the ÖGB executive and the Cabinet both ratified the Agreement. Despite its denials of talks in April and early May, the ÖGB was insistent that the negotiations for the new Agreement should be seen to have been conducted in full view of the public.

It is noteworthy that, in contrast to the Fourth Wages and Prices Agreement, it was the ÖGB leaders who pressed most vigorously for a Fifth Agreement. There are indications that by this time they believed that they had the power to achieve greater protection for real wages by minimising price increases and adjusting income tax laws to ensure that any increase in gross pay would go directly to swell wage packets. Without doubt, the 1951 Agreement was more complex than its predecessors. Wholesale prices for grains and dairy products were raised by 40–50 per cent, with prices in the shops rising on average by 50 per cent; gas prices went up by 74 per cent, electricity by 35 per cent, and the cost of postage was doubled. There were also increases in the cost of rail and tram travel and in social insurance contributions. But the Fifth Wages and Prices Agreement also included a complicated economic formula designed to convince workers that, despite previous disappointments, these price increases would not lead to a decline in real wages. Great stress was laid on raising the tax threshold, as a result of which, according to the *Arbeiter-Zeitung*, workers would receive a wage increase of 140 Schillings per month tax free; the increase in child allowances was also highlighted.[23] But labour leaders had made one concession which the newspaper did not announce immediately. The unions and the SPÖ had agreed to discussions on the lifting of the rent controls which had first been introduced in 1916. Rent control had been central to the whole Socialist electoral strategy in Red Vienna in the 1920s and, indeed, to the Socialists' policy of cheap workers' housing.[24] Its agreement to the removal of these controls was one indication of the distance which the labour movement had travelled since that time.

The increase in prices which followed the Fifth Wages and Prices Agreement was the highest since the economic crisis of 1947.[25] Yet workers responded to the announcement with mute resignation rather than outright hostility, and Communist attempts to rekindle the anger of September 1950 were ignored. There were no demonstrations or strikes. Moreover, there was little protest when unemployment continued to rise, reaching record levels in 1953 when the official figure was 8.5 per cent, 2.5 per cent higher than it had been in 1950.[26] The initial promise which labour leaders had made to workers when the First Wages and Prices Agreement was announced in 1947, and which they repeated in defence of each subsequent Agreement, was that a co-ordinated wages and prices policy would ensure full employment. Uncontrolled wage claims would be counter-productive, since runaway wage increases would merely fuel inflation. By 1953 it was clear that full employment had not been achieved, but by this time ÖGB leaders had consolidated their control over the trade union movement, increasing the grip of their organisation's bureaucracy and effectively stifling all stirrings of grass-roots militancy. Under Böhm's direction, the ÖGB had also established a statutory right to participate in economic policy formation through its membership of the Economic Directorate. The Austrian Trade Union Federation had thereby achieved a goal to which many other European labour movements could only aspire.[27] But this victory was soon under threat from the Constitutional Court, backed by the Chamber of Business, which in June 1952 ruled that the Law on Foreign Trade was unconstitutional on the grounds that it bound government ministers to follow the advice given by the Economic Directorate and therefore violated the sovereignty of parliament.[28] The Directorate itself only survived this ruling until 1954, when it was wound up.

Had the story ended there, the conclusion of this book would have been that the specific conditions which confronted Austria in the immediate post-war years led to a temporary situation in which politicians and the major economic interest groups secured the country's survival by constructing a system of joint decision-making and presenting this to the occupying powers and the general public as a successful exercise in consensus politics. The greatest external threat to the security of the new state was Soviet expansion; the greatest domestic threats were economic instability and labour militancy. The power of the trade union leaders rested on their ability to control the actions of their members and this they did in return for a seat, or several seats, at the high table of economic policy formation. However, once the threat of working-class protest had subsided, the employers withdrew their support for consensus politics and undermined the post-war culture of consensus by challenging the newly won legal status of the Economic Partnership. Indeed, in 1955, when the ÖGB Congress met for the third time, consensus appeared to have gone down in defeat. At this meeting, which took place after the State Treaty had been signed and the occupying forces had finally agreed to leave Austria, and at a moment when inflation was rising, delegates were more vocal than ever before in their criticisms of the leadership. They challenged Böhm's position on wages, his insistence that wage rises should be linked to increased productivity, and the failure of the ÖGB either to protect its members against unemployment or to win political support for new legislation on the length of the working day. There were also indications of schisms within the ÖGB itself, as members of the Socialist faction accused the ÖVP of sponsoring 'yellow' (i.e. company) unions, which would have undermined the unity and centralisation of the trade union movement.[29]

But the demise of the Economic Directorate did not after all mark the end of the ÖGB's hopes of gaining an institutional role for itself in economic policy formation. The main business of the Third Congress was to discuss a ten-point Action Programme drawn up by the Federation's executive committee that included the demand for the creation of a new institution comprising the Chambers and trade unions, which would draw up suggestions and advise the government on economic questions. The Action Programme was approved, but at this stage neither the government nor the Chamber of Business was prepared to resurrect the Economic Commission. Within less than a year, however, the presidents of the Chambers of Business and of Agriculture changed their minds after a boom in the economy had led to the dangerous combination of a shortage of skilled labour and rising prices. The result was a wave of industrial strikes and renewed demands from the ÖGB for the revival of the Economic Commission, which duly met in the autumn of 1956. Shortly thereafter the government set up a sub-committee composed of the Ministers of the Interior and of Finance and one representative each of the ÖGB and of the Chambers, to make recommendations on price policy. In 1957 the ÖGB offered to 'exert a strongly moderating influence' on wage claims in return for the setting up of a new joint commission to advise the government on measures to stabilise the economy.[30] The Joint Commission on Prices and Wages, or Parity Commission, was set up on 27 March 1957 with, initially, a nine-month mandate. It became a permanent institution in 1963 and its remit was extended to cover social welfare issues, taxation and fiscal policy, as well as wages and prices. It subsequently provided the framework for the extensive, institutionalised and centralised system of collective elite decision-making which is the Austrian Social Partnership, otherwise known as Austro-corporatism or 'consociationalism', and it accorded labour leaders an unusually powerful role in economic policy formation.[31]

By the later 1950s, the Austrian labour movement had travelled a long road since the fractious days of the First Republic and the repression which followed the civil war. Under Böhm's leadership, the ÖGB had emerged as the major force behind the consensus politics which became embedded in the political culture of the Second Republic. It had been the chief advocate of parity and the recognition of shared goals across the political and economic divide. In order to arrive at this position, its leaders had redefined the role of the unions, rejecting the principle that the interests of workers depended on their ability to win wage increases and replacing this with the doctrine that any significant improvement in living standards required sustained economic growth and constant monitoring of economic policy. Union leaders had begun to preach patience to their members as early as 1945, when living standards were abysmal and labour was in short supply. They continued to do so when the economy began to grow in response to Marshall Aid, but the constraints imposed by the terms of that Aid, the impact of the occupation on the domestic economy, and Austria's inability to trade successfully on the world market, all combined to widen the gap between prices and wages. As a result, labour leaders were admitted to the hallowed halls of economic decision-making. But when the patience of their members evaporated, as it did in 1950, the power of the ÖGB was momentarily threatened; that it emerged unshaken was due to the Soviet military presence, the bungled actions of the KPÖ and the fact that Austrian workers felt they had more to fear from the alleged Communist putsch than they did from wage restraint. The ÖGB's trump card remained its ability to control its membership. In the longer term, this was enough to persuade employers and the government to support the Social Partnership.

The political culture of the Second Republic was the product of an unusual set of circumstances. Austria experienced a protracted occupation in which from the outset the occupiers were divided among themselves. For ten years it was a state whose autonomy was ambiguous and whose leaders were forced to negotiate and bargain with the local representatives of two mutually hostile superpowers, the USSR and the USA. Those leaders found it necessary to present a united front in public and, to this end, they introduced procedures which emphasised consensus and harmony. Although the facade of unity sometimes tottered, most notably during election campaigns, it was successfully kept in place until the end of the occupation, by which time the concept of the Social Partnership had taken firm root. But the new and existing economic structures also affected the political culture. While there is no question that the Austro-corporatism of the post-war period laid the foundations for a peaceful and affluent society with little overt civil strife, this system of economic decision-making concentrated power in the hands of the peak interest groups and was run by an intricate network of committees and sub-committees. There was little direct accountability and an unhealthy level of patronage. It was, in effect, an oligarchy. Decisions continued to be hammered out in private sessions and presented to the general public as unanimously agreed policy. The lack of accountability weakened public debate on crucial issues. The 'victim' thesis and the 'putsch' myth both became enshrined in the public memory, laying Austrians open to ill-considered accusations of hypocrisy and an inability to confront their own past. The consensus culture was based on myopia. It was this failure to address the complexities of recent history that was exposed by both the Waldheim Affair and the Haider Phenomenon.

Notes

1 'Eine infamere Verdrehung der Tatsachen hat sich in Österreich ausser dem Naziregime wohl noch niemand geleistet', *Stenographische Protokolle*, 31. Sitzung des Nationalrates der Republik Österreich, 12 October 1950, 1096.

2 'mehr oder weniger schwer verletzt', *ibid.*, 1098–103.

3 The Donawitz shop stewards were exonerated by the Leoben Conciliation Board on 19 December, which ruled that, 'Nor has it been shown that the opponents of the petition formed a combination with the object of undermining the independence, the constitutionally established state and/or governmental structures, or the constitutional arrangements pertaining in Austria in contravention of the law, or of illegally preventing or hampering the implementation of laws, decrees, decisions or regulations laid down by the authorities.' (Es ist ferner nicht erwiesen, daß die Antragsgegner eine Verbindung gegründet hätten, deren Zweck es war, auf ungesetzliche Weise die Selbständigkeit, die verfassungsmässig festgestellte Staats- oder Regierungsform oder verfassungsmässige Einrichtungen Österreichs zu erschüttern, die Vollziehung von Gesetzen, Verordnungen, Entscheidungen und Verfügungen der Behörden gesetzwidrig zu verhindern oder zu erschweren), reprinted in *Wahrheit*, 21 December 1950.

4 'The Communist Attempt to promote a General Strike in Austria', NA, RG 59, 8, (OIR) Report No. 5461.

5 For example, in a telegram sent by the State Department to the Austrian Mission on 1 August 1951: 'Finally, it should not be overlooked that the main-

tenance of political and economic stability in Austria and the repelling of the totalitarian menace constitute an active contribution of this country to the defense of the free world.' NA, RG 84, Box 13, file 560.1.

6   The United States High Commissioner for Austria (Keyes) to the Department of the Army, 4 October 1950, *FRUS, 1950: Central and Eastern Europe; the Soviet Union*, vol. IV (Washington: Government Printing Office, 1980), 407–9.

7   'Memorandum of Conversations', NA, RG 84, Box 3, file 350. Donnelly's official title was Envoy Extraordinary and Minister Plenipotentiary. He took up his post on 20 September 1950.

8   Olah maintains that his movement had no links with similar organisations set up by the Americans in Europe, and that he made his initial contacts in the USA while there as part of the ÖGB delegation to the American Federation of Labor convention in 1948. Olah, *Die Erinnerungen*, 132, 143–9. Further questions were raised in 1996 when it became known that the Americans had set up secret arms stashes in Austria in the 1950s. See *Falter* (4/98), 8–9; Konrad and Lechner, '*Millionenverwechslung*', 63–87; Daniele Ganser, 'Terrorism in Western Europe: An Approach to NATO's Secret Stay-Behind Armies', *Whitehead Journal of Diplomacy and International Relations*, vol. VI, no.1, Winter/Spring 2005, 82–3.

9   'Aus dem Arbeitsbericht der Abteilung für innere Angelegenheiten der SČSK für Österreich für das Jahr 1950, 19. Jänner 1951', Suppan *et al.*, *Sowjetische Politik in Österreich*, 1945–1955. Donnelly advised Figl to stand firm on this issue. United States High Commissioner (Donnelly) to the Secretary of State, 7 December 1950, *FRUS 1950*, vol. IV, 426–7.

10   Klenner, *Die österreichischen Gewerkschaften*, 1476.

11   Gruber, 'Der Massenstreik gegen das 4. Lohn- Preisabkommen', 346–8.

12   'Annual Labor Report for Austria, 1950', dated 6 June 1951. NA, RG 84, NND 560, vol. 1, 14.

13   Austrian Labor Report, September 1950, appendix A, dated 23 October 1950. NA, RG 84, file 560, vol. 1.

14   Unsigned telegram, dated 6 December 1950, NA, RG 59, 863.06/12–1450.

15   'Information on Unemployment', Austrian Legation Washington D.C., 12 February 1951, *ibid*.

16   Böhm and Proksch to Donnelly, 20 January 1951, NA, RG 84, Box 16, file 560.1. This file also contains Donnelly's reply, in which he offers 'to assist in every way possible', as well as a memorandum recording that the issue letter had been sent.

17   The ÖGB continued to remind them of this. Later that year Proksch wrote to the International Confederation of Free Trade Unions asking members to lobby politicians in their respective countries in support of Austrian requests for increased economic assistance from the United States. The letter criticises the Secretary of State, Dean Acheson, for failing to pay enough attention to the 'special nature of the Austrian situation': 'It should not be overlooked that the maintenance of political and economic stability in Austria and the repelling of the totalitarian menace constitute an active contribution of this country to the defence of the free world. . . . This genuine contribution to defence can, however, only be undertaken by the Austrian workers if they have the assurance that their special position will be taken into account and that the free world is doing everything in its power to defend their economic, social and political

interests.' The letter was forwarded to the State Department, which produced the temporising response that 'the questions raised by Proksch are under active consideration by the Legation and the ECA Mission in Vienna'. Proksch to the ICFTU, 1 August 1951, NA, RG 84, Box 16, file 560.1

18 *Arbeiter-Zeitung*, 14 February 1951.

19 *Arbeiter-Zeitung*, 11 March 1951; Emmerich Tálos, 'Sozialpartnerschaft: Zur Entwicklung und Entwicklungsdynamik kooperativ-konzertierter Politik in Österreich', in Peter Gerlich, E. Grande, and W.C. Müller, *Sozialpartnerschaft in der Krise: Leistungen und Grenzen des Neokorporatismus in Österreich* (Vienna: Böhlau, 1985), 65–7. The KPÖ and VdU both opposed the new legislation on the grounds that the Directorate would undermine the authority of parliament.

20 'The Fifth Wage-Price Agreement', American Legation Report dated 24 July 1951, NA, RG 84, Box 14, file 500.2.

21 Austrian Labor Report dated 22 May 1951. NA, RG 59, 863.06/5–2251. Karl Renner died on 30 December 1950. There were four candidates in the first election for his successor, which was held on 6 May, namely Burghard Breitner (VdU), Gottlieb Fiala (KPÖ), Theodor Körner (SPÖ) and Heinrich Gleißner (ÖVP). Gleißner obtained 40.1 per cent of the vote and Körner 39.2 per cent. Körner won the run-off election on 27 May, despite coming first only in Vienna, Carinthia and Styria, in the last by just 54 votes.

22 *Ibid.*

23 *Arbeiter-Zeitung*, 12 July 1951.

24 Lewis, 'Red Vienna: Socialism in One City, 1918–27', 335–54.

25 Zimmermann, 'Wirtschaftsentwicklung in Österreich 1945–51', 321.

26 Kammer für Arbeiter und Angestellte für Wien, *Wirtschafts- und Sozialstatistisches Handbuch 1945–1969* (Vienna: Verlag der Kammer für Arbeiter und Angestellte für Wien, 1970), table II.26, 276.

27 The significance of the fact that the Economic Directorate had its basis in statute was clearly recognised during the debate on the national economy at the second congress of the ÖGB. See *Stenographisches Protokoll des II. Kongresses des Österreichischen Gewerkschaftsbundes vom 1. bis 5. Oktober 1951 im Wiener Konzerthaus* (Vienna: Verlag des Österreichischen Gewerkschaftbundes, 1951), 130–8.

28 Tálos, 'Sozialpartnerschaft: Zur Entwicklung und Entwicklungsdynamik kooperativ-konzertierter Politik in Österreich', 66. The case was brought before the court by the provincial government of Vorarlberg.

29 *Stenographisches Protokoll des III. Kongresses des Österreichischen Gewerkschaftsbundes vom 18. bis 22.Oktober 1955 im Wiener Konzerthaus* (Vienna: Verlag des Österreichischen Gewerkschaftbundes, 1955), 193–246.

30 Emmerich Tálos and Bernhard Kittel, 'Roots of Austro-Corporatism: Institutional Preconditions and Cooperation before and after 1945', in Bischof and Pelinka (eds), *Austro-Corporatism, Past, Present and Future*, 41–2.

31 Lewis, 'Austria in Historical Perspective: From Civil War to Social Partnership', 19–22. The significance of the Social Partnership diminished after the collapse of the Eastern Bloc and Austria's admission to the European Union in 1995.

Bibliography

Archives

Austria
Österreichisches Staatsarchiv, Archiv der Republik, (AdR)
  Bundeskanzleramt (BKA) (including Ministerratsprotokolle/MRP)
  Bundeskanzleramt/Auswärtige Angelegenheiten (BKA/AA)
  Bundesministerium für Inneres (BMfI)
  Bundesministerium für Soziale Verwaltung (BMfsV)
Verein der Geschichte der Arbeiterbewegung,
  SPÖ Akten
  Adolf Schärf Nachlaß
  Oskar Helmer Nachlaß
Zentrales Parteiarchiv der KPÖ
Kammer für Arbeiter und Angestellte, Vienna
  Dokumentationsarchiv des österreichischen Widerstand (DÖW)

The United Kingdom
The National Archives (TNA) (London): Public Record Office (PRO)
  Foreign Office (FO)
  Labour and Employment Office: Austria (LAB)

The United States
National Archives, Washington DC (NA)
  State Department
  Records of the Department of State Relating to the Internal Affairs of Austria
    (RG 59)
  Political Advisers (POLAD) (RG 84)

Russia
Russian State Archive of Socio-Political History (RGASPI)
Foreign Policy Archive of the Russian Federation (Austrian Section) (AVP RF)

208   *Bibliography*

Published records

Tätigkeitsbericht des Österreichischen Gewerkschaftsbundes: 1945–47; 1950; 1951; 1955; 1959.

Stenographisches Protokoll des II. Kongresses des Österreichischen Gewerkschaftsbundes vom 1. bis 5. Oktober 1951 im Wiener Konzerthaus (Vienna: Verlag des Österreichischen Gewerkschaftsbundes, 1951).

Stenographisches Protokoll des III. Kongresses des Österreichischen Gewerkschaftsbundes vom 18. bis 22. Oktober 1955 im Wiener Konzerthaus (Vienna: Verlag des Österreichischen Gewerkschaftsbundes, 1955).

ÖGB Bildungsfunktion: Nov.–Dec. 1953; Jan.–Feb. 1956; Jan.–March 1958; Jan.–March 1960.

Arbeiterkammer Wien, Jahrbuch: 1947; 1948; 1949; 1950; 1964.

Arbeiterkammer in Innsbruck, Jahresbericht: 1947; 1948; 1949; 1950; 1951.

Foreign Relations of the United States, Diplomatic Papers (FRUS), 1944, vol. I, *General* (Washington: Government Printing Office, 1966).

FRUS, 1945, vol. III, *European Advisory Commission; Austria; Germany* (Washington: Government Printing Office, 1968).

FRUS, 1950, vol. IV, *Central and Eastern Europe; the Soviet Union* (Washington: Government Printing Office, 1980).

Report on Vienna Mission 3 June 1945 to 13 June 1945, reprinted in Siegfried Beer and Eduard G. Staudinger, 'Die "Vienna Mission" der Westalliierten im Juni 1945', in *Studien zur Wiener Geschichte, Jahrbuch des Vereins für Geschichte der Stadt Wien*, vol. 50 (Vienna, 1994), 317–412.

Wirtschafts- und sozialstatistisches Handbuch, Kammer für Arbeiter und Angestellte für Wien: 1945–1969 (Vienna: Verlag der Kammer für Arbeiter und Argestellte für Wien, 1970).

Protokoll des Achten Arbeiter Kammertages abgehalten am 18. und 19 März 1948 (Vienna, 1948), 32–5.

Protokolle des Kabinettsrates der Provisorischen Regierung Karl Renner, Gertrude Enderle-Burcel *et al.* (eds)
   Volume 1, *29. April 1945 bis 10. Juli 1945* (Vienna: Verlag Österreich, 1995).
   Volume 2, *17. Juli bis 5. September 1945* (Vienna: Verlag Österreich, 1995).
   Volume 3, *12. September bis 17. Dezember 1945* (Vienna: Verlag Österreich, 2003).

Die Ergebnisse der österrichischen Volkszählung rom 22. März 1934 (Vienna: Verlag der österrichischen Staatsdruckerei, 1935).

Documents on German Foreign Policy, 1918–1945, Series C, vol. V (London: HMSO, 1966).

Documents on German Foreign Policy, 1918–1945, Series D, vol. I (London: HMSO, 1949).

Report mandated by the XIV members of the European Union through the President of the European Court of Human Rights to look at the commitment of the Austrian Government to the common European values, in particular concerning the rights of minorities, refugees and immigrants. Written by Martti Ahtisaari, Jochen Frowein and Marcelino Oreja, submitted and accepted on 8 September 2000 (Paris: 2000).

The Waldheim Report submitted to Federal Chancellor Dr Franz Vranitzky by the International Commission of Historians designated to Establish the Military

Service of Lieutenant/1st Lieutenant Kurt Waldheim (Copenhagen: Museum Tusculanum Press, 1993).

Rot-Weiss-Rot-Buch. Darstellungen, Dokumente und Nachweise zur Vorgeschichte und Geschichte der Okkupation Österreichs (nach amtlichen Quellen) (Vienna: Verlag der österreichischen Staatsdruckerei, 1946).

Christine Klusacek and Kurt Stimmer (eds), *Dokumentation zur österreichischen Zeitgeschichte 1928–1933*, 2 vols. (Vienna: Jugend und Volk, 1982).

Wolfgang Mueller, Arnold Suppan, Norman Naimark and Gennadji Bordjugov (eds), *Sowjetische Politik in Österreich 1945–1955. Dokumente aus russischen Archiven* (Vienna: Verlag der Österreichischen Akademie der Wissenschaften, 2005).

Stefan Karner, Barbara Stelz-Marx and Alexander Tschubarjan (eds), *Die Rote Armee in Österreich. Sowjetische Besatzung 1945–1955*, vol. 1, *Dokumente*; vol. 2, *Beiträge* (Graz: Oldenbourg, 2005).

Newspapers

Alpenruf
Arbeiter-Zeitung www.arbeiter-zeitung.at (for issues published from 5 August 1945).
Falter
Kleines Volksblatt
Neue Zeit (Graz)
Neue Zeit (Linz)
Neues Österreich
Österreichische Volksstimme
profil
Stern
Volksstimme
Weg und Ziel
Zukunft

Websites

Wien im Rückblick www.wien.gv.at/ma53/45jahre/inhalt.htm
Arbeiter-Zeitung www.arbeiter-zeitung.at
Yalta Agreement www.yale.edu/lawweb/Avalon/wwii/yalta.html

Exhibition catalogues

Susanne Breuss (ed.), *Die Sinalco-Epoche. Essen, Trinken, Konsumieren nach 1945* (Vienna: Czernin Verlag/Wien Museum, 2005).

Frauenleben 1945. Kriegsende in Wien. Sonderausstellung des Historischen Museums der Stadt Wien (Vienna: Eigenverlag der Museen der Stadt Wien, 1995).

Hans Petschar, *Die junge Republik. Alltagsbilder aus Österreich 1945–1955* (Vienna: Ueberreiter, 2005).

Printed sources

75 Jahre Kammern für Arbeiter und Angestellte (Vienna: Verlag des Österreichischen Gewerkscharftbundes, 1995).

Arnberger, Heinz, Winfried R. Garscha and Christa Mitterrutzner (eds), *'Anschluß' 1938. Eine Dokumentation* (Vienna: Österreichischer Bundesverlag, 1988).

Ausch, Karl, *Erlebte Wirtschaftsgeschichte. Österreichische Wirtschaft seit 1945* (Vienna: Europa Verlag, 1963).

Bauer, Otto, *Zwischen zwei Weltkriegen? Die Krise der Weltwirtschaft, der Demokratie und des Sozialismus* (Bratislava: E. Prager, 1936).

Berg, Matthew Paul (ed.), in collaboration with Jill Lewis and Oliver Rathkolb, *The Struggle for a Democratic Austria. Bruno Kreisky on Peace and Social Justice* (New York and Oxford: Berghahn, 2000).

Böhm, Johann, *Erinnerungen aus meinem Leben* (Vienna: Europa Verlag, 1964).

Buttinger, Joseph, *In the Twilight of Socialism: A History of the Revolutionary Socialists of Austria* (London: Weidenfeld and Nicolson, 1953).

Clare, George, *Last Waltz in Vienna: The Destruction of a Family, 1842–1942* (London: Macmillan, 1981).

Deutsch, Julius, *Ein weiter Weg* (Vienna: Amalthea Verlag, 1960).

Eden, Anthony, *The Eden Memoirs*, vol. 3, *The Reckoning* (London: Cassell, 1965).

Figl, Leopold, *Reden für Österreich* (Vienna: Europa Verlag, 1965).

Fischer, Ernst, *The Rebirth of my Country: A series of broadcasts on Austria over Moscow radio* (London: Austrian Centre, 1944).

Fischer, Ernst, *Das Jahr der Befreiung. Aus Reden und Aufsätzen* (Vienna: Stern Verlag, 1946).

Fischer, Ernst, *An Opposing Man*, trans. P. and B. Ross (London: Allen Lane, 1969).

Fischer, Ernst, *Das Ende einer Illusion. Erinnerungen 1945–1955* (Vienna: Molden, 1973).

Gedye, G.E.R., *Fallen Bastions: The Central European Tragedy* (London: Victor Gollancz, 1939).

Haider, Jörg, *Die Freiheit, die ich meine. Das Ende des Proporzstaats. Plädoyer für eine Dritte Republik* (Frankfurt/Main: Ullstein, 1993).

Helmer, Oskar, *50 Jahre Erlebte Geschichte* (Vienna: Verlag der Wiener Volksbuchhandlung, 1957).

Hitler, Adolf, *Mein Kampf*, with an introduction by D.C. Watt (London: Hutchinson, 1969).

Karner, Stefan, Barbara Stelz-Marx and Alexander Tschubarjan (eds), *Die Rote Armee in Österreich. Sowjetische Besatzung 1945–1955*, vol. 1, *Dokumente*; vol. 2, *Beiträge* (Graz: Oldenbourg, 2005).

Klenner, Fritz, *Putschversuch – oder nicht?* (Vienna: Pressereferat des österreichischen Gewerkschaftsbundes, 1951).

Knight, Robert (ed.), *'Ich bin dafür, die Sache in die Länge zu ziehen.' Wortprotokolle* (Frankfurt am Main: Athenäum, 1988).

Layton, W.T., and Charles Rist, *The Economic Situation of Austria. Report presented to the Council of the League of Nations by W.T. Layton, C.H., and Charles Rist* (Geneva: League of Nations, 1925).

Lothar, Ernst, *Returning to Vienna* (New York: Doubleday, 1949).

Migsch, Alfred, *Anschlag auf Österreich. Ein Tatsachenbericht über den kommunistischen Putschversuch im September – Oktober 1950* (Vienna: Zentralsekretariat der SPÖ, 1950).

Muchitsch, Max, *Die Partisanengruppe Leoben-Donawitz* (Vienna: Europa Verlag, 1966).

Mueller, Wolfgang, Arnold Suppan, Norman Naimark and Gennadji Bordjugov (eds), *Sowjetische Politik in Österreich 1945–1955. Dokumente aus russischen Archiven* (Vienna: Verlag der Österreichischen Akademie der Wissenschaften, 2005).

Olah, Franz, *Die Erinnerungen* (Vienna: Amalthea, 1995).

Rathkolb, Oliver, *Gesellschaft und Politik am Beginn der Zweiten Republik. Vertrauliche Berichte der US-Militäradministration aus Österreich in englischer Originalverfassung* (Vienna: Böhlau, 1985).

Rathkolb, Oliver, *Washington ruft Wien. US-Großmachtpolitik und Österreich 1953–1963; mit Exkursen zu CIA-Waffenlagern, NATO-Connection, Neutralitätsdebatte* (Vienna: Böhlau, 1997)

Renner, Karl, *Denkschrift über die Geschichte der Unabhängigkeitserklärung Österreichs und die Einsetzung der Provisorischen Regierung der Republik* (Vienna: Österreichische Staatsdruckerei, 1945).

Renner, Karl, *An der Wende zweier Zeiten* (Vienna, Danubia Verlag, 1946).

Renner, Karl, *Österreich von der Ersten zur Zweiten Republik* (Vienna: Wiener Volksbuchhandlung, 1953).

Scharf, Erwin, *Ich darf nicht schweigen* (Vienna: self-publishing, 1948).

Scharf, Erwin, *Ich hab's gewagt mit Sinnen. Entscheidungen im anti-faschistischen Widerstand. Erlebnisse in der politischen Konfrontation* (Vienna: Globus, 1988).

Schärf, Adolf, *April 1945 in Wien* (Vienna: Verlag der Wiener Volksbuchhandlung, 1948).

Schärf, Adolf, *Österreichs Erneuerung 1945–1955. Das erste Jahrzehnt der zweiten Republik* (Vienna: Verlag der Wiener Volksbuchhandlung, 1955).

Schärf, Adolf, *Erinnerungen aus meinem Leben* (Vienna: Wiener Volksbuchhandlung, 1963).

Schöner, Josef, *Wiener Tagebuch 1944/1945* (Vienna: Böhlau, 1992).

Schuschnigg, Kurt, *Austrian Requiem* (London: Victor Gollancz, 1947).

Shtemenks, S.M., *The Soviet General Staff at War, 1941–1945* (Moscow: Progress Publishers, 1970).

Sturzeis, Fritz, *Österreich 1945. Drittes Reich – Kriegsende – 2. Republik. Langersehnte Nachrichten und ausgewählte Dokumente von Menschen, die es erlebt haben* (Vienna: Verlag Pollischansky, 2001).

Wachs, Walter, *Kampfgruppe Steiermark* (Vienna: Europa Verlag, 1968).

Wagnleitner, Reinhold (ed.), *Understanding Austria: The Political Reports and Analyses of Martin F. Herz, Political Officer of the US Legation in Vienna 1945–1948* (Salzburg: Neugebauer, 1984).

Wagnleitner, Reinhold (ed.), *Diplomatie zwischen Parteiproporz und Weltkonflikt: Briefe, Dokumente und Memoranden aus dem Nachlaß Walter Wodaks, 1945–1950* (Salzburg: Neugebauer, 1980).

Books

Ableitinger, Alfred, Siegfried Beer and Eduard G. Staudinger, *Österreich unter alliierter Besatzung 1945–1955* (Vienna: Böhlau, 1998).

Albrich, Thomas, Klaus Eisterer, Michael Gehler and Rolf Steininger (eds), *Österreich in den Fünfzigern* (Innsbruck: Österreichischer Studienverlag, 1995).

Ardelt, Rudolf G., Wolfgang J.A. Huber and Anton Staudinger (eds), *Unterdrückung und Emanzipation: Festschrift für Erika Weinzierl* (Vienna: Geyer, 1985).

Bader, William, *Austria Between East and West, 1945–1955* (Stanford, CA: Stanford University Press, 1966).

Bader, W.B., *A Communist Failure: Occupied Austria 1945–1950* (PhD Dissertation, New Jersey, 1964).

Balfour, Michael, and John Mair, *Four-Power Control in Germany and Austria, 1945–1946* (London: Oxford University Press, 1956).

Bauer, R. (ed.), *The Austrian Solution* (Charlottesville, VA: University Press of Virginia, 1982).

Baumgartner, Marianne, '*Jo, des waren halt schlechte Zeiten . . .*'. *Das Kriegsende und die unmittelbare Nachkriegszeit in den lebensgeschichtlichen Erzählungen von Frauen aus dem Mostviertel* (Frankfurt am Main: Peter Lang, 1994).

Berger, Stefan, and Hugh Compston (eds), *Policy Concertation and Social Partnership. Lessons for the 21st Century* (New York/Oxford: Berghahn, 2002).

Bischof, Günter, Anton Pelinka and Dieter Stiefel, *The Marshall Plan in Austria* (New Brunswick, NJ: Transaction, 2000).

Bischof, Günter, and Josef Leidenfrost (eds), *Die bevormundete Nation. Österreich und die Alliierten* (Vienna: Haymon Verlag, 1988).

Bischof, Günter, *Austria in the First Cold War. The Leverage of the Weak* (Basingstoke: Macmillan, 1999).

Bischof, Günter, and Anton Pelinka (eds), *Austria in the Nineteen Fifties* (New Brunswick, NJ: Transaction, 1995).

Bischof, Günter, and Anton Pelinka (eds), *Austro-Corporatism: Past, Present and Future*, (New Brunswick, NJ: Transaction, 1996)

Bischof, Günter, Anton Pelinka and Alexander Lassner (eds), *The Dollfuss/ Schuschnigg Era in Austria. A Reassessment* (New Brunswick, NJ: Transaction, 2003).

Blinkhorn, Martin (ed.), *Fascists and Conservatives: the Radical Right and the Establishment in Twentieth-Century Europe* (London: Unwin Hyman, 1990).

Böhmer, Peter, *Wer konnte, griff zu. Arisierte Güter und NS-Vermögen im Krauland-Ministerium, 1945–1949* (Vienna: Böhlau, 1999).

Botz, Gerhard, *Wien vom 'Anschluß' zum Krieg* (Vienna: Jugend und Volk, 1978).

Botz, Gerhard, *Der Nationalsozialismus in Wien. Machtübernahme und Herrschafts-sicherung* (Vienna: Buchloe, 1988).

Breuning, Eleonore, Jill Lewis and Gareth Pritchard, *Power and the People: A Social History of Central European Politics* (Manchester: Manchester University Press, 2005).

Bukey, Evan Burr, *Hitler's Hometown: Linz, Austria, 1908–1945* (Bloomington, IN: Indiana University Press, 1986).

Bukey, Evan Burr, *Hitler's Austria* (Chapel Hill, NC: University of North Carolina Press, 2000).

Bullock, Alan, *The Life and Times of Ernest Bevin*, vol. 3, *Foreign Secretary 1949–1951* (New York/London: Norton, 1983).

Bushell, Anthony (ed.), *Austria 1945–1955: Studies in Political and Cultural Re-emergence* (Cardiff: University of Wales Press, 1996).

Carew, Anthony, *Labour under the Marshall Plan* (Manchester: Manchester University Press, 1987).

Crampton, R.J., *Eastern Europe in the Twentieth Century – and after* (2nd edn, London: Routledge, 1997).

Cronin, Audrey Kurth, *Great Power Politics and the Struggle over Austria* (Ithaca, NY: Cornell University Press, 1986).

Deák, István, Jan T. Gross and Tony Judt (eds), *The Politics of Retribution in Europe: World War II and its Aftermath* (Princeton, NJ: Princeton University Press, 2000).

Ducynska, Ilona, *Workers in Arms* (New York: Monthly Review Press, 1978).

Duchen, Claire, and Irene Bandhauer-Schöffmann, *When the War was Over: Women, War and Peace in Europe, 1945–1956* (Leicester: Leicester University Press, 2000).

Epler, Ernst, *Der grosse Streik* (Vienna: Stern-Verlag, 1965).

Erickson, John, *The Road to Berlin: Stalin's War with Germany*, vol. 2 (New Haven, CT: Yale University Press, 1999).

Feichtlbauer, Hubert, *The Austrian Dilemma: An Inquiry into National Socialism and Racism in Austria* (Vienna: Holzhausen, 2001).

Fröschl, Erich, Maria Mesner and Helge Zoitl (eds), *Die Bewegung. Hundert Jahre Sozialdemokratie in Österreich* (Vienna: Passagen Verlag, 1990).

Fulbrook, Mary, *The Fontana History of Germany 1918–1990: The Divided Nation* (London: Fontana, 1991).

Gehl, Jürgen, *Austria, Germany and the Anschluss, 1931–1938* (Oxford: Oxford University Press, 1963).

Gerlich, Peter, E. Grande and W.C. Müller, *Sozialpartnerschaft in der Krise. Leistungen und Grenzen des Neokorporatismus in Österreich* (Vienna: Böhlau, 1985).

Goode, D.F., M. Grandner and M.J. Maynes (eds), *Austrian Women in the Nineteenth and Twentieth Centuries: Cross-Disciplinary Perspectives* (Providence, RI: Berghahn, 1996).

Gruber, Ronald, 'Der Massenstreik gegen das 4. Lohn-Preisabkommen im September/Oktober 1950' (PhD Dissertation, University of Vienna, 1975).

Gruber, Ronald, and Manfred Hörzinger, *... bis der Preistreiberpakt fällt. Der Massenstreik der österreichischen Arbeiter im September/Oktober 1950* (Vienna: Alois Wieser Gesellschaft, 1975).

Gulick, C.A., *Austria from Habsburg to Hitler*, 2 vols. (Berkeley, CA: University of California Press, 1948).

Hanisch, Ernst, *Der lange Schatten des Staates. Österreichische Gesellschafts-geschichte im 20. Jahrhundert* (Vienna: Ueberreuter, 1994).

Hannak, Jacques, *Karl Renner und seine Zeit* (Vienna: Europa Verlag, 1965).

Hannl, Margarete, 'Mit den Russen leben'. *Ein Beitrag zur Geschichte der Besatzungszeit im Mühlviertel* (Diplomarbeit, University of Salzburg, 1988).

Hautmann, Hans, Winfried Garscha and Willi Weinert, *Die Kommunistische Partei Österreichs: Beiträge zu ihrer Geschichte* (Vienna: Globus Verlag, 1987).

Herz, Martin F., *Beginnings of the Cold War* (Bloomington, IN: Indiana University Press, 1966).

Höbelt, Lothar, *Von der Vierten Partei zur Dritten Kraft. Die Geschichte der VdU* (Graz: Leopold Stocker Verlag, 1999).

Hobsbawm, Eric, *The Age of Extremes in the Short Twentieth Century* (London: Michael Joseph, 1994).

Hogan, Michael, *The Marshall Plan: America, Britain and the reconstruction of Western Europe, 1947–1952* (Cambridge: Cambridge University Press, 1987).

Jagschitz, Gerhard, and Klaus Dieter Mulley (eds), *Die 'wilden' fünfziger Jahren. Gesellschaft, Formen und Gefühle eines Jahrzehnts in Österreich* (St Pölten: Verlag Niederösterreichisches Pressehaus, 1985).

Judt, Tony, *Postwar: A History of Europe since 1945* (London: Penguin, 2005).

Kater, Michael, *The Twisted Muse: Musicians and their Music in the Third Reich* (London/New York: Oxford University Press, 1997).

Keyserlingk, Robert H., *Austria in World War II* (Kingston/Montreal: McGill-Queens University Press, 1988).

Kindermann, Gottfried Karl, *Hitler's Defeat in Austria: Europe's first Containment of Nazi Expansionism* (London: Hurst, 1988).

Kirk, Timothy, *Nazism and the Working Class in Austria* (Cambridge: Cambridge University Press, 1996).

Klein, Erich (ed.), *Die Russen in Wien. Die Befreiung Österreichs, Wien, 1945: Augenzeugenberichte und über 400 unpublizierte Fotos aus Russland* (Vienna: Falter Verlag, 1995).

Klenner, Fritz, *Die österreichischen Gewerkschaften*, 2 vols. (Vienna: Verlag des Österreichischen Gewerkschaftsbundes, 1953).

Knight, Robert, *British Policy towards Occupied Austria 1945–1950* (PhD dissertation, University of London, 1986).

Konrad, Helmut, and Manfred Lechner, *'Millionenverwechslung'. Franz Olah. Die Kronenzeitung. Geheimdienste* (Vienna: Böhlau, 1992).

Kos, W., *Eigenheim Österreich: Zu Politik, Kultur und Alltag nach 1945* (Vienna: Sonderzahl, 1994).

Kos, Wolfgang, and Georg Rigele (eds), *Inventur 1945/55. Österreich im ersten Jahrzehnt der Zweiten Republik* (Vienna: Sonderzahl, 1996).

Kreissler, Felix, *Der Österreicher und seine Nation. Ein Lernprozess mit Hindernissen* (Vienna: Böhlau, 1984).

Krohn, Claus Dieter, and Patrik von zur Mühlen (eds), *Handbuch der deutschsprachigen Emigration 1933–1945* (Darmstadt: Primus Verlag, 1998).

Leichter, Otto, *Österreichs Freie Gewerkschaften im Untergrund* (Vienna: Europa Verlag, 1963).

Leichter, Otto, *Zwischen zwei Diktaturen. Österreichs Revolutionäre Sozialisten 1934–1938* (Vienna: Europa Verlag, 1968).

Lewis, Jill, *Fascism and the Working Class in Austria 1918–1934* (Oxford: Berg, 1991).

Luther, K.R., and Peter Pulzer, *Austria 1945–95: Fifty Years of the Second Republic* (London: Ashgate, 1998).

Luža, Radomir, *Resistance in Austria, 1938–1945* (Minneapolis, MN: University of Minnesota Press, 1984).

Luža, Radomir, *Austro-German Relations in the Anschluss Era* (Princeton, NJ: Princeton University Press, 1975).

Mähr, Wilfried, *Der Marshallplan in Österreich* (Graz: Verlag Styria, 1989).

Maimann, Helene, *Politik im Wartesaal. Österreichische Exilpolitik in Großbritannien 1938–1945* (Vienna: Böhlau, 1975).

Malia, Martin, *The Soviet Tragedy: A History of Socialism in Russia, 1917–1991* (New York: Maxwell Macmillan International, 1994).

März, Eduard, *Österreichs Wirtschaft zwischen Ost und West. Eine sozialistische Analyse* (Vienna: Europäische Perspektiven, 1965).

Mausbach, Wilfried, *Zwischen Morgenthau und Marshall: Das wirtschaftspolitische Deutschlandkonzept der USA 1944–1947. Forschungen und Quellen zur Zeitgeschichte* (Düsseldorf: Droste, 1996).

Milward, Alan, *The Reconstruction of Western Europe* (London: Methuen, 1984).

Mitten, Richard, *The Politics of Antisemitic Prejudice: The Waldheim Phenomenon in Austria* (Boulder, CO: Westview Press, 1992).

Mueller, Wolfgang, Suppan, Arnold, Naimark, Norman and Bordjugov, Gennadji, (eds), *Sowjetische Politik in Österreich 1945–1955. Dokumente aus russischen Archiven* (Vienna: Verlag der O-Sterreichischen Akademie der Wissenschaften, 2005).

Mulley, Ludwig, Dieter Klaus and Robert Streibel, *Der Oktoberstreik 1950* (Vienna: Picus Verlag, 1990).

Naimark, Norman, *The Russians in Germany: A History of the Soviet Zone of Occupation, 1945–1947* (Cambridge, MA: Yale University Press, 1995).

Naimark, Norman, and Leonid Gibianskii (eds), *The Establishment of Communist Regimes in Eastern Europe, 1944–1949* (Boulder, CO: Westview Press, 1997).

Oxaal, Ivaar, Michael Pollak and Gerhard Botz (eds), *Jews, Anti-Semitism and Culture in Vienna* (London: Routledge & Kegan Paul, 1987).

Parkinson, F. (ed.), *Conquering the Past: Austrian Nazism Yesterday and Today* (Detroit, MI: Wayne State University Press, 1989).

Pelinka, Anton, *Modellfall Österreich. Möglichkeiten und Grenzen der Sozialpartnerschaft* (Vienna: Braumüller, 1981).

Pelinka, Peter, *Erbe und Neubeginn: Die Revolutionären Sozialisten in Österreich 1934–1938* (Vienna: Europa Verlag, 1981).

Pelinka, Anton, *Karl Renner zur Einführung* (Hamburg: Junius, 1989).

Pelinka, Anton, *Austria: Out of the Shadow of the Past* (Boulder, CO: Westview Press, 1998).

Pick, Hella, *Guilty Victim: Austria from the Holocaust to Haider* (London: I.B. Taurus, 2000).

Pittaway, Mark, *Eastern Europe 1939–2000* (London: Arnold, 2004).

Portisch, Hugo, and Sepp Riff, *Österreich II. Die Wiedergeburt unseres Staates* (Vienna: Kremayr and Scherlau, 1985).

Priester, Eva, *Der grosse Streik. Tatsachenbericht über den Oktoberstreik 1950* (Vienna: Globus, no date).

Rabinbach, Anson, *The Crisis of Austrian Socialism: from Red Vienna to Civil War 1927–1934* (Chicago, IL: University of Chicago Press, 1983).

Rauchensteiner, Manfried, *Der Krieg in Österreich 1945* (Vienna: Österreichischer Bundesverlag, 1984).

Rauchensteiner, Manfried, *Der Sonderfall. Die Besatzungszeit in Österreich 1945–1955* (Graz: Verlag Styria, 1995).

Rauchensteiner, Manfried, and Wolfgang Etschmann (eds), *Österreich 1945. Ein Ende und viele Anfänge* (Graz: Verlag Styria, 1997).

Rauscher, Walter, *Karl Renner. Ein österreichischer Mythos* (Vienna: Ueberreuter, 1995).

Rothschild, K.W., *The Austrian Economy since 1945* (Aberdeen: Royal Institute of International Affairs, 1950).

Safrian, Hans, and Hans Witek (eds), *Und keiner war dabei. Dokumente des alltäglichen Antisemitismus in Wien 1938* (Vienna: Picus Verlag, 1988).

Schapiro, Leonard, *The Communist Party of the Soviet Union* (London: Eyre and Spottiswoode, 1960).

Schleicher, Barbara, *Heißes Eisen. Zur Unternehmenspolitik der Österreichisch-Alpine Montangesellschaft in den Jahren 1918–1933* (Frankfurt am Main: Peter Lang, 1999).

Schmidl, Erwin, *Österreich im frühen Kalten Krieg. Spione, Partisanen, Kriegspläne* (Vienna: Böhlau, 2000).

Shell, Kurt L., *The Transformation of Austrian Socialism* (Albany, NY: State University of New York Press, 1962).

Spitzer, Rudolf, *Karl Seitz. Waisenknabe – Staatspräsident – Bürgermeister von Wien* (Vienna: Franz Deuticke, 1994).

Stadler, Karl, *Österreich 1938–1945. Im Spiegel der NS-Akten* (Vienna: Herold, 1966).

Stadler, Karl, *Austria* (London: E. Benn, 1971).

Stadler, Karl, *Adolf Schärf. Mensch – Politiker – Staatsmann* (Vienna: Europa Verlag, 1982).

Stearman, William Lloyd, *The Soviet Union and the Occupation of Austria (an analysis of Soviet policy in Austria, 1945–1955)* (Bonn: Verlag für Zeitarchive, 1960).

Steininger, Rolf, *Der Staatsvertrag. Österreich im Schatten von deutscher Frage und Kaltem Krieg 1938–1955* (Innsbruck: Studien Verlag, 2005).

Steininger, Rolf, Günther Bischof and Michael Gehler, *Austria in the Twentieth Century* (New Brunswick/London: Transaction, 2002).

Rodney Stiefbold *et al.* (eds), *Wahlen und Parteien in Österreich*, vol. 4, *Nationalratswahl* (Vienna: Jugend und Volk, 1966).

Stiefel, Dieter, *Entnazifizierung in Österreich* (Vienna: Europa Verlag, 1981).

Stourzh, Gerald, *Geschichte des Österreichischen Staatsvertrages 1945–1955: Österreichs Weg zur Neutralität* (Graz: Verlag Styria, 1985).

Svoboda, Wilhelm, *Die Partei, die Republik und der Mann mit den vielen Gesichtern. Oskar Helmer und Österrreich II, eine Korrektur* (Vienna: Böhlau, 1993).

Svoboda, Wilhelm, *Franz Olah, Eine Spurensicherung* (Vienna: Promedia, 1990).

Swain, Geoffrey, and Nigel Swain, *Eastern Europe since 1945* (3rd edn, London: Macmillan, 2003).

Sweeney, Jim, Josef Weidenholzer and Jeremy Leaman (eds), *Austria: A Study in Modern Achievement* (Aldershot: Avebury, 1988).

Tálos, Emmerich, *Sozialpartnerschaft. Kontinuität und Wandel eines Modells* (Vienna: Verlag für Gesellschaftskritik, 1993).

Emmerich Tálos, 'Sozialpartnerschaft: Zur Entwicklung und Entwicklungsdynamik kooperativ-konzertierter Politik in Österreich', in Peter Gerlich, E. Grande and W.C. Müller (eds), *Sozialpartnerschaft in der Krise. Leistungen und Grenzen des Neokorporatismus in Österreich* (Vienna: Böhlau, 1985).

Tálos, Emmerich, Ernst Hanisch and Wolfgang Neugebauer (eds), *NS-Herrschaft in Österrreich 1938–1945* (Vienna: Verlag für Gesellschaftskritik, 1988).

Thaler, Peter, *The Ambivalence of Identity: the Austrian Experience of Nation-building in a Modern Society* (West Lafayette, IN: Purdue University Press, 2001).

Thurnher, Armin, *Das Trauma, ein Leben. Österreichische Einzelheiten* (Vienna: Zsolnay Verlag, 1999).

Thurnher, Armin, *Heimniederlage. Nachrichten aus dem neuen Österreich* (Vienna: Zsolnay Verlag, 2000).

Timms, Edward, *Karl Kraus: Apocalyptic Satirist: Culture and Catastrophe in Habsburg Vienna* (New Haven, CT: Yale University Press, 1986).

Tweraser, Kurt, *U.S.-Militärregierung in Oberösterreich, 1945–1950*, vol. 1, *Sicherheitspolitische Aspekte der Amerikanischen Besatzung in Oberösterreich-Süd, 1945–1950* (Linz: Oberösterreichisches Landesarchiv, 1995).

Ungváry, Krisztián, *The Battle for Budapest* (London: I.B. Taurus, 2003).

Utgaard, Peter, *Remembering and Forgetting Nazism: Education, National Identity and the Victim Myth in Postwar Austria* (New York/Oxford: Berghahn, 2003).

Wall, Irwin, *French Communism in the Era of Stalin: the Quest for Unity and Integration, 1945–62* (Westport, CT: Greenwood Press, 1983).

Wall, Irwin, *The United States and the Making of Post-war France, 1945–54* (Cambridge: Cambridge University Press, 1991).

Wallisch, Paula, *Ein Held stirbt* (Graz: Verlag der Sozialistischen Partei Landesleibung Steiermark, 1946).

Weber, Fritz, *Der Kalte Krieg in der SPÖ. Koalitionswächter, Pragmatiker und Revolutionäre Sozialisten 1945–1950* (Vienna: Verlag für Gesellschaftskritik, 1986).

Zeman, Zbynek, *The Masaryks* (London: Weidenfeld and Nicolson, 1976).

Zimmermann, Hannes, 'Wirtschaftsentwicklung in Österreich 1945–1951, am Beispiel der Lohn-Preis-Abkommen und des Marshallplans' (PhD Dissertation, University of Vienna, 1983).

Articles

Bandhauer-Schöffmann, Irene, 'Women's Fight for Food in Post-War Vienna', in Claire Duchen and Irene Bandhauer-Schöffmann (eds), *When the War was Over: Women, War and Peace in Europe 1945–1956* (Leicester: Leicester University Press, 2000), 71–86.

Bandhauer-Schöffmann, Irene, and Ela Hornung, 'Geschlechtsspezifische Auswirkungen von Hungerkrise und "Freßwelle"', in Thomas Albrich, Klaus Eisterer, Michael Gehler and Rolf Steininger (eds), *Österreich in den Fünfzigern* (Innsbruck: Österreichischer Studienverlag, 1995), 15–19.

Bandhauer-Schöffmann, Irene, and Ela Hornung, 'Der Topos des sowjetischen Soldaten in lebensgeschichtlichen Interviews mit Frauen', in *Dokumentationsarchiv des österreichischen Widerstandes (DÖW) Jahrbuch* 1995, 28–44.

Baumgartner, Marianne, 'Vergewaltigungen zwischen Mythos und Realität. Wien und Niederösterreich im Jahr 1945', in *Frauenleben 1945. Kriegsende in Wien. Sonderausstellung des Historischen Museums der Stadt Wien* (Vienna: Eigenverlag der Museen der Stadt Wien, 1995), 59–71.

Beer, Siegfried, 'Die Besatzungsmacht Großbritannien in Österreich', in Alfred Ableitinger, Siegfried Beer and Eduard G. Staudinger (eds), *Österreich unter alliierter Besatzung 1945–1955* (Vienna: Böhlau 1998), 41–70.

Beer, Siegfried, and Eduard G. Staudinger, 'Die "Vienna Mission" der Westalliierten im Juni 1945', in *Studien zur Wiener Geschichte, Jahrbuch des Vereins für Geschichte der Stadt Wien*, vol. 50 (Vienna, 1994), 317–412.

Berg, Matthew Paul, 'Challenging Political Culture in Postwar Austria: Veterans' Associations, Identity, and the Problem of Contemporary History', *Central European History*, vol. 30, no. 4, 1997, 513–44.

Biddiscombe, Perry, 'Dangerous Liaisons: the Anti-fraternization Movement in the US Occupation Zones of Germany and Austria, 1945–1948', *Journal of Social History*, vol. 34, Spring 2001, 611–47.

Bischof, Günter, ' "Prag liegt westlich von Wien": Internationale Krisen im Jahre 1948 und ihr Einfluss auf Österreich', in Günther Bischof and Josef Leidenfrost (eds), *Die bevormundete Nation. Österreich und die Alliierten* (Vienna: Haymon, 1988), 314–45.

Bischof, Günter, 'Die Instrumentalisierung der Moskauer Erklärung nach dem Zweiten Weltkrieg', *Zeitgeschichte*, 20, Heft/11–12, 1993, 345–66.

Bischof, Günter, 'Restoration, not Renewal: From Nazi to Four Power Occupation. The Difficult Transition from Dictatorship to Democracy in Austria after 1945' *Hungarian Studies*, 2000, vol. 14 no.2, 207–31.

Denscher, Bernhard, 'Die Werbungen in Wien für die Nationalratswahl am 25. November 1945', *Studien zur Wiener Geschichte, Jahrbuch des Vereins für Geschichte der Stadt Wien*, 42, 1986, 119–40.

Erickson, Eric, 'The Zoning of Austria', *Annals of the American Academy of Political and Social Science*, vol. 267, January 1950, 106–13.

Ganser, Daniele, 'Terrorism in Western Europe: An Approach to NATO's Secret Stay-Behind Armies', *Whitehead Journal of Diplomacy and International Relations*, vol. VI, no.1, Winter/Spring 2005, 69–95.

Gehler, Michael, and Wolfram Kaiser, 'A study in Ambivalence: Austria and European Integration 1945–1995', *Contemporary European History*, vol. 6, part 1, March 1997, 75–100.

Gulick, C.A., 'Austria's Socialists in the Trend toward a Two-Party System: An Interpretation of Postwar Elections', *The Western Political Quarterly,* vol. 11, issue 3, September 1958, 539–62.

Haas, Hans, 'Österreich 1949: Staatsverhandlungen und Wiederbewaffnungsfrage', *Jahrbuch für Zeitgeschichte*, 1978, 175–200.

Hautmann, Hans, 'Oktoberstreik in Österreich. Der Platz des Oktoberstreiks in der Geschichte', www.kpoenet.at/bund/geschichte/oktoberstreik.htm. September 2000.

Honner, F., 'Der Streik als Waffe', in *Weg und Ziel* IZ/1950, 845.

John, Michael, 'Das "Haarabschneiderkommando" von Linz', *Historisches Jahrbuch der Stadt Linz 1995 – Entnazifizierung und Wiederaufbau in Linz*, 1996, 335–59.

Judt, Tony, 'The Past is another Country: Myth and Memory in Postwar Europe', in István Deák, Jan T. Gross and Tony Judt (eds), *The Politics of Retribution in Europe. World War II and its Aftermath* (Princeton, NJ: Princeton University Press, 2000), 293–323.

Kaiser,Wolfram, 'Integration 1945–1995', *Contemporary European History*, vol. 6, part 1, March 1997, 75–100.

Kepplinger, Brigitte, and Josef Weidenholzer, 'Die Rekonstruktion der Sozial-demokratie in Linz 1945–1950', *Historisches Jahrbuch der Stadt Linz 1995 – Entnazifizierung und Wiederaufbau in Linz*, 1996, 13–67.

Kirk, Tim, 'Fascism and Austrofascism', in Günther Bischof, Anton Pelinka and Alexander Lassner (eds), *The Dollfuss/Schuschnigg Era in Austria: A Reassessment* (New Brunswick, NJ: Transaction, 2003), 10–31.

Knight, Robert, 'The Waldheim Context: Austria and Nazism', *The Times Literary Supplement*, 30 October 1986.

Konrad, Helmut, 'Zur politischen Kultur der Zweiten Republik am Beispiel des "Falles Olah"', *Geschichte und Gegenwart*, 1/86, 31–53.

Kopeczek, Arnold, 'Die amerikanischen Waffenlager, die "Einsatzgruppe Olah" und die Staatspolizei im Kalten Krieg der fünfziger Jahre', in Erwin Schmidl (ed.), *Österreich im frühen Kalten Krieg* (Vienna: Böhlau, 2000), 101–19.

Lewis, Jill, 'Red Vienna: Socialism in One City, 1918–27', *European History Quarterly* (formerly *European Studies Review*), vol. 13, no. 3, July 1983, 335–54.

Lewis, Jill, 'Conservatives and Fascists in Austria, 1918–34', in Martin Blinkhorn (ed.), *Fascists and Conservatives: The Radical Right and the Establishment in Twentieth Century Europe* (London: Unwin Hyman, 1990), 98–117.

Lewis, Jill, 'Austria in Historical Perspective: from Civil War to Social Partnership', in Stefan Berger and Hugh Compston (eds), *Policy Concertation and Social Partnership in Western Europe: Lessons for the 21st Century* (New York/Oxford: Berghahn, 2002), 19–33.

Mattl, Siegfried, 'Frauen in Österreich nach 1945', in Rudolf G. Ardelt, Wolfgang J.A. Huber and Anton Staudinger (eds), *Unterdrückung und Emanzipation: Festschrift für Erika Weinzierl* (Vienna: Geyer, 1985), 101–26.

Moser, Johannes, 'Erinnern und Vergessen – Schuld und Scham. Eine verdrängte Geschichte von Zwangsarbeit unf Judenvernichtung in der Steiermark', www.kakanien.ac.at/beitr/fallstudie/jmoser1.pdf.

Schmidl, Erwin, 'The Airlift that Never Was: Allied Plans to Supply Vienna by Air 1948–1950', *Army History Bulletin of Arms History*, Winter 1998, 12–23.

Staudinger, Anton, 'Zur Geschichte der B-Gendarmerie', *Österreichische Militärische Zeitschrift*, vol. 5, 1972, 343–48.

Tálos, Emmerich, and Bernhard Kittel, 'Roots of Austro-Corporatism: Institutional preconditions and co-operation before and after 1945', in Günter Bischof and Anton Pelinka (eds), *Austro-Corporatism: Past, Present and Future* (New Brunswick, NJ: Transaction, 1996), 21–52.

Tálos, Emmerich, and Bernhard Kittel, 'Austria in the 1990s: the Routine of Social Partnership in Question', in Stefan Berger and Hugh Compston (eds), *Policy Concertation and Social Partnership in Western Europe: Lessons for the 21st Century* (New York/Oxford: Berghahn, 2002), 35–50.

Thaler, Peter, '"Germans" and "Austrians" in WW2. Military History and National Identity', *Center for Austrian Studies Occasional Paper*, September 1999. www.cas.umn.edu/wp991.pdf.

Index

Note: 'n.' after a page reference indicates the number of a note on that page.

Lightning Source UK Ltd.
Milton Keynes UK
UKOW07f1559150115

`4509UK00003B/41/P